A HANDBOOK TO
DANTE STUDIES

BY

UMBERTO COSMO

TRANSLATED BY

DAVID MOORE

BASIL BLACKWELL
OXFORD
1950

Printed in Great Britain for Basil Blackwell & Mott, Limited
by A. R. Mowbray & Co. Limited, London and Oxford

PREFACE

THIS *Handbook to Dante Studies* is Umberto Cosmo's last work. When I requested him to undertake the task of writing it for the firm of De Silva he at first hesitated. But he gladly returned once more to his beloved Dante to make what was almost a re-capitulatory survey, and he applied himself with ever-increasing zeal to a labour in which the burden of his days was eased and forgotten. To whom else could I have turned for just such guidance as this? He brought to his task a boundless wisdom— Barbi, too, wanted him to assist in the work of editing the text of the *Comedy*, unaware that his new associate was already too old for an undertaking that would still demand so much time and labour. More than this, he brought to it the mind of one who had always found in Dante avenues of experience, compounded of sorrows and hopes, similar to his own, and he had a thorough understanding of the rich life which underlay the poetry and gave it birth. Finally, he had a mind that could handle formidable and complicated materials—a mind that far transcended the arid, mechanical talent of ordinary scholars.

This book was needed to make the most recent studies of Dante complete. It must, I think, supersede even the most estimable 'guides' that other teachers have provided, not only because it naturally brings our information up to date, but also in virtue of its instructional value, and it is bound to become a standard work. Despite its compendious nature, it constitutes an integrative, personal survey of countless problems to which numerous scholars have bent their energies. Lastly, it is, as it were, the testament bequeathed by a teacher to pupils who are by now grown old and who had become his friends, as well as to unknown pupils of the future.

'One by one the masters leave the stage, but the way that they have opened up remains. Now we look to the young men, and to be successful they have only to follow in their predecessors' footsteps.'

Umberto Cosmo left the stage, having completed this work,

iii

which he knew instinctively to be his last, but without having been able to put the finishing touches to it. While he was living in his retreat at Corio Canavese his heart was broken by the news of a violent incident in the underground war.

His *Handbook to Dante Studies*, which is now published, has been completely revised by a faithful and able old pupil, Professor Felice Arese, who brought to his task an *élan* inspired by affection and a sense of duty. I thank him, and I must also thank, as the greatly-loved teacher would have done, Professor Giuseppe Vidossi, who from time to time helped Cosmo in this work, and whose many suggestions have contributed to its perfection.

FRANCO ANTONICELLI.

July, 1947.

TRANSLATOR'S NOTE

The translator gratefully acknowledges his indebtedness to Mr. C. Grayson for reading the text and offering many helpful suggestions for its improvement.

D. C. M.

CONTENTS

Contents

A HANDBOOK TO DANTE STUDIES

I

GENERAL AIDS

Bibliographies and General Aids

For more than six centuries the life and works of Dante Alighieri have been the subject of single-minded and persistent research. Though the researches have often deviated from the true path, and errors have been frequent, many facts have been established, and much light has been shed on the poet's life, thought and art. Mere factual information does not constitute knowledge. We are truly knowledgeable about a given fact only if we are aware of the process by which it has been established. Hence, the student ought to know where he may obtain information about the work that has been done. In Dante's case this, happily, is easy. Indeed, few writers command so vast a bibliography. And where the bibliography is deficient the specialist periodicals and reviews come to our aid.

For the early researches up to 1870 and a little later aid is always forthcoming from De Batines and Ferrazzi. Of these the former is the more systematic and far the more orderly; his descriptions of the Dante manuscripts, the editions of his works and the commentaries are still most valuable. Ferrazzi's writings are something of a hotchpotch in which there is a merging of the encyclopaedic and the bibliographical; yet—and this is especially true of his summaries—he helps the student to form an idea of the nature of Dante criticism immediately after 1850.

COLOMB DE BATINES, *Bibliografia dantesca, ossia catalogo delle edizioni, traduzioni, codici, manoscritti e commenti della Divina Commedia e delle Opere minori di Dante, seguito dalla serie dei biografi di lui.* Prato, 1845–6, in two parts (three volumes).

A. BACCHI DELLA LEGA, *Indice generale della bibliografia dantesca compilata dal visconte C. De Batines,* Bologna, 1883.

G. Biagi, *Giunte e correzioni inedite alla bibliografia dantesca del visconte C. De Batines*, Florence, 1888.

G. I. Ferrazzi, *Manuale dantesco*, Bassano, 1865–77. Bibliography in Vols. II, IV and V.

Since the inauguration of the specialist reviews and periodicals investigation has become easier; no subsequent publication of any value has escaped notice.

L'Alighieri, edited by F. Pasqualigo, Verona and Venice, 1889–93.

Il Giornale dantesco, edited by G. L. Passerini, Florence, Olschki, 1893–1915. Indexes, each covering a period of twenty-two years, to the reviews *L'Alighieri* and *Il Giornale dantesco* under the supervision of G. Boffito, Florence, Olschki, 1916.

Il nuovo Giornale dantesco, critical and bibliographical review of Dante literature, Florence and Milan, 1917–21, five volumes.

Il Giornale dantesco, edited by L. Pietrobono, Florence, Olschki, since 1921.

Indexes to *Il Giornale dantesco* from the nineteenth to the thirtieth years of publication (1911–27), under the supervision of L. Pietrobono, Florence, Olschki, 1931. Beginning at Volume XXXI the journal has appeared once a year with the sub-title of *Annuario.*

N. D. Evola, *Bibliografia dantesca* (1920–30), Florence, Olschki, 1932.

Bibliografia dantesca, under the supervision of H. Wieruszowski, in *Giornale dantesco* (Vol. XXXIX (1938), pp. 341–410 for the years 1931–7, and Vol. XLI (1940), pp. 221–50 for the years 1938–9).

Evola, *Bibliografia dantesca, 1931–4,* in *Bibliografia degli studi sulla letteratura italiana,* Milan, Vita e Pensiero, 1938, Part I, pp. 291–333; Evola, *Bibliografia dantesca, 1935–9,* in *Aevum,* XV (1941), pp. 91–149; Siro A. Chimenz, *Rassegna critica degli studi danteschi in Italia dal 1940 al 1945,* in *Orientamenti culturali,* II (1946), *sq.*

Covering the years 1891–1900 there are also:

G. L. Passerini and C. Mazzi, *Un decennio di bibliografia dantesca, 1891–1900,* Milan, Hoepli, 1905. (But see *Bullettino della Società dantesca italiana,* New Series, XII (1905), pp. 179–81).

But for the years 1889–1921 the student should constantly consult in particular the *Bullettino della Società dantesca italiana,* Florence, 1890–1921: First Series, Nos. 1–15, critical bibliography compiled by M. Barbi, covering the years 1889–93; New Series, edited first by M. Barbi and subsequently by E. G. Parodi (Vols. I–XXVIII), critical review of publications on Dante during the years 1893–1921. Copious yearly indexes. Index covering ten years (1893–1903) compiled by F. Pintor, Florence, 1912; this is an exemplary piece of work.

The *Bullettino* has been continued in *Studi danteschi,* edited by M. Barbi, Florence, Sansoni, 1920 and following years. Volume XX (1937) contains an *Indice analitico dei primi venti volumi* (pp. 141–96).

Although not concerned with Dante in particular because its scope embraces the whole of Italian literary history, the *Giornale storico della letteratura italiana* will also prove very useful by virtue of the many articles and reviews and copious notices bearing on our subject which have appeared in it since its inauguration (1883). It will be even more useful when the long-awaited *Indice generale* is published.

Dante articles and reviews, often important, have constantly been published in addition by the other Italian reviews (*Rassegna,* edited by D'Ancona and his successors, Percopo and Zingarelli's *Rassegna, Nuova Antologia, Rivista d'Italia, La Cultura,* etc.). For this reason it will always be advantageous to consult their indexes.

For the German bibliography the student should refer to SCARTAZZINI, *Dante in Germania, bibliografia dantesca alemanna dal secolo XIV ai giorni nostri,* Vol. II, Milan, 1881–3. A supplement (*Bibliografia dantesca alemanna dell'ultimo decennio,* 1883–93) appears in *Giornale dantesco,* I (1893), pp. 174–87. Also the *Deutsches Dante-Jahrbuch* in its successive issues.

The *Annual Report of the Dante Society* (Cambridge, Mass.) contains the *Additions* to the Harvard College collection of works on Dante.

But the most extensive and complete bibliography of Dantesque literature is that compiled by T. WESLEY KOCH, *Cornell University Library—Catalogue of the Dante Collection Presented by W. Fiske,* Ithaca, N.Y., 1898–1900. Two large volumes containing a bibliography of Dante's works and of writings on Dante, arranged in alphabetical order of authors, an index of subjects and passages of the *Divine Comedy* on which the author has provided a commentary, and an iconographical appendix.

M. FOWLER has since published a volume of *Additions, 1898–1920*, Ithaca, 1921.

Despite a number of omissions, G. MAMBELLI's *Gli annali delle edizioni dantesche* (Bologna, Zanichelli, 1931) makes a useful contribution to our knowledge of the editions of Dante's works. It contains much information about the writings which each edition has evoked, and an excellent *Saggio bibligrafico per la storia della fortuna di Dante*. Here, in addition, is a list of some useful dictionaries and catalogues, omitting those which are merely intended for schools:

L. G. BLANC, *Vocabolario dantesco*, Leipzig, 1852 (Italian translation by G. Carbone, Florence, 1859).

G. POLETTO, *Dizionario dantesco di quanto si contiene nelle opere di Dante Alighieri con richiami alla Somma teologica di San Tommaso, con l'illustrazione dei nomi propri e delle questioni più controverse*, Siena, 1885–92.

G. A. SCARTAZZINI, *Enciclopedia dantesca, dizionario critico e ragionato di quanto concerne la vita e le opere di Dante Alighieri*, Milan, Hoepli, 1896–9, two volumes. A. FIAMMAZZO subsequently added a third volume: *Vocabolario concordanza delle opere latine e italiane*, Milan, 1905.

P. TOYNBEE, *A Dictionary of Proper Names and Notable Matters in the Works of Dante*, Oxford, Clarendon Press, 1898. Of much greater value than the preceding works and very helpful in view of the reliability of the information, which is derived directly from the sources. Cf. BARBI, *Bullettino della Società dantesca italiana*, VI (1899), pp. 201–17, and COSMO, *Giornale dantesco*, VII (1899), pp. 310–26. Toynbee is also responsible for a *Concise Dictionary*, Oxford, 1914.

A useful *Indice analitico dei nomi e delle cose* which occur in the works of Dante has been compiled by M. CASELLA for the edition of the *Opere di Dante* sponsored by the *Società dantesca italiana*, Florence, Bemporad, 1921.

The Dante Society of Cambridge, Mass., has published three very useful volumes of concordances:

Concordance of the Divine Comedy (E. A. FAY), Boston and London, 1888.

Concordanza delle opere italiane in prosa e del Canzoniere di Dante Alighieri (E. S. SHELDON, with the assistance of A. C. WHITE), Oxford, 1905.

Dantis Alighieri Operum latinorum Concordantiae (E. K. RAND and E. H. WILKINS, with the collaboration of A. C. WHITE), Oxford, 1912.

Historical Aids

Men and their works, to be fully understood and realistically appraised, must always be set in the historical environment in which they developed. This is all the more necessary in the case of a man such as Dante, who took part in the artistic life of his own locality, and derived from it in his early youth the blue-print of his own art. Later he became involved in the party strife which rent his city, but rose above the personal misfortunes which were its sequel to meditate upon the political life of Europe as a whole, with his intellect free to study and contemplate all the scientific, philosophical and religious problems that vexed the minds of his contemporaries. The thirteenth century was not a century of uniformity: its progress towards the establishment of its own way of thought was characterized by hot disputes in university, monastery and curia. The *Comedy* was born of this vexation of spirit and was, as it were, its mirror. A schooling in the history—civil, philosophical, religious and poetical—of the century is thus necessary for the understanding, enjoyment and appraisal of the work as a whole.

I call attention here to just a few books of a general character but furnished with full bibliographies covering the various relevant matters for the use of any who desire to intensify their researches.

For the ideas that informed medieval history the student should consult G. FALCO's book, *La santa romana repubblica*, a historical outline of the Middle Ages, Naples, Ricciardi, 1945 (published in 1942 under the name of G. FORNASERI), with a

select bibliography covering each period. There is a summary
in about twelve pages of the period 1285–1314, with an excellent
bibliography, in *Gebhardts Handbuch der deutschen Geschichte*
(Stuttgart).

L. SALVATORELLI, *L'Italia comunale dal secolo XI alla metà del
secolo XIV*, Milan, Mondadori, undated (actually published in
1940), a detailed record of events with bibliographical references
both of a general nature and embracing each individual period.

R. CAGGESE, *Duecento-Trecento. Dal concordato di Worms alla
fine della prigionia di Avignone (1122–1377)*, Turin, Utet, 1939.
The part that concerns Florence is particularly detailed.

The two volumes published earlier by Salvatorelli and Caggese
will contribute to a fuller understanding of the Middle Ages.

C. BARBAGALLO, *Il medioevo*, Turin, Utet, 1935, including a
bibliography. I would also call attention to two non-Italian
series which are, however, readily obtainable:

From the *Histoire générale*, edited by G. Glotz: Vol. IV, *L'Allemagne et l'Italie de 1125 à 1273*, by E. JORDAN; Vol. V, *La décadence
de la papauté—L'Allemagne et l'Italie de 1273 à 1492*, by E. PERRIN;
Vol. VIII, *La civilisation occidentale au moyen âge du XIe au milieu
du XVe siècle*, by H. PIRENNE, G. COHEN and H. FOCILLON.

From the series *Peuples et civilisations*: Vol. VI, *L'essor de l'Europe
(XIe-XIIIe siècles)*, by L. HALPHEN, and Vol. VII, *La fin du
moyen âge*, by H. PIRENNE and others (first three chapters).

With special reference to the history of Florence the student
should read:

F. T. PERRENS, *Histoire de Florence*, Paris, 1877–80 (the early
volumes); P. VILLARI, *I primi due secoli della storia di Firenze*,
Florence, Sansoni, 1905; R. DAVIDSOHN, *Geschichte von Florenz*,
Berlin, 1896–1927, four volumes.

The history of Florence is completed by the same author in his
book, *Florence in the Time of Dante*, a picture of Florentine society
in the poet's lifetime, just as in the last chapter of the first volume
of the *Geschichte* we have a picture of the age of Cacciaguida.

In addition the student should constantly refer to DAVID-
SOHN's *Forschungen zur Geschichte von Florenz*, Berlin, 1896–
1908, four volumes. The information in this book with a special

bearing on culture was summarized by S. DEBENEDETTI in the *Giornale storico della letteratura italiana*, LVI (1910), pp. 165–86.

R. CAGGESE, *Firenze dalla decadenza di Roma al risorgimento d'Italia*, Florence, Bemporad, 1912–21 (Vol. I, *Dalle origini all'età di Dante*; Vol. II, *Dal priorato di Dante alla caduta della repubblica*); the same author's *Roberto d'Angiò e i suoi tempi*, Florence, Bemporad, 1922–31; G. SALVEMINI, *Magnati e popolani in Firenze dal 1280 al 1295*, Florence, Carnesecchi, 1898. 'Farfetched in its interpretation of history on the basis of economics and social distinctions' (Salvatorelli), but a standard text-book of the period; see A. S. BARBI's article in the *Bullettino della Società dantesca italiana*, VII (1900), pp. 237–58.

Salvemini's thesis is opposed by N. OTTOKAR in *Il comune di Firenze alla fine del Dugento*, Florence, Vallecchi, 1927. 'Useful by virtue of its observations on individual questions, but inadequate in its general interpretation of history and politics' (Salvatorelli).

A book that must be read at all costs is I. DEL LUNGO's *I Bianchi e i Neri, pagine di storia fiorentina da Bonifazio VIII ad Arrigo VII per la vita di Dante*, Milan, Hoepli, 1921.

Reference may be made to the heading *Firenze ai tempi di Dante* in the index to *Studi danteschi* (Vol. XX).

But modern historians, despite the exactitude and the completeness of their information, and the sureness with which they correct the mistakes of the ancient chroniclers, cannot represent the spirit of the age in the same way as contemporary writers. Let me quote an instance which is none the less illuminating for being comparatively unfamiliar. Everyone knows how proud Dante was of his family's Roman origin, and how skilfully he conveys this feeling in the episodes of Brunetto and Cacciaguida. Whatever the truth with regard to the family's origin, such a sentiment might well seem childish to a modern mind; but all who read in Villani, or better still in Malispini, the eulogies of the great Florentine families of Roman descent will understand how the ultimate roots of that sentiment are set in the consciousness of the men of that time. Now Dante in his thoughts freely explored the infinite, yet he shared the feelings of his age. Hence, it is not enough to be acquainted with the best-founded conclusions of critics of history; it is also essential that one should be aware of what Dante may have known of his times and of the past, and of how he regarded them and felt towards them. What we in the event find to have been his mistakes were to him truths.

I mention here the names of those few chroniclers who best enable us to situate the poet in his environment and to understand his life and works. Compagni and Villani are indispensable reading to the student of Dante. All the better if he acquires in addition a knowledge of the other chroniclers who are, as it were, complementary to these two.

The non-specialist reader of Compagni may find his needs met by DEL LUNGO's school edition, *Cronica di Dino Compagni delle cose occorrenti nei tempi suoi*, Florence, Le Monnier, 1889. The research student should consult the same authority's critical edition, which includes a very full commentary and is published in the new series of the *Rerum Italicarum Scriptores*, Vol. IX, Part 2, Città di Castello, Lapi, 1913–16; this work supersedes Del Lungo's original edition published by Le Monnier. There is no critical edition of Villani, whose works, originally in Lami's hands, are now receiving the attentions of Luiso. There are good editions by Magheri (Florence, 1823) and by F. Gherardi Dragomanni (Florence, Coen, 1844–7). Lloyd's edition (Trieste, 1861) is convenient.

The so-called *Cronaca dello Pseudo Brunetto* may be read in Villari, *I primi due secoli della storia di Firenze*, Florence, 1898, II, pp. 185 *sq.* Text verified in SCHIAFFINI, *Testi fiorentini del dugento e dei primi del trecento*, Florence, Sansoni, 1926, pp. 82–150.

The critical edition of the *Storie pistoresi*, under the supervision of A. S. BARBI, in the new *Rerum Italicarum Scriptores*, Vol. XI, Part 5, Città di Castello, Lapi, 1907.

For Ricordano Malispini's *Cronica*, pending the publication of the critical edition which Morghen is preparing for the series *Rerum Italicarum Scriptores*, the student may consult Follini's edition, Florence, 1816.

There is a full selection of these chronicles in *Cronisti del trecento* edited by R. PALMAROCCHI, Milan, Rizzoli, 1935.

All expositions of scholastic philosophy help one to acquire a knowledge of Dante's thought. I mention here only a few works of a general character which contain full bibliographies answering every individual need.

In the *Grundriss der Geschichte der Philosophie* by F. UEBERWEG and B. GEYER, the volume entitled *Die patristische und scholastische Philosophie*, Berlin, 1928.

M. DE WULF, *Histoire de la philosophie médiévale*, Sixth Edition, Louvain, 1934-6: Vol. I, *Des origines jusqu'à la fin du XIIe siècle*; Vol. II, *Le XIIe siècle*.

For a description of the intellectual background of scholastic philosophy and theology consult C. BAEUMKER, *Die patristische Philosophie*, in P. Hinneberg's *Kultur der Gegenwart*, Third Edition, Leipzig, 1923.

E. GILSON, *La philosophie du moyen âge des origines patristiques à la fin du XIVe siècle*, Paris, 1944 (new edition, re-arranged and enlarged, of *La philosophie au moyen âge*, Paris, 1922).

E. GILSON, *L'esprit de la philosophie médiévale*, Paris, Vrin, 1932, two volumes. At the end of each volume there are 'notes bibliographiques pour servir à l'histoire de la notion de philosophie chrétienne.'

G. DE RUGGIERO, *Storia della filosofia*, Part II: *La filosofia del Cristianesimo*, Fourth Edition, Bari, Laterza, 1946.

G. GENTILE, *I problemi della scolastica e il pensiero italiano*, Bari, Laterza, 1923.

U. MARIANI, *La scolastica negli inizi del secolo XIII — La scolastica nella seconda metà del secolo XIII*, in *Giornale dantesco*, XL (1939), pp. 55–85, and XLII (1941), pp. 9–41. In the Middle Ages philosophy and theology go hand in hand, often merging into each other. Valuable for its information—well-founded even if rather superficial—and for the completeness of its bibliography is M. GRABMANN's *History of Catholic Theology from the End of the Patristic Age down to Our Own Times*. The student should also consult Grabmann's *Die Geschichte der scholastischen Methode*, Freiburg i. B., 1909.

Father F. CAYRÉ's *La patrologie et l'histoire de la théologie* is also useful for its clear exposition and bibliography. For our purposes the second volume is interesting. For individual points the student should constantly have recourse to the great *Diction-naire de théologie catholique*, Paris, 1905 and following years. For the religious movement see the bibliography in Salvatorelli, *op. cit.*, under the heading *Storia ecclesiastica*, p. 854; also Chap. VII, p. 860, and Chap. X, p. 863.

Here I would simply mention that the old book by Tocco, *L'eresia nel medio evo* (Florence, Sansoni, 1884), is always useful. The student would do well to co-ordinate it, making the necessary corrections, with the many writings which the author has since published—in particular *Quel che non c'è nella Divina Commedia*, Bologna, Zanichelli, 1899. Also the histories of the inquisition by Lea and Guiraud.

G. Volpe, *Movimenti religiosi e sette ereticali nella società medievale italiana*, Florence, Vallecchi, 1926. An agreeable and useful book is E. Gebhart's *L'Italie mystique*; also G. Monticelli, *Vita religiosa italiana nel secolo XIII*, Turin, Bocca, 1932.

There is a rapid and reliable survey of the Franciscan movement and its evolution during the thirteenth century in P. Gratien, *Histoire de la fondation et de l'évolution de l'ordre des Frères Mineurs au XIIIᵉ siècle*, Paris, 1928. See also my *Rassegne francescane* in *Con Madonna Povertà* (Bari, Laterza, 1940, pp. 176–303), which contains many details of the trends prevailing during the late thirteenth and early fourteenth centuries.

A. De Stefano, *Federico II e le correnti spirituali del suo tempo*, Rome, 1922.

What is the relationship of Dante's art to that of the writers who preceded him or were his contemporaries? To what extent was he in their debt for the material of his own art and for the form in which it was expressed? These are questions which every serious student of Dante should be able to answer. Hence, anyone can see that a thorough knowledge of the literary history of the thirteenth century must be acquired before his works can be fully understood—and I would add to this a knowledge of Provençal literature and something of French. To understand Dante fully we ought to be acquainted with the full range of his studies.

Detailed references will be given in their proper place when

I speak of the poet's youth; here it must suffice to refer the reader
to a few books of a general character containing copious refer-
ences. Together with the volumes that comprise BARTOLI's *Storia
della letteratura italiana* (Florence, Sansoni) and the first volume of
GASPARY (Turin, Loescher) I would therefore mention *Le origini*
by NOVATI and MONTEVERDI and the new edition by VISCARDI,
BERTONI's *Duecento* and the early chapters of SAPEGNO's *Trecento*.
All these last-named works form part of Vallardi's series entitled
Storia letteraria. Vol. I of the *Manuale* by D'ANCONA and BACCI
(Florence, Barbèra, First Edition 1892) and Vol. I of ROSSI's
Storia della letteratura italiana (Milan, Vallardi, First Edition 1900),
though intended for schools, are useful because of the reliability
of the information they contain. The chapter on Dante in
D'Ancona is provided with a full bibliography which, even if it
is not strictly select, may prove useful, especially as an indication
of the state of Dante criticism at the time when the distinguished
teacher compiled it.

In conclusion I would mention besides two works by G. A.
Scartazzini which were written with an object similar to my own,
and which, while they enable one to get to know the ideas of a
distinguished Dantologist, serve to throw light on the state of
Dante criticism some fifty years ago:

G. A. SCARTAZZINI, *Prolegomeni della Divina Commedia, intro-
duzione allo studio di Dante Alighieri e delle sue opere*, Leipzig,
Brockhaus, 1890. This work should be co-ordinated, the
necessary corrections being made, with V. ROSSI's review in the
Giornale storico della letteratura italiana, XVI (1890), pp. 383 *sq.*,
and with that by F. TORRACA in the *Nuova Antologia*, October
16th, 1890, reprinted in *Studi danteschi*, Naples, Perrella, 1912,
pp. 9–42.

G. A. SCARTAZZINI, *Dantologia*, Milan, Hoepli, 1883, 1894,
1906. See BARBI, *Bullettino della Società dantesca italiana*, II (1894),
pp. 2–24.

But after consulting these works the student should read
Barbi's study published in 1893 in the first part of the *Giornale
dantesco*, viz. *Gli studi danteschi e il loro avvenire in Italia* (*Problemi
di critica dantesca*, Series I, Florence, Sansoni, 1934, pp. 1–18), and
the same author's preface (*Dieci anni dopo*) to the first ten-yearly

B

Index of the *Bullettino della Società dantesca italiana* (1903), reprinted in part in *Problemi*, I, pp. 18–27.

What, then, has been the course of Dante studies in Italy during the last fifty years? The young student who wishes to form an idea of it should see M. BARBI's outline, *Un cinquantennio di studi danteschi*, in the volume entitled *Un cinquantennio di studi sulla letteratura italiana*, Florence, Sansoni, 1937, I, pp. 111–35. This was reprinted in part in *Studi danteschi*, XX (1937), pp. 129–34, and will appear as an epilogue to the third volume of *Problemi di critica dantesca* by the same writer.

Two attempts to summarize all these studies have been made by N. ZINGARELLI in the work that he wrote for Vallardi. First edition: *Dante*, Milan, Vallardi, 1899–1903 (see the most important reviews by BARBI in the *Bullettino della Società dantesca italiana*, XI (1904), pp. 1–58, now reproduced in *Problemi* (cited above), I, pp. 29–85, and by ROCCA in *Giornale storico della letteratura italiana*, XLVI (1905), pp. 136–76). Second edition: *La vita, i tempi e le opere di Dante*, ib., 1931, in two parts, 1338 pp. Apropos of this book see COSMO's article in *La Cultura*, X (1931), pp. 956–75.

This is a massive work, with abundant bibliographical references. It is fantastic in design and often obscure, for Zingarelli passed very easily from the subject of discussion to another that was in the back of his mind, and the reader has to divine his meaning by following the turn of his thought rather than the strict grammatical sense. Yet with all its peculiarities and mistakes it is a monumental work, and one to which the young student should constantly refer.

Another great work which, though to a great extent outmoded, it may prove helpful to consult, especially the part dealing with religious and artistic matters, is F. X. KRAUS's *Dante, sein Leben, sein Werk, seine Verhältnisse zur Kunst und zur Politik*, Berlin, 1897. V. CIAN, *Bullettino della Società dantesca italiana*, V (1898), pp. 113–61.

There is a select bibliography, limited naturally by the scope of the work, in M. BARBI's *Dante*, Florence, Sansoni, 1940.

II

LIFE — SOURCES

SOURCES for the study of Dante's life are: (*a*) the information about himself which the poet left in his works; (*b*) the information emerging from extant public instruments and deeds which refer to him and his family; (*c*) a few items of information supplied by the ancient commentators; (*d*) the oldest biographies.

(*a*) References to the autobiographical indications may easily be found in Toynbee's *Dictionary* under 'Dante' and in the *Indice analitico dei nomi e delle cose* which Casella compiled for the Società dantesca's edition of the *Opere di Dante*. These indications are certainly extremely valuable, and in their absence it would be impossible to reconstruct Dante's life, but they cannot be accepted without objection. We must not confuse Dante's artistic representation of himself with the historical reality, nor the ideal man with the real. And it behoves us always to distinguish that which Dante was from that which throughout his life he aspired and strove to be. He succeeded in realizing his ideal of himself only after courageous efforts, at the end of his life.

(*b*) Information about Dante and his family was first collected from public instruments by learned Florentines of the seventeenth century, led by Carlo Strozzi. A large number of documents was assembled mid-way through the eighteenth century by Giuseppe Pelli in his *Memorie per servire alla vita di Dante*; and the harvest has been growing richer ever since. At the end of the last century Guido Biagi and G. Lando Passerini conceived the idea of assembling the whole in a *Codice diplomatico dantesco*. They launched it in a sumptuous edition in 1895 (Florence, Landi); but the work was left half-finished in 1911. Happily the *Codice diplomatico dantesco* now exists in a complete form, having been compiled on the basis of criteria of an infinitely more scientific kind by Renato Piattoli (Florence, L. Gonnelli e figli, 1940). As regards the period from December 9th, 1189— 'date of the oldest document which refers with absolute certainty to members of the Alighieri family'—to April 21st, 1364, when 'the most long-lived of Dante's sons closed his eyes in Treviso', or rather until September 21st, 1371, when 'Master Donato, doctor of rhetoric and grammar, as the heir of Sister Beatrice, daughter of the late Dante Alighieri, made over to the Monastery of Santo Stefano degli Ulivi in Ravenna the sum of three golden ducats, on behalf of a friend who was, and felt himself to be, obliged to make the gift', all the information which may be inferred from public and legal documents, and which in any way concerns the Alighieri family, has been carefully sifted and transcribed, and assembled in a single volume. Nor is there any lack of repeated bibliographical references for those who wish to seek fuller elucidation from the original publishers of any given document. When in 1895 Biagi and Passerini issued the first part of their *Codice* it seemed to Carducci that 'the firm foundations of the definitive history of Alighieri and his times' were being laid. No definitive histories are ever written, particularly of men whose thought has embraced the whole world and probed the infinite. Yet in Piattoli's *Codice* we have a precious instrument with which to work; save in special cases we should constantly have recourse to it, and it alone need be quoted.

(*c*) The information which may be gleaned from the ancient commentators is not plentiful; yet something may be inferred from the writer of the *Ottimo Commento*, who knew Dante and seems to have had a good knowledge of Florentine affairs, and from Benvenuto. The former, for instance, confirms that the poet went on a mission to Rome, and sheds a ray of light on a stormy episode of his exile. As for Benvenuto, Bartoli has already observed that his information needs to be carefully sifted. He does not deny that it may contain elements of truth; he says that it should be examined with a critical eye.

(*d*) The ancient biographers to whom the student should refer are Giovanni Villani, Boccaccio and Leonardo Bruni. When in the course of his narrative he came to the year 1321 Villani commenced a new section designed 'to create in his chronicle an everlasting memorial' to his great fellow-citizen. Though he belonged to the opposite faction to the man whose life he was recalling he was conscious of his transcending superiority, and the information that he gives—an obituary rather than a biography—is evidence of what was known in Florence of the great exile a few years after his death. The chronicler occasionally fell into error, as with regard to the month in which the poet died (July instead of September); but we cannot reject the other information that he gives—as regards, for instance, the poet's journey to Paris—without a careful examination that leads inevitably to a different conclusion.

The devotion which Boccaccio professed for Dante is well known—a devotion that he manifested throughout his righteous life in the imitation of his works, the transcription of part of his writings, his researches into the *Epistole* and the poet's lesser known compositions, and the *Vita* that he several times rewrote.

Whatever his source—the 'trustworthy' person who told him the story of Beatrice, or the poet's friends whom he questioned about his sojourn in Ravenna—Boccaccio sought always to verify the information that he gradually accumulated. He obeyed the preconceived maxim that if a devotee of learning is to give his whole attention to his task he should neither marry nor take any part in public life. He allowed himself to be so carried away by his imagination that he embellished his narrative with fanciful descriptions, but where he was ignorant, as of the early years of Dante's exile, he preferred silence to invention. And his information on the last years and the sojourn in Ravenna he obtained direct from the poet's friends. Hence it is natural that modern critics should be inclined to attribute to him far more authority than their predecessors. Never satisfied, he was always amending and recasting his little book, and the researches of Barbi and Vandelli have shown that from the *Elogio* he proceeded to the more concise version known as the *Compendio*, and thence to other versions yet. 'The number of these transcriptions is to-day hard to determine, even supposing that they were all equal as regards the number and the order of the writings collected, but there were certainly four: the first in the *Vita*, the second in the *Compendio*, and the other two in the *Compendio abbreviato*' (Barbi).

To Leonardo Bruni, however, it seemed that Boccaccio, wholly intent on emphasizing the loves and longings of the poet, had 'left out of account the serious and truly important aspects of his life. Bruni, a student of Florentine history, had access to letters and writings of Dante which now, unfortunately, are irretrievably lost, as for instance the famous letter written from exile to the people of Florence, in which he alludes to his activities as a combatant at Campaldino. He also deduced from the letter other information which need not be recorded here, but which may be found in the note added to the *Epistole* in the edition of the Società dantesca (pp. 447–49). As a source for the study of the poet's life Bruni's writings are therefore of the highest importance.

The lives of Filippo Villani—nephew of the great chronicler— and of Giannozzo Manetti are unimportant. Still, in summarizing extracts from the work of his uncle and of Boccaccio, Villani added a few items of information, such as the poet's mission to Venice. Subsequent lives are of even less importance; indeed, they are wholly negligible.

The work of Pelli in the eighteenth century, says Bartoli, 'marks the beginning of critical inquiry into the history of Dante's life'. But in connection with the 'Lives of Dante' the student should refer to the chapter in Bartoli (*Storia della letteratura italiana*, Vol. V, Chap. XX), and for the oldest lives he should consult the well-balanced study by Moore. The whole of Bartoli's volume, even if it may appear largely out-of-date, deserves to be read attentively by the young student. It administered the *coup de grâce* to the romantic legend created by Troya and Balbo.

But if the conclusions which the critic reached were to a great extent negative, his inquiries were not in effect systematic negations of the kind that we associate with Imbriani and, to some extent, with Scartazzini. They took the form of a careful revision of what were regarded as known facts. Now if progress was to be made it was necessary that critical awareness should be sharpened in the face of blind faith in tradition. It was in this revision that the reconstruction of the poet's life had its source. And it is greatly to the credit of the historians that they initiated it, as they initiated the revision of our entire literary history. The pioneers of our studies were Todeschini, Comparetti, D'Ancona, Carducci, Del Lungo, Bartoli. Youthful scholars who really desire to progress in historical and critical studies should not forget the fact.

I shall recall a number of their writings in the course of this treatise. Many others I shall have no opportunity to mention. This does not mean that they are any less important, whether they concern the poet's life or whether they throw light on his work. Accordingly, the young student should try to become familiar with them all. There is always something to be learned from each; they all have it in them to inspire the zeal which gives the impetus to progress in historical research. The fact that this or that study has been superseded in the course of further research, or that in one or another some error is found, means nothing. Even more than in the truth that he discovers, the teacher's value consists in the training he provides in the art of discovery. And these great teachers, like Galileo, have furnished their disciples with the compass that enables them to advance ever further in all kinds of historical and critical research.

For the allusion in the *Ottimo* to Dante's mission see ZINGAR-ELLI, *Dante* (cited above), Second Edition, I, p. 408.

Apropos of VILLANI's special section in *Cronica*, IX, p. 136, the student may still gain something—despite the numerous exaggerations—from the study of V. IMBRIANI's essay, *Sulla rubrica dantesca nel Villani*, in *Studi danteschi*, Florence, Sansoni, 1891, pp. 1–175. Much important information on this section, as well as on Boccaccio and Dante's *Epistole*, has been assembled by O. ZENATTI in a carelessly written but noteworthy book which may always be consulted with profit, viz. *Dante e Firenze, prose antiche*, Florence, Sansoni, 1903.

The text of the Toledo and Chigi autograph MSS. of Boccaccio's *Vita* and *Compendio* may be consulted in BOCCACCIO, *Il commento alla Divina Commedia e gli altri scritti intorno a Dante*, Bari, Laterza, 1918, edited by D. Guerri.

G. VANDELLI, G. *Boccaccio editore di Dante*, Florence, Ariani, 1923 (excerpt from the *Atti della Reale Accademia della Crusca*, 1921–2); M. BARBI, *Sulla 'fededegna persona' che rivelò al Boccaccio la Beatrice dantesca*, in *Problemi*, II, pp. 415–20; the same author's *Qual è la seconda redazione della 'Vita di Dante' del Boccaccio?* in *Problemi* (cited above), I, pp. 395 sq. And cf. VANDELLI's article in *Bullettino della Società dantesca italiana*, XXIV (1917), pp. 125–42.

Bruni's *Vita* has also been reprinted on numerous occasions as a preface to commentaries on the *Divine Comedy*. The three 'lives', with others written in the fourteenth century, have been assembled by G. L. PASSERINI in *Le vite di Dante scritte da G. e F. Villani, da G. Boccaccio, L. Aretino e Giann. Manetti*, Florence, Sansoni, 1918. Cf. VANDELLI, *Bullettino della Società dantesca italiana*, XXIV (1917), pp. 125–42. It is useful to compare the *Vita* with LEON. ARETINUS, *Historiarum florentini populi lib. XII*, edited by Santini and Di Pierro, *Rerum Italicarum Scripta*, Vol. XIX, Part 3, Città di Castello, Lapi, 1914. As regards the value of the *Vita* see Santini's *La produzione volgare di Leonardo Bruni e il suo culto per le tre corone fiorentine*, in *Giornale storico della letteratura italiana*, LX (1912), pp. 320–6.

E. MOORE, *Dante and His Early Biographers*, London, Rivington, 1890.

For Troya's *Veltro* see Cosmo's article in *La Cultura*, XI, Part 4 (October–December, 1932), pp. 689–94.

III

YOUTH

Early Days

Dante makes many references to the antiquity and nobility of his family, and by means of skilful allusions conveys the impression that it was of Roman origin (*Inf.*, XV, 74-8; *Par.*, XVI, 44). He celebrates a great-great-grandfather who was knighted by the 'Emperor Currado', and died on a crusade in the Holy Land (*Par.*, XV, 139-48); he alludes to the pride of a great-grandfather (*ib.*, 91-4); to the blood-feud which resulted in the death of a cousin who was a spreader of scandal (*Inf.*, XXIX, 19-21); and he employs the self-same words in which the mob blessed Christ to praise his mother (*Inf.*, VIII, 44-5). He mentions a sister who was beautiful and kind (*Vita Nuova*, XXIII). Only to his father does he make no reference. The acquisition of a knowledge of his family is therefore a way of integrating one's knowledge of his personality, and this purpose is served on the one hand by the relevant passages in the *Comedy* and the *Vita Nuova*, on the other by the legal documents assembled in the *Codice diplomatico*.

At times we have to content ourselves simply with the poet's word. This is so in the case of his first ancestor and the latter's wife. Is the Cacciaguida, *filius olim Adami*, unearthed by Davidsohn, Dante's ancestor? Piattoli does not record the document in the *Codice* because he could produce no evidence of its authenticity. The same observation holds good in the case of his wife. 'My lady came to me from the valley of the Po,' says Cacciaguida; but 'the valley of the Po' is an extremely general term, and Dantologists have indulged their fancy in determining the locality. Was it Parma, Bologna or Ferrara? Probably it was the last, as Del Lungo would have it; but this is no more than a probability.

On the other hand, though some deny it, the family's nobility is certain, for the belt of the militia would not have been accorded to him by the Emperor had he not been of noble birth. It was not, however, included among the *Grandi*, which is not the same thing.

As the poet skilfully implies (*Par.*, XVI, 40–5), the family was descended from the Elisei, and its livelihood was drawn substantially from the profession of moneylending. But to his father there are merely a few vague allusions, which emerge principally from the sarcastic remarks of Forese in the tenson in which he engages with the youthful Dante. Hence the many conjectures, all more or less rash, of which he has been the subject. For the most likely of the possible theories the student should consult Barbi's commentary on the tenson. At all events he was a man of little account, and this explains, at least in part, his son's silence.

As regards Dante's birth, to-day all are agreed that it took place in 1265. But in the past there have been long discussions which it may be profitable to examine. The date is deduced from the first lines of the *Comedy* (mid-way of life=age 35, date of the journey=1300; 1300 − 35=1265). If we correlate this to the allusion to Gemini in *Par.*, XXII, 112–7, we may locate it more accurately between the middle of May and the middle of June. The objection that in 1265 the Guelfs had not yet returned to Florence is not valid, for only the 'caporali' of the party went into exile, and Dante's father, insignificant as he was, inevitably passed unnoticed. If, however—as was maintained with a wealth of astronomical data by Angelitti—the journey took place in 1301, it is patent to all that the date of Dante's birth would be altered by a year to 1266, and the objections of those who oppose the commonly-accepted date would accordingly be silenced. But, apart from the many arguments which tempt one to accept the hypothesis that the journey took place at the beginning of the century, decisive encouragement is lent to the advocates of 1265 by the testimony, recorded by Boccaccio, of Piero Giardini, who heard the tale of the poet's years from his own lips as he lay on his death-bed.

His mother died young, and his father contracted a second marriage, by which he had nine children; but as to the family and its economic circumstances it is best to seek reliable information in the *Codice*, where the indications that we need abound.

Of the young Dante's early years and early studies we know nothing, but we can form some idea of them if we reflect on the educational conditions prevalent in the Florence of those days. Adequate for that purpose is the information vouchsafed to us by Davidsohn. All the while the life of the Commune was unfolding before the young man's eyes. What repercussions did it have on his mind? At this stage it is very profitable to read the chroniclers, and also the indications given by the mature poet in the *Comedy*, though these should be interpreted cautiously. For instance, the ruins of the houses of the Uberti, which lay in heaps in the Gardingo, must have caused the figure of Farinata to stand out like a colossus in the feverish imagination of the boy.

But above all it is important to study the youthful Dante's evolution as a poet. He says that he taught himself the art of writing verse (*Vita Nuova*, III); but poets in their youthful essays have the same experience as all artists: they remain under the influence of the school in which they grow up. Thus Dante is tied to the old Tuscan school, which was unrefined and mannered. Yet it is well to be familiar with this school through those who represent it if one desires to appraise accurately the development of the young poet, who must have been very precocious. The sonnet which is commonly regarded as his first—written when he was about eighteen—was in all probability not the first that he composed. Of what I will term the 'learner's exercises' of these years only a small proportion has come down to us, but the poems which may with certainty be attributed to Dante include a number of sonnets which in view of their obscurity of language, arbitrariness of form and intricacy of syntax must be regarded as having been composed before, if only a little before, the sonnet in the *Vita Nuova*. Among these is the so-called tenson on the pains of love.

The study of the Sicilian and Tuscan poetry of the thirteenth century is thus indispensable as a training for the comprehension and appraisal of Dante's art. One must re-create the literary atmosphere of Florence and Tuscany, become familiar with the whole of that farrago of indifferent poetry in its every detail, from Guittone and Guinizelli to Cavalcanti, and make a thorough study of the language used as a means of expression. The literary histories and critical essays, though extremely useful, are not enough; what is required is a direct acquaintance with the original writings. No history, for example, can define the influence that was exerted by Cavalcanti on the young poet as he made his first tentative efforts. It is essential to form a clear idea of the poetry of the one and to have traced its development in order to throw light on the other. Now such an object can only be achieved by reading the poems at first hand and comparing them. If we study those which preceded the *canzone* 'Donne ch'avete intelletto d'amore' we are in effect studying the artistic evolution of the young poet.

We see him progressively, but quickly, refining his art. Under the influence of his Florentine friends he breaks away from the old school; he enters the new circle and in doing so enters the world of poetry. Thus the pattern of his life is created. It is the life of an artist and a gentleman, consisting in amusement and gallantry rather than in love-affairs. It is probable that to this period belong the sonnet *Sonar bracchetti* and the *serventese* in celebration of the sixty fairest women in the city.

Beatrice has not yet appeared on his poetical horizon. This is evident from the sonnet 'Guido, i' vorrei che tu e Lapo ed io'. Here the third young woman—Dante's lady—who takes her place with Monna Vanna and Monna Lagia, i.e. with the ladies of Cavalcanti and Lapo Gianni, and who is supposed to sail with them and the lovers in the vessel, is the one who in the *serventese* was 'Number 30'. This assuredly is not Beatrice, who, as we know from the *Vita Nuova* (VI), occupied the ninth place in that composition. This place was assigned to her by pure chance, for the number nine had not yet assumed in Dante's mind that mysterious meaning and value which it took on later when he came to idealize Beatrice.

At all events the women whose praises are sung during this period betoken not so much love in the full sense as a bent for gallantry. Yet in their names we perceive the influence of Cavalcanti. The *senhal* of Madonna Vanna was Spring, but if she was adorned with 'flowers and verdure', Dante's ladies were flowers pure and simple: Fioretta, Violetta.

THE FAMILY.—For the information that may be derived from

Dante's works not merely about the author but about his family the student should consult the *Indice analitico* in the edition of the *Opere* sponsored by the Società dantesca (Florence, Bemporad, 1921). Such facts as emerge from the documents are assembled in the *Codice diplomatico*, which also contains the necessary bibliographical references. See also the bibliographical references in my *Vita di Dante*. All the varied information which Barbi has given about the family is now assembled in *Problemi di critica dantesca*, Second Series, Florence, Sansoni (1941), pp. 324–45 and 347–70. As regards the date of Cacciaguida's birth, his participation in the crusade and the lady who came to him from the valley of the Po, it is well to read the views of the more cautious commentators. For all questions relating to the surname Alighieri see P. RAJNA, 'Il casato di Dante', in *Studi danteschi*, III (1921), pp. 59–88, and BARBI, 'Un altro figlio di Dante?' in *Studi danteschi*, V (1922), pp. 23–31, reproduced in *Problemi*, II, pp. 347 *sq.*

For Dante's earliest years the student should constantly consult SCHERILLO's *Alcuni capitoli della biografia di Dante*, Turin, Loescher, 1896.

Death of Dante's Father—Marriage

This period saw the death of Dante's father. The exact date we do not know, but from a legal document which records the sale by Dante of a small security inherited from his father it emerges that by 1283 the latter was dead. Dante was eighteen, and by the statutes of the city—being an orphan—he now became of age. Not long afterwards—a year more or less—he must have married Gemma di Manetto Donati. Boccaccio is a great authority where his knowledge is certain; where it was not he worked by a process of induction. He took the narrative of the *Vita Nuova* to be absolutely true, and quite logically deduced that Dante could only have married after the death of Beatrice. His effort to discover a psychological motive which would explain the fact led him to think that the young poet's parents provided their son with a wife in the hope of consoling him for the loss of the woman he loved. But we should be guided by the implications of the documents and of the customs of the time. Now it is apparent from one deed that Manetto Donati had settled his little daughter Gemma's dowry as early as 1277; and normally the dowry was settled when a marriage was in prospect. At times children were betrothed in their infancy. Dante's father and Manetto probably intended to marry off their two children without delay, and that was why Manetto settled his daughter's dowry at such an early date. We know, on the other hand, that young men who had become of age through the death of their fathers were wont to embark on family life without delay. Hence everything encourages us to think that in Dante's case also this was what happened. It is, indeed, not apparent on what grounds he should have failed to conform to the customs of his time. But for that very reason the young man's marriage was one that bore no relation to his life as a poet.

MARRIAGE.—The *instrumentum dotis* is not extant, but the fact of its existence is definitely established by the deeds 'which Dante's widow had to execute in order to claim her dotal rights with respect to her husband's possessions, which had reverted to the State' (Barbi). The text of the deed appears in the *Codice diplomatico*, No. 146, and in DAVIDSOHN's *Geschichte von Florenz* (cited above), pp. 341-5. As regards these infant marriages and the technical terminology of the subject see DEL LUNGO, *Storia esterna, vicende, avventure d'un piccolo libro dei tempi di Dante*, Milan, Albrighi e Segati, 1917-8, II, pp. 98-108. On the independence of marriage and love even in the Tuscan poets consult DEL LUNGO, *Beatrice nella vita e nella poesia del secolo XIII* (pp. 112-5 in the Bemporad edition of *La donna fiorentina del buon tempo antico*, Florence, 1905).

The Tenson with Forese

It was, in my opinion, during these years that Dante engaged in his tenson with Forese Donati. Forese belonged to a family of much higher standing than Dante's, but thanks to the marriage which the latter had contracted, or was on the point of contracting, with Gemma he had become, or was on the point of becoming, a relative of his, albeit a distant one—and furthermore a friend. The tenson is commonly ascribed to the so-called period of aberration which Dante is supposed to have passed through after the death of Beatrice. We shall see in due course

how this aberration should be interpreted. It is well, however, to make it clear at the start that the years subsequent to 1292 are the most fruitful as regards the man's early philosophical and poetical development and his spiritual regeneration. That the tenson should have taken place during these years, when his spiritual life was being renewed under the influence of his philosophical studies, is incomprehensible. On the other hand it may be fully explained if we ascribe it to a period not much later than the death of his father, when, in consequence of that event, the family was beginning to find itself in the straitened circumstances with which Forese twits his friend. The poet alludes to his father as to one but lately dead whose identity is known to all. After another ten or twelve years that insignificant man must have been already forgotten. The abortive 'eaglet's vengeance' with which Forese reproaches Dante—and all the indications are that its cause was something of little importance—does not suffice to make of Dante's father a Geri del Bello who awaits vindication 'by one who is a partner in his shame' (*Inf.*, XXIX, 33). After so great a lapse of time—even in view of Florentine sentiment—the jibe would have been meaningless, and Forese was too shrewd a master of fence to reproach his adversary with something which by virtue of its triviality must by then have been forgotten.

Opponents of this simple thesis cite Dante's allusion to Forese in the *Purgatorio*:

> From such a life my heart was turned away
> By him who walks before me. . . .
>
> (XXIII, 118–9)

i.e. from the life of sin into which, in the pictorial fiction of the *Comedy*, Dante lapsed after the death of Beatrice. But if the tenson marks an ugly episode in Dante's life it could only have been assigned in the fiction of the *Comedy* to the period of his supposed aberration. To imagine that Dante had sunk as low as he did when he exchanged those sonnets with Forese and descended to jibes and insults of the most vulgar kind—even to the expedient of blackening the name of Forese's mother—and to make out that this was his moral condition when Beatrice—the Beatrice, be it understood, of the poetic fiction—sustained him with her presence and 'led him on a rightward course' (*Purg.*, XXX, 121–3), would be a travesty of the fiction itself.

The tenson contains obscurities which not even Del Lungo and Barbi, with their great diligence and their expert knowledge of Florentine affairs, have succeeded in clarifying. It should be studied especially in Barbi's edition, with its exhaustive commentary.

For the rest, to whatever stage in the poet's life one chooses to ascribe the tenson it is of singular importance for the understanding of the man, because it reveals to us that sarcastic and malignant, not to say disreputable, manner which was later to be subdued by chivalrous love and spiritual refinement, but which from time to time comes to the surface in the *Inferno*. But it is even more important because it enables us to appraise his exquisite awareness of his guilt—an awareness which contributed so much to his reformation. Hence, even more than because it affords us a glimpse of certain episodes in his life as a young man, the tenson is of essential importance to us for psychological reasons. Having achieved his spiritual reformation Dante became fully sensible of the abject state into which he had sunk, and he repented it bitterly. Those who for love of Dante sought to minimize the savagery of the tenson and almost wished to reduce it to the level of a jest obscured the intricate beauty of his soul even as they thought to excuse him. Having made peace with his friend he bitterly lamented his death and awaited with a quaking heart the hour when he might in some measure wipe out the guilt which, as his spiritual reformation became more complete, seemed to him ever more horrifying. He freed himself from its shackles, as the kings of poesy alone can, by exalting to the highest realms of art those whom he had made a target for so much derision and filthy abuse. From such a frame of mind sprang the episode of Forese in Purgatory, and with it the glorification in Paradise of Piccarda, the only Florentine woman to share with Beatrice so lofty a station. He could not redeem Monna Tessa from the infamy with which he had covered her save by a confession that he had lied, in other words by bringing his name into utter disrepute, which would have been ridiculous. But she had a daughter, Piccarda, the purest flower of goodness and charity, and the virtues of the daughter shed their lustre even upon the woman who bore her.

BARBI, *Studi danteschi*, V (1922), p. 10; *Problemi*, II, p. 353.

On the Florentine and Tuscan versifiers of Dante's early youth see DAVIDSOHN, *Geschichte von Florenz* (cited above), Chap. IV, pp. 310 *sq.*; ZINGARELLI, *Dante*, Chap. VI; TORRACA, *Studi sulla lirica italiana del Duecento*, Bologna, Zanichelli, 1902, pp. 154–62; S. DEBENEDETTI, *Nuovi studi sulla Giuntina*, Città di Castello, Lapi, 1912, pp. 15–33; R. PALMIERI, 'Studi di lirica toscana anteriore a Dante', in *Giornale dantesco*, XXIII (1915), pp. 118–40 and 191–6. On the period in general see the literary histories.

THE 'RIME'.—Dante's *Rime* have been assembled in the edition of the *Opere* sponsored by the Società dantesca italiana; but death unhappily prevented M. Barbi from publishing the critical text and commentary at which he laboured for so many years. It is to be hoped that the two volumes of the *Vita Nuova* and the *Canzoniere* will not be long in appearing under the editorship of his devoted followers. All who desire to form an idea of the state of the *Canzoniere*—so to term it—would do well to read BARBI's work with the specific title *Studi sul Canzoniere di Dante*, Florence, Sansoni, 1915, and some of his minor studies published in wedding presentation collections or in *Studi danteschi*. (A bibliography is to be found in Vol. XX of *Studi danteschi*.)

G. CONTINI has added a useful recapitulatory note on the subject to his commentary on the *Rime* (Turin, Einaudi, 1939; Second Edition, 1946). Earlier commentaries are of little help; the most useful among them is Santi's.

Zonta has derived the best part of his commentary from his essay which we shall cite later (Turin, Paravia, 1923). As an interpretation it is poor. The only commentary of which we can make use for philological purposes is Contini's. The latter's edition also contains an 'essential bibliography'. Here I give a few references apropos of questions which relate to the period under review.

On the early stages of the poet's career see CARDUCCI, *Delle rime di Dante* (*Opere*, VIII, pp. 14–23). For Dante da Maiano and his correspondence with Dante, DEBENEDETTI, *Nuovi Studi*

C

sulla Giuntina (cited above), pp. 9–14 and 45–6; F. PELLEGRINI, 'La tenzone del duolo d'amore,' in *Bullettino della Società dantesca italiana*, XXIV (1917), pp. 160–8, and V. CRESCINI, ib., XXV (1918), pp. 78–85.

For all points arising from the tenson with Forese see BARBI, 'La tenzone di Dante con Forese,' in *Studi danteschi*, IX (1924), pp. 5–149, and XVI (1932), pp. 69–103, now included in *Problemi*, II, pp. 87–214. In this essay the author drives home his conclusions in face of the opposition of D. GUERRI, who in *La corrente popolare nel Rinascimento—Berte, burle e baie nella Firenze del Brunellesco e del Burchiello*, Florence, Sansoni, 1931, denied that the sonnets were written by Dante. For the date consult G. A. VENTURI, 'Il canto XXIII del Purgatorio', in *Giornale dantesco*, XVIII (1910), pp. 5 *sq.*, and V. ROSSI, *Bullettino della Società dantesca italiana*, XI (1904), pp. 302–4.

Still of prime importance for its effect on the chronology of Dante's loves is BARBI's little book, *Un sonetto e una ballata d'amore nel Canzoniere di Dante*, Florence, Landi, 1897 (cf. *Bullettino della Società dantesca italiana*, IV (1897), p. 160). On Merlin, the 'good enchanter', and the linking of the sonnet *Guido, i' vorrei* with the *Mare amoroso* (vv. 214–7, 228–31, MONACI, *Crestomazia*, p. 134) see RAJNA, 'Dante e i romanzi della Tavola rotonda', in *Nuova Antologia*, June 1st, 1920, pp. 241–3. MAZZONI's article, 'Sul numero de le trenta', in *Almae luces malae cruces* (Bologna, Zanichelli, 1941) pp. 131–4, is unconvincing.

For general comments on the *Rime* see, in addition to the ever-useful essay by Carducci (cited above), PARODI, 'Le Rime', in *Dante*, Milan, Treves, 1921; ZONTA, 'La lirica di Dante', in *Giornale storico della letteratura italiana*, 1922 supplement; CROCE, *La poesia di Dante*, Bari, Laterza, 1921 (Fifth Edition, 1943); CIAFARDINI, *Tra gli amori e tra le rime di Dante*, Naples, P. Federico e G. Ardia, 1919; SAPEGNO, 'Le rime di Dante', in *La Cultura*, October, 1930; L. PIETROBONO, 'Note sul Canzoniere', in *Giornale dantesco*, XXXVIII (1936), pp. 27–63.

New Studies—Brunetto Latini

The present phase is characterized by savage irony, vulgarity and moral turpitude—but at the same time the poet was setting himself a standard of achievement that nothing could satisfy. While he paid court to noble ladies and indulged in knightly exercises, he was striving zealously to refine his art. In order to give expression to the world that surged within him he felt it necessary to master completely the technique of style. The key to this attainment was provided by the *artes dictandi*, the study of which was an essential part of a literary man's culture. The professor of such studies in Florence was Ser Brunetto Latini, the great 'cultivator'—as Villani described him—of his fellow-citizens, to whom he taught the art of rhetoric and—because of the connection which the man of the Middle Ages saw between the two—the statesman's art.

We need not sketch an outline of him here. I am not writing a life of Dante: I am merely indicating the knowledge which students of the poet should have if they are to appreciate his work to the full. The verses in which Dante eulogized the old professor, recalling that he had taught him 'how man achieves immortality' (*Inf.*, XV, 82-4), have been the subject of much discussion. To-day, generally speaking, no one doubts that Dante, when a young man, received instruction—occasionally at least—from Ser Brunetto, and that he derived from it encouragement to face life. Brunetto's word must have whetted his youthful appetite for more ambitious studies, and this very probably accounts for his visit to Bologna. There the study of the *artes* flourished, and famous professors had occupied the university chair. There was frequent intercourse between Bologna and Florence, and Florentines were to be found in Bologna in great numbers. It is therefore very likely that Dante lingered there for some time, even if—for reasons unknown to us—he did not complete what is termed a regular course of study. Incidentally, a sonnet of his—playful in tone—that has come down to us in the transcription of a notary provides curious evidence of his stay, which is confirmed by a number of allusions in the *Comedy*.

The environment in which Dante formed his cultural background was thus expanding. 'I counsel thee to read my *Trésor*,' says Ser Brunetto to his pupil as he leaves him; and the student of Dante cannot afford to be ignorant of the *Trésor* and the *Tesoretto* in view of the influence which they exerted on the poet's cultural development and the benefits which he derived from them as an artist. But the third book of the *Trésor* contains Brunetto's theory of Rhetoric, which Dante knew well, we may say, during his formative period. And this was the hey-day of the *Summae artis dictaminis*, the school in which, especially at Bologna, he refined his technique as a poet and paved the way for the doctrine of the *De Vulgari Eloquentia*. Now a knowledge, partial at least, of the theory of Rhetoric and the *Summae* is indispensable to all who desire to appraise not only the poet and the teacher but the author, who in the *Vita Nuova* begins to carry out the precepts and rules which they prescribe and in the *Convivio* adapts them with shrewder skill to the requirements of his own prose.

For the oldest bibliography of Brunetto Latini see D'Ancona's *Manuale*, I, pp. 86–9. That Brunetto taught Dante was denied by V. Imbriani in 'Che Brunetto Latini non fu maestro di Dante', in *Studi danteschi*, Florence, Sansoni, 1891, p. 333. A moderate opinion was subsequently formulated by Scherillo in his essay in *Alcuni capitoli* (cited above), Turin, Loescher, 1896, p. 157. Next see F. Novati's 'Le epistole', in *Lectura Dantis*: *Le opere minori di Dante Alighieri*, Florence, Sansoni, 1906, pp. 283–310, reproduced in *Freschi e Minii*, Milan, Cogliati, 1925; Parodi, *Poesia e storia nella Divina Commedia*, Naples, Perrella, 1921, pp. 211 *sq.*; Walter Goetz, 'Dante und Brunetto Latini', in *Deutsches Dante-Jahrbuch*, XX (1938), pp. 78–99.

As regards Dante's residence at Bologna see Ricci, 'Dante a Bologna', in *Ore e ombre dantesche*, Florence, Le Monnier, 1924, pp. 3–42, and 'Dante scolaro a Bologna,' in *Cogliendo biada o loglio*, Florence, Le Monnier, 1924, pp. 93–135; F. Filippini, *Dante scolaro e maestro* (*Bibl. Archivium Romanicum*, Vol. XII), Chaps. 1–3. The latter also contains a bibliography. For the residence of Tuscans and in particular of Florentines at Bologna see G. Livi, *Dante, suoi primi cultori, sua gente in Bologna*, Bologna, Cappelli, 1918, *passim*, and the recapitulatory pages in Zaccagnini's 'Guido Guinizelli e le origini bolognesi del dolce stil novo', in *Documenti e studi pubblicati per cura della R. Dep. di storia patria per le province di Romagna*, IV (1922), pp. 13–61.

There is a bibliography of the sonnet on the Garisenda in

FILIPPINI, *Dante scolaro e maestro* (cited above), p. 4 (note), and in LOVARINI, 'Il sonetto di Dante per la Garisenda', in *Archiginnasio*, XV (1910), pp. 199–210; see also the latter's *Per madonna Garisenda*, ib., XXXIII (1938), pp. 263–71, and G. MAZZONI, 'I risguardi belli', in *Almae luces* (cited above), pp. 123–5.

The original text of the *Trésor* may be seen in CHABAILLE's edition, *Li livres dou Trésor*, Paris, 1863; but in general the student of Dante may rest content with the Italian version of Giamboni, edited by L. GAITER, Bologna, Romagnoli, 1878–83. For the *Tesoretto* see WIESE's edition, Strasbourg (*Bibl. romanica*, Nos. 94–5). For the cases in which Dante is indebted to the *Trésor* see A. DOBELLI, 'Il "Tesoro" nelle opere di Dante', in *Giornale dantesco*, IV (1896), pp. 310–49, and L. M. CAPELLI, 'Ancora del "Tesoro" nelle opere di Dante', in *Giornale dantesco*, V (1897), pp. 548–56.

For the Italian theory of Rhetoric see F. MAGGINI, *La Rettorica italiana di Brunetto Latini*, Florence, 1912, and the same writer's *La Rettorica di Brunetto Latini*, critical text, Florence, 1915.

For the *Artes Dictandi* see MARIGO's Introduction to his edition of the *De Vulgari Eloquentia*, Florence, Le Monnier, 1938, pp. xxx–xl, and BERTONI's *Duecento*, Third Edition, 1939, Chap. XIV, pp. 253–8 and 275–6. But these writings provide only preliminary indications for further study.

The composition of the *Fiore* would fall within this period if that work were by Dante. 'Everything that could be adduced in favour of Dante's authorship has been stated by Mazzoni and D'Ovidio (G. MAZZONI, 'Se possa il Fiore essere di Dante Alighieri,' in *Raccolta D'Ancona*, Florence, 1901, pp. 657–92; F. D'OVIDIO, 'Se possa il Fiore essere di Dante Alighieri,' in *Nuovi studii danteschi*, Naples, 1932, pp. 253–86); there is, I think, little else that may be added' (BARBI, 'La questione del Fiore,' in *Studi danteschi*, III (1921), pp. 154–5). But Morpurgo's demonstration that the poet of the *Fiore* is also the poet of the *Detto d'amore* settles the question once and for all. See DEBENEDETTI, *Studi danteschi*, VIII (1924), pp. 140–50.

IV

THE DISCOVERY OF BEATRICE

WHEN Dante was at Bologna—and, whatever the reason, he cannot have stayed there long, nor did he complete there what we term a regular course of study—Beatrice had not yet appeared on his poetical horizon. True, he had mentioned her as being among the sixty fairest women in Florence, and in his eulogy she had been allotted the ninth place, but the number was quite fortuitous and without any of those special significations which Dante later chose to attach to the number nine. The discovery of Beatrice was a revelation; but if we wish to appreciate to the full how the poet proceeded from the first eulogy to the resolve which marks the close of the *Vita Nuova*—namely to say nothing more of that blessed one until he should be able to write of her what had never been said of any woman—we must seek the development of his thought not so much in the prose-passages of the little book as in the poems considered independently of the prose that illustrates them. The latter, indeed, was written at a time when the poet was giving effect to an idea which he had evolved after the lady's death, or rather after the crisis of the *donna gentile*. And above all we must take as our starting-point those poems which, because they are not included in the *Vita Nuova*, constitute the most authentic clue to that idea. For this purpose especial importance attaches to the two *canzoni* 'E' m'incresce di me sì duramente' and 'Lo doloroso amor che mi conduce'.

The first of these, in the opinion of a critic of high standing, Luigi Pietrobono, refers to the *donna gentile*. I am not convinced. In the first place the reasons he gives ought to be carefully sifted if it is desired to form an opinion based on personal experience, and not on the authority of another. To me the poet seems in the two *canzoni* to be still under the influence of Cavalcanti, and therefore to have a lugubrious vision of life and love. These *canzoni* mark the beginning of that self-liberation and self-assertion which were to find expression in 'Donne ch'avete intelletto d'amore'.

But the last-named poem brings with it other problems which likewise demand a solution. When a critic comes to examine a man's soul, what he does is to probe its deepest recesses so that he may visualize and solve all the problems that vex it—the more so when he is concerned with a great soul which, as was Dante's, is continually developing and maturing. If he adopts this procedure he is not faced with the meretricious lure of allegories and symbols which has made the understanding of the *Vita Nuova* such a wearisome task. However lofty the ideal that she personifies, Beatrice remains a living creature. The thesis that she did not really exist may arise from the prose of the *Vita Nuova*, but not from its poetry. This does not mean that the poet has not at times gone too far and here and there, when the form was unpropitious, reduced her to a type. This is the explanation of the thesis put forward by Bartoli, who so inflexibly maintained that Beatrice was not a concrete personage but rather Woman exalted to angelic status. Bartoli's thesis is not to be confused with the exaggerations of the allegorists and the symbolists, and hence his book still makes an extremely valuable contribution to our understanding of the 'new Tuscan lyrical poetry'. In criticism there is no place for dogmatic assertions. Idealists, allegorists and symbolists may indeed have exaggerated, but their researches have not been entirely useless. They have revealed all the complexities of Dante's art and examined every aspect of the problem, so that to-day it seems less difficult to arrive at a concrete solution. Beatrice has, so to say, a twofold history: that which is unfolded in Dante's poetry, from the moment when she is first discovered to her transfiguration in the *Comedy*, and that which, I would almost say, has suffered as a result of critical inquiry, in the process of which it has assumed the most varied forms. But a thorough knowledge of the second is essential for a better understanding of the first.

The initial problem that arises when we read the *canzone* 'Donne ch'avete'—and it arises in all its vastness—is the problem of the *stil novo*; and it is proper that we should appreciate it to the full with the aid of the *Vita Nuova* (XVIII–XIX) and the episode of Bonagiunta in the *Purgatorio* (XXIV, 49–63). It would, however, be an error—one, unfortunately, into which nearly all students of the subject have fallen—to think that the young poet was able in 1290 to formulate his ideas on art as clearly and rigorously as he did some fifteen years later. After his art had reached its full maturity the poet in his answer to Bonagiunta condensed into one trenchant phrase the result of his experiences and of his meditation upon them. It is therefore fitting that we should always distinguish clearly between Dante as he was in his successive phases and Dante as he saw himself, and as he wished that others should see him, when he contemplated himself from the heights to which he ultimately climbed.

But the account which Dante gives in the prose-passages of the *Vita Nuova* of the manner in which he conceived and wrote the *canzone*, satisfying as it does all the conditions of credibility, enables us to enjoy a glimpse of the manner in which the poet obeyed his inspirations and went to work. After the first intuition, which was the result of hard toil, the basic idea was slowly elaborated in the poet's imagination until the verses began to trickle forth of their own accord ('my tongue spoke as though prompted by some innate power'). Then he would meditate afresh until his material fired his brain and enabled his hand to transcribe, so to say, what was by now written in the book of his memory. It took him a long time to elaborate an idea in his imagination, but he wrote quickly.

The second stanza of the *canzone*, containing God's answer to the angel who had entreated Him to summon Beatrice to heaven ('Diletti miei'), has provided several reputable critics with grounds for wondering whether they should not see in it the original germ of the *Comedy*. I do not think their view is correct, and among the various interpretations placed upon those tortured lines the one to which I still pin my faith is D'Ancona's, the more so if it is correlated with lines 29–42 of the *canzone* 'Lo doloroso amor'. But even if it be denied that we should see in this stanza the ultimate and original germ of the *Comedy*, we ought to note how Dante's spirit, albeit unconsciously, embarks on the journey that ends with this work. Dante's imagination knows no bounds, and he transports the scene of action to whatever sphere necessity demands—whether it be earth, paradise or hell. Hence a knowledge of what has been written on the subject, even if a number of critics in their desire to read too much between the lines have erred in the direction of excessive subtlety, is always useful if one desires, as one always should, to grasp the problem in all its aspects. The student should persuade himself—and for that reason I can never labour the subject too much—that the solution of a problem never carries conviction unless one is aware of the process by which it has been reached.

After the *canzone* 'Donne ch'avete' the development of the figure of Beatrice follows its logical course: eulogy of her ever-increasing spiritual beauty; her death, or rather her transition from earth to heaven; the poet's grief, in the midst of which, however, he derives comfort from the thought that she has grown rich in spiritual beauty. By now the sight of Beatrice is for the poet a sight of heaven.

Military Interlude—Campaldino and Caprona

It would, however, be a grave error, while on the subject of Beatrice, to think that Dante's whole life was given up to love. Side by side with the poet's imaginative life was his life as a citizen, which, as we shall see, was soon to claim his attention. For the moment there was the life of a gentleman, for the young man continued to frequent gay society, and there was the obligation to perform military service. As early as a year or so before the death of Beatrice we find him taking part in the Battle of Campaldino (June 11th, 1289) against the Aretines, and shortly afterwards in the siege of Caprona, where his adversaries were the Pisans. Evidence of the first-named episode is furnished by a letter, written by Dante himself to the Government of Florence during the first years of his exile, in which he proudly claims credit for having fought on behalf of the Guelf Commune—in the front rank. Nor can we doubt the authenticity of the letter even though it has been lost, for Leonardo Bruni solemnly declares that he saw it. Again, as regards the question of whether Dante took part in the siege of Caprona, he himself asserts that he did so in the *Comedy* (*Inf.*, XXI, 91–6), and hence there is no reason for doubt.

The Donna Gentile

With the figure and the problem of Beatrice are linked the figure and the problem of the *donna gentile*—one of the most difficult problems in Dante. Its solution would throw light on one of the most obscure episodes and one of the gravest spiritual crises in Dante's life. But neither the far-fetched inferences of Pietrobono nor the analytical simplicity of Barbi carry conviction. Here, as with Beatrice, to form an opinion of our own we are bound to draw a distinction. We must distinguish between what Dante says in his poems and what he tells us about the matter in the prose-passages of the *Vita Nuova* and the *Convivio*. The prose came later—in the case of the *Convivio* much later. Moreover, in each case it tends to transform the truth—in the *Vita Nuova*, following a sudden intuition of the 'wondrous vision', and in the *Convivio*, as a result of the new and pressing exigency arising from the poet's exile. It must be added that the two accounts do not tally, and are therefore suspect. I would say, indeed, that the astronomical data given in the *Convivio* are not included for the purpose of throwing light on the facts.

If, immediately after studying the four sonnets to the merciful lady that are inserted in the *Vita Nuova*, we read the *canzone* 'Voi che 'ntendendo', we feel that we are involved in the same emotional situation. It is a situation which continues to develop logically, and which is accordingly dramatized in the conflict between the persistent recollection of the beloved dead and the fresh attachment that grows deeper every day. Not all the shrewd skill in the use of allegory which Dante exhibits in the *Convivio* avails to convince the reader that while the dead woman preserves her identity, the merciful lady, at the very moment when she dominates her lover's heart most completely, has dissolved into a philosophical abstraction.

'Voi che 'ntendendo', therefore, is not, as has been asserted, the first of the philosophical *canzoni*—even if the philosophical studies in which he was at this period engaged are reflected in its form—but the first of the poems in which Dante, dramatizing the conflict in his soul, unyieldingly affirms his love. Later, therefore, when the conflict was renewed, to be resolved with the triumph of

Beatrice, the poet, conscious of the 'travail' that he had endured in loving that woman so deeply, if not of his error in believing that she loved him, was able to assert that his song of love for her began with that *canzone*:

> *Parole mie che per lo mondo siete,*
> *Voi che nasceste poi ch'io cominciai*
> *A dir per quella donna in cui errai*
> *'Voi che 'ntendendo il terzo ciel movete'.*[1]

And if 'erred' is not an appropriate word to indicate the travail of love, it does at all events signify an error due to a woman, and to her alone. Philosophy does not come into the question. How can Dante have erred in this instance? In a theoretical way? So far as we know he did not fall into any error of this kind. By showing an excessive love for science? This over-indulgence was only to reveal itself in the *Convivio*, that is at least ten years later, and then it was praised as a virtue, not decried as an error. The philosophical poetry cannot therefore have begun with the *canzone* 'Voi che 'ntendendo', and the fact that it is impossible to offer a philosophical interpretation of the 'error' is the best proof of the fact. If the sonnet alluded to an error of such a kind it would be incomprehensible that the lover's feelings should have undergone such changes that, a few days later, enticed by heaven knows what hope, he should have been able to repudiate, so to say, words that had escaped his lips in an hour of sadness and unease, and that he should have desired to return to the lady, having cast her aside the day before, flattering her now, and desiring her always. Such a state of mind is characteristic of a lover, not of a philosopher.

We too, however, should be falling into error if we claimed to have solved the problem of the *donna gentile*. In order to find something like a credible solution we ought at least to make sure which poems really were written in her honour. Opinions differ widely. Some scholars limit them to the few contained in the *Vita Nuova* and the *Convivio* and one or two more, while others lump these together with the verses written in honour of the *pargoletta* and

---

[1] 'My words, that echo throughout the world, you that *were born* after I began to say in honour of that lady *on whose account I erred*: "You who through your understanding move the Third Heaven".'

even with those inspired by Madonna Pietra. This is obviously going too far.

As to the lady's identity all conjectures are idle since the poet has not even mentioned her name. Hence all the hypotheses suggested by the various critics—Gemma Donati, Matelda, etc.—are without foundation, and the student may freely leave them out of account.

Rather should we try to see whether we can fix the period at which 'Voi che 'ntendendo' was written. Since Dante causes Charles Martel to mention it to him in the *Paradiso* (VIII, 36-7), it is usually connected with their encounter during the early months of 1294 in Florence, whither Charles had come to meet his father and mother on their return from France. There is, however, nothing to prove that the *canzone* must have been composed at that precise time and not rather several months before. Dante was surrounded by the glamour that attaches to a love-poet, and such a powerful expression of the conflict between his affection for a dead woman and a new love must have made him even more interesting to the young prince, who had been brought up in the gay intellectual tradition of Provence. Of all the poems that he ultimately composed it was certainly the most original, and it must surely have been read or recited to the prince as a love-poem—a fresh proof, if it were needed, that the philosophical allegory is a belated accretion.

At all events the problem of the *donna gentile* is one of the most important for the reconstruction of Dante's life, and its solution depends on nothing less than the interpretation placed upon the group of poems which refer to this episode. Philology in that case proves to be an indispensable factor in our historical reconstruction and aesthetic appreciation.

The Return to Beatrice—The Vita Nuova

The struggle between the living and the dead ended, as is well known, in the victory of the dead. This is understandable. We do not know the reasons for Dante's estrangement from the *donna gentile*, but we do know that, although she moved Dante to write poetry, she did not awake in him any higher inspiration. The loftiest of all these poems, 'Voi che 'ntendendo', is an expression of the conflict and is at bottom inspired by the dead Beatrice. The poems that Dante wrote during this period did not furnish him with the inspiration he needed in order to attain those heights to which his soul aspired—we can see this when he transforms them by the use of allegory into a glorification of philosophy—nor did they excel in their formal qualities those written in honour of Beatrice. Had they done so, the poet would probably have dismissed Beatrice from his mind. It was not to be, and Beatrice returned to be the fount of Dante's inspiration and of his poetry. What brought him back to her was his infinite dissatisfaction with his art and his longing to reach the heights.

The return to Beatrice thus signalizes a peak of creative fervour which hitherto Dante had never attained. The rebirth of his spirit is expressed in the sonnet 'Oltre la spera che più larga gira'. The lugubrious sonnets 'Lasso! per forza di molti sospiri' and 'Deh peregrini che pensosi andate' may have been written even before the return to Beatrice, being as they are an expression of his grief at her death. 'Oltre la spera' marks the resumption of a train of thought of which there had been indications several times already: the desire of the Blessed to have Beatrice among their number; her virtue, which fills the eternal Lord God with wonder, so that He summons this vessel of salvation into His presence; her transformation into a symbol of great spiritual beauty, to which all the Blessed do honour, with the result that her zealot has but one desire—to die, so that he may join her. This mood, epitomized in the second stanza of 'Voi che 'ntendendo', is recaptured in 'Oltre la spera', where it is expressed in all its implications: Beatrice among the angels in heaven, in the presence of God, and the spirit of the poet exalted by a new understanding into her company. It is the beginning of a new style of poetry—a new state of grace in which all the untried forces of the past flow once more in the poet's veins, magnified by his overriding need to persuade himself and others that he had always loved one woman and one woman only, and that this one woman had been and was Beatrice. The idea is all-embracing, and the fictions beloved of the troubadours make the task simpler. Beatrice takes on new lines, more slender, more virginal. She is no longer merely Woman exalted to angelic status; she is, if the expression may be allowed, a communicator of that status, because she raises her lover to the region inhabited by the beings that are elect of God. Hence the religious, and at times mystical, tone of the book in which Dante assembles his experiences, and the simplicity of style that springs from it and is in complete harmony with it. Because of this he must have written the book when in a state of almost mystical exaltation, as well as in a short space of time.

But when? The old view that he wrote it in 1300 is now hopelessly discredited, and no one to-day would wish to revive it. It was based on a reading (*Vita Nuova*, XL, 1) which has now been proved false. Nor, for that matter, has any support been forthcoming for the view, so vehemently maintained by Luigi Pietrobono, that after making a first draft the poet essayed a second, the present one, carrying out considerable alterations, especially towards the end; for not more than one draft of the little book has ever been discovered. However, there is one point in Pietrobono's thesis which still holds good—namely that the return to Beatrice marks a turning-point in Dante's spiritual life, and that thereafter the celebration of other loves was an impossibility—their *celebration*, I mean: the possibility of other loves in real life was not ruled out. It is to Pietrobono's credit that he saw this and demonstrated the significance of the *donna gentile* in Dante's life. The poet barely alludes to the episode, yet it developed into a dramatic struggle and a spiritual crisis fraught with decision.

The view most commonly held assigns the work to the years 1292–3, and there is certainly no lack of arguments in favour of this assumption. But to accept such a date one would have to admit that 'Voi che 'ntendendo' was written after the *Vita Nuova*—in other words that Dante's heart may have been rent by the conflict here described after his return to Beatrice, which seems absurd. After the *Vita Nuova* there could no longer be a place for the *donna gentile* in Dante's heart. I therefore think that the date should be put forward to 1294. At all events, when Dante entered political life in 1295 it had already been written.

Those who are content merely with aesthetic enjoyment have only to abandon themselves to the pleasure of reading the book, satisfied to live again the artistic reality that is created in its pages.

And there is no objection to such a course. But the student who would appreciate to the full a work like the *Vita Nuova* should distinguish the elements which have gone to its making. In other words, he should distinguish between the historical truth of some of those elements and the transformation to which others have had to be subjected so that they may blend with them. This is no freak of fancy, but the submission of reality to the fiction of a Beatrice who had been in sympathy with the poet ever since he was nine years old, and who from that day forth was sole mistress of his heart. Several poems which could not be fitted into the story were therefore summarily rejected. The sonnet 'Guido, i' vorrei' is an outstanding example. In the artistic fiction women who had in actual fact been wooed and extolled underwent, if the expression may be allowed, a change of role and, just as in the poetry of the troubadours, became a screen for the truth or means by which the poet could conceal from the profane his love for Beatrice.

Other poems which lent themselves more readily to Dante's requirements were forced to say what in point of fact they did not mean. So much is clear from the very first sonnet. Originally it was a general address by the young poet to his brother artists on the theme of the heart that is devoured. This theme, which occurs frequently in the culture of the troubadours, lent itself to a variety of interpretations, and in the little book it is made to signify the mysterious, fatal quality of Dante's love for Beatrice. And it is easy to convince oneself that the meaning has been forced when one passes from the verse with its vagueness to the prose with its far deeper meaning.

Hence the importance of the prose. Interpreting and sometimes altering the meaning of the verse, it forms, with a sprinkling of poems, written at various periods, a united whole, on which its fresh tone confers an unmistakable semblance of originality. For just as the poet altered the meaning at the beginning of the work and interpreted it in the middle, making the facts conform to his plans—as with the date of Beatrice's death—so he altered it at the end.

It would be ingenuous to believe that the battle between the old love and the new for the merciful lady lasted only 'a few days' and ended merely because of 'a vivid picture' which formed in his mind of Beatrice as a child. Dante looked before everything to the aims of his art. The central figure in this new glorification was to be Beatrice, and Beatrice alone. In a nutshell, Dante's experience with the *donna gentile* was broadly similar to Manzoni's with the figure of the Nun of Monza. Logic would have prescribed for her character that fuller development which it was accorded in the first draft. But such a development conflicted with that of the novel because it created a second novel within it. Apart from moral considerations, therefore, Manzoni obeyed his shrewd artistic intuition and suppressed the second part of his narrative, condensing it—and so affording a glimpse of its further development—into a phrase: *La sventurata rispose.*[1] So it is in Dante, as we see from the similarly abrupt break in the narrative just when it was on the point of reaching its full development. Artistically, the episode regarded as a separate entity suffered from this break, but the book as a whole profited, because if the episode had been further developed on any large scale the reader's attention would have been distracted from the person in whose honour the book was written. Thus the episode of the merciful lady was in the event accorded scarcely more prominence than that of the *donne dello schermo*. Historical truth suffered in the process, but artistic truth profited. If we forget that where Dante is telling his own story he is above all an artist who is prepared to sacrifice factual truth to the truth that he creates in his poetry, not only do we fail to comprehend his work, but there is a danger that we may not understand his life.

The simplicity of the form is such that many readers overlook the studied art of the writer. His culture at the time when he wrote was not so slight as some have thought; we see the poet striving to ally himself to the classical writers and to enter, so to say, the ranks of the classical poets. It is necessary to study the lines along which his genius developed: the traditional elements and the new element which gradually develops out of them and becomes independent of them. As regards the prose—the habit of repeating certain words, the position accorded to certain members of the sentence—the ability to analyse it enables one to picture the

[1] The unfortunate replied.

author's schooling in the *Artes dictandi*, and from occasional allusions one gathers that he has already embarked on his philosophical studies. The horizon broadens. The poet reveals a fondness for subtleties of expression, and seeks analogies which it requires an effort on our part to grasp. Critics who have tried to follow them up—for example, those relating to the architecture of the physical organism—have merely exaggerated tendencies which Dante himself exhibits. It is more profitable to seek resemblances to contemporary poets—and not merely to Guido—always with the object of fully elucidating the text. As regards the first sonnet it is well to know the three replies to it that have come down to us, even the vulgar, derisive one from the aged Dante da Maiano.

The same remark applies to the *canzone* 'Donne ch'avete'. There has come down to us a *canzone*—'Ben aggia l'amoroso e dolce core'—written in the name of the women to whom that poem was addressed. Some have even contrived to attribute this *canzone* to Dante himself, but neither he nor Guido Cavalcanti wrote it. Just as it is impossible to read the chapter (XXIX) on the day and year of Beatrice's death without reverting to the analogy with Alfragano drawn by Toynbee, who proves in a conclusive manner the day and even the hour of her passing, so we should read the consolatory poem written by Cino da Pistoia to comfort his friend ('Avegna ched el m'aggia più per tempo'). And when we come to his description of 'his abject life' following the death of his most gentle lady, it is fitting that we should contrast Guido's sonnet, 'I' vegno il giorno a te 'nfinite volte', which throws so much light on that period of profound dejection. If we desire to account for everything we must neglect nothing—not even the sonnet 'Dante Allaghier, Cecco il tuo servo e amico', by Cecco Angiolieri, who tries to catch him in the act of contradicting what he had asserted in the final tercet of the sonnet 'Oltre la spera'.

The last chapter of the *Vita Nuova* has been the subject of much discussion, and scholars have been at pains to inquire into the nature of the 'wondrous vision' which inspired the poet with the resolve to write no more of that most gentle lady until he was able to do so in a worthy manner. It was, one appreciates, the

D

original seed from which the *Comedy* sprang; but in saying this we have said all. If we wonder whether that seed should be sought in Beatrice's appearance in the Earthly Paradise or whether, basing our reasoning on the sonnet 'Oltre la spera', we should not rather look for it in the scene that is set in the Empyrean, we are certainly indulging in a curious form of inquiry, but not one that can yield any definite result. By which I do not mean that our time is entirely wasted if, even as we complete the inquiry, we remember that its scope is limited and content ourselves with noticing the vaguely relevant notions which take shape in the poet's unconscious mind and which one day, perhaps, will reach their full development in his masterpiece.

For the precise moment when Dante discovered Beatrice, and the first poems of which she is the subject, see COSMO, *Vita di Dante*, Chap. II, expressly entitled 'La scoperta di Beatrice'. The verse writings that should be ascribed to the period of the *Vita Nuova* and are not included in it have been assembled in the edition of Dante's *Opere* sponsored by the Società dantesca. This edition also contains the verses which various poets exchanged with Dante.

As regards the figure of Beatrice it is a good thing to read I. DEL LUNGO's essay, *Beatrice nella vita e nella poesia del secolo XIII* (Milan, Hoepli, 1891), completing the picture of the historical background with the same author's *La donna fiorentina del buon tempo antico* (Florence, Bemporad, 1906). This volume also contains a reprint of the essay on Beatrice.

As regards the 'trustworthy' person who provided Boccaccio with his information about Beatrice see BARBI's article in *Studi danteschi*, I (1920), pp. 148–55, reprinted in *Problemi*, II, pp. 415–20. See also DAVIDSOHN, 'Beatrice, Simone und Musciattino de' Bardi', in *Deutsches Dante-Jahrbuch*, I (1928), pp. 12 *sq.*

For Beatrice's father see DEL LUNGO, op. cit., pp. 1–12 and 107–38.

For the *canzone* 'E' m'incresce di me sì duramente' see BARBI's article in *Bullettino della Società dantesca italiana*, XI (1904), pp. 5–6 (now reproduced in *Problemi*, I, pp. 32–3). For a contrary view see PIETROBONO's article, 'Se la canzone di Dante "E' m'incresce ..." si possa ritenere scritta per Beatrice', in *Giornale dantesco*,

XXIX (1926), pp. 53–6, and XXXVII (1936), pp. 27–63; but consult BARBI's article in *Studi danteschi*, XIX (1935), pp. 97–116 (now reproduced in *Problemi*, II, pp. 253 *sq.*).

For the *canzone* 'Lo doloroso amor che mi conduce' see BARBI, *Bullettino della Società dantesca italiana*, IV (1896), p. 9; X (1903), p. 98; *Problemi*, II, p. 263.

The *canzone* 'Donne ch'avete' has naturally given rise to a great deal of discussion, especially as regards the second stanza. A summary of the various opinions expressed has been furnished by Melodia on pp. 140–6 of his edition. See besides the 'Indice decennale' (1893–1903) of the *Bullettino della Società dantesca italiana*, p. 143, and BARBI, *Problemi*, I, pp. 107–9.

For the *canzone* 'Ben aggia l'amoroso e dolce core'—written in reply to 'Donne ch'avete'—which Salvadori (*La poesia giovanile e la canzone d'amore di Guido Cavalcanti*, Rome, 1895, pp. 76 *sq.*) and Federzoni (*Studi e diporti danteschi*, Bologna, Zanichelli, 1902) wrongly insisted on ascribing to Dante, see BARBI, *Problemi*, I, pp. 109–12. The last-mentioned passage also contains observations on and corrections to Federzoni's 'shrewd and valuable' commentary.

Next see BARBI's article, 'A proposito delle cinque canzoni del Vaticano 3793 attribuite a Dante', in *Studi danteschi*, X (1925), pp. 5–42, now reproduced in *Problemi*, II, pp. 277–304.

The literature—to use the customary term—on the *dolce stil novo* is extremely copious. CORDIÉ's book, *Dolce stil novo* (Milan, Bianchi Giovini, 1942) contains a most detailed bibliography, dealing not only with the problem in general but with the individual poets referred to in the volume. Here I will content myself with drawing attention to V. ROSSI's 'Il dolce stil novo', in *Le opere minori di Dante* ('Lectura Dantis'), Florence, Sansoni, 1930, I, pp. 9–90; F. FIGURELLI's *Il dolce stil novo*, Naples, Ricciardi, 1933 (cf. CASELLA, *Studi danteschi*, XVIII (1933), pp. 103–26); and PARODI's 'Il dolce stil nuovo', in *Poesia e storia nella Divina Commedia*, Naples, Perrella, 1921, pp. 211–29.

As regards the philosophy that informs the poetry of these writers the student may now consult B. NARDI, 'Filosofia dell'amore nei rimatori italiani del Duecento e in Dante', in *Dante e la cultura medievale*, Bari, Laterza, 1942, pp. 1–88.

The foremost edition of the *Vita Nuova*, to which reference should constantly be made, is *La Vita Nuova di Dante Alighieri* (critical edition prepared by M. BARBI, Florence, Bemporad, 1932). It contains a description of the manuscripts, a classification of the different texts, an estimate of previous editions, and a discussion on the book's orthography and language. The first edition of Barbi's work was published at Florence in 1907. For the editions of the *Vita Nuova* see also MAMBELLI, *Gli annali delle edizioni dantesche* (already cited), pp. 229–56. These editions are numerous, and mainly intended for school use. I would first of all mention D'ANCONA's, Pisa, Nistri, 1884 (and in this connection D'OVIDIO's 'La Vita Nuova ed una recente edizione di essa', in *Nuova Antologia*, March 15th, 1884, reprinted in *L'ultimo volume dantesco*, Rome, 1926 (Vol. V of the *Opere* of FRANCESCO D'OVIDIO), and R. RENIER's article in *Giornale storico della letteratura italiana*, II (1883), pp. 366–94, are still worth consulting); CASINI's (Florence, Sansoni, 1885), because of the many comparisons made with ancient texts (this edition has now been brought up to date by Pietrobono (ib., 1932), although he has given it a different colouring); and MELODIA's (Milan, Vallardi, 1905). For our purposes the editions prepared by SCHERILLO (Milan, Hoepli, 1911), GUERRI (Naples, Perrella, 1922) and SAPEGNO (Florence, Vallecchi, 1931) are also worth consulting. The first-named is especially valuable for the analogies that it points in Provençal texts. The student should also read the prefaces to the editions of Guerri and Sapegno.

Referring to Beatrice, Mazzoni made the following excellent observation: 'At this time of day denial of the reality of Beatrice is an expression of would-be scepticism rather than of a reasonable doubt.' Yet it is an advantage to have a clear idea of the whole question. There is a lucid résumé of the various interpretations (symbolistic, idealistic, realistic) which have been offered of the figure of Beatrice in MOORE, *Studies in Dante*, Oxford, Clarendon Press, 1889, II, pp. 79–151. Concise summaries are also to be found in the *Discorso su Beatrice* which forms the introduction to D'ANCONA's edition (pp. xxv–xli) and in PICCIOLA's 'La Vita Nuova' ('Le opere minori di Dante,' in *Lectura Dantis*, Florence, Sansoni, 1906, pp. 118 *sq.*). Of those works in which the symbolistic theories are upheld, *La Beatrice svelata* by F. Perez (Palermo, 1865) deserves to be read: this writer saw in Beatrice the personification of the active intellect. The allegorical fantasies of Mandonnet are confuted by E. Gilson, *Dante the Philosopher* (tr. D. C. Moore), London, Sheed & Ward, 1948, Chap. I. The idealistic interpretation has been upheld principally by A. Bartoli in the fourth volume of his history, *La nuova lirica toscana*, which still deserves to be read also for its observations on the poets who were contemporary with Dante. Bartoli is supported strongly by R. Renier in *La Vita Nuova e la Fiammetta*, Turin, Loescher, 1879, and with even greater effect in a large number of reviews published in his *Giornale storico*.

As regards the allegorist thesis E. V. Zappia's *Studi sulla Vita Nuova: Della questione di Beatrice* (Rome, Loescher, 1904) is 'deserving of special consideration'. Apropos of this book the student should see Barbi's article, 'La questione di Beatrice', in *Bullettino della Società dantesca italiana*, XII (1905), pp. 204–23, now reproduced in *Problemi*, I, pp. 113–32, and also the reviews of the books by C. Grasso and A. Scrocca contained in an appendix (pp. 132–9). In addition, there are reviews of those by Scarano and Gargano Cosenza in *Bullettino della Società dantesca italiana*, X (1903), pp. 413–4.

All the books cited refer in general terms to the real and imaginary elements in the *Vita Nuova*; but see especially L. Pietrobono, 'Realtà e idealità nella Vita Nuova', in *Giornale dantesco*, XLII (1941), pp. 107–18, and Bertoni, 'La Vita Nuova,' in *Nuova Antologia*, CDXV (1941), pp. 254–63.

The *donne dello schermo* are discussed by E. Sicardi, 'Amore e schermi d'amore nell'antica poesia', in *Nuova Antologia*, April 1st, 1909.

As regards the vein of mysticism which runs through the book see Pascoli, *La mirabile visione*, Messina, Muglia, 1902; G. Salvadori, *Sulla vita giovanile di Dante*, Rome, Società Dante Alighieri, 1906; A. Marigo, *Mistica e scienza nella Vita Nuova di Dante*, Padua, Drucker, 1914; Pietrobono, *Il Poema sacro*, Bologna, Zanichelli, 1915; Barbi, 'Razionalismo e misticismo in Dante', in *Studi danteschi*, XVII (1933), pp. 6–44 and XXI (1937), pp. 5–91, now included in *Problemi*, II, pp. 1–86. For Pietrobono see also below.

For the date of composition every student should read the old essay by RAJNA, 'Per la data della Vita Nuova e non per essa soltanto', in *Giornale storico della letteratura italiana*, VI (1885), pp. 113–62, and BARBI, *Problemi*, I, pp. 100 *sq.* Even if one cannot subscribe to Pietrobono's thesis one should none the less read 'Intorno alla data delle opere minori', in *Giornale dantesco*, XLII (1941), pp. 45–68. Also by PIETROBONO: 'Il rifacimento della Vita Nuova e le due fasi del pensiero dantesco', in *Giornale dantesco*, XXXV (1934), pp. 1–82, and ib., XXXIV (1933), pp. 113–37, the preface to Casini's larger edition of the *Vita Nuova* brought up to date.

GENERAL STUDIES: The prefaces to their respective editions by Cesareo (Messina, Principato, 1914) and D'Ancona; PASCOLI, *La mirabile visione*, Messina, Muglia, 1902; G. PICCIOLA, 'La Vita Nuova di Dante Alighieri', in 'Lectura Dantis', *Le opere minori*, Florence, Sansoni, 1906, pp. 118 *sq.*; SCHERILLO, 'La Vita Nuova', in *Dante*, Milan, Treves, 1921; SHAW, *Essays on the Vita Nuova*, Princeton, 1930 (see *Studi danteschi*, XV (1931), pp. 111–6); BIONDOLILLO, *Il problema critico della Vita Nuova*, Palermo, Trimarchi, 1932 (cf. *Giornale storico della letteratura italiana* (1932), pp. 298–9). There are some useful observations in L. SPITZER's *Bemerkungen zu Dantes Vita Nuova* (*Publications de la Faculté des Lettres de l'Université d'Istanbul*, II, Istanbul, 1937, pp. 162–208); see *Studi danteschi*, XXV (1940), pp. 189–92. As regards the design of the *Vita Nuova* (argument, poetry, apportionment of material), see P. RAJNA, 'Lo schema della Vita Nuova', in *Biblioteca scuole italiane*, June 1st, 1890; the same author's 'Per le divisioni della Vita Nuova', in *Strenna dantesca*, Florence, 1902; CRESCINI, *Giornale storico della letteratura italiana*, XXXII (1898), pp. 463–4.

On the symmetrical arrangement of the poems, which had already been noticed by Norton in his translation of the *Vita Nuova*, Boston, 1867 (v. SCARTAZZINI, *Enciclopedia*, II, pp. 2159–60), see the article by J. EARLE in the *Biblioteca storico-critica*, edited by Papa and Passerini, Bologna, Zanichelli, 1899; but cf. MAZZONI, *Bullettino della Società dantesca italiana*, VI (1899), pp. 57–63.

See also pp. 467 *sq.* in Scherillo's edition. For imitations of the Provençal poets see SCHERILLO, 'Alcune fonti provenzali della Vita Nuova', in *Atti R. Acc. archeol. lett. e belle arti*, Società Reale di Napoli, XIV (1889–90), pp. 201–316; SCARANO, 'Fonti provenzali e italiane della lirica petrarchesca', in *Studj di filologia romanza*, VIII (1901), pp. 250–360; SANTANGELO, *Dante e i trovatori provenzali*, Catania, Giannotta, 1921.

As regards the language of the *Vita Nuova* and the structure of the prose see Chap. V of Barbi's Introduction to his critical edition and the notes written to justify the text preferred (*v.* the special index). Also useful as an aid to forming an idea of the studies that should be undertaken if one desires to fathom the problem is Barbi's long note on p. cclxxx, which indicates a large number of texts with which it is convenient to be familiar. A good foundation is provided by SCHIAFFINI's book, *Testi fiorentini del Dugento e dei primi del Trecento*, Florence, Sansoni, 1926. Next consult LISIO, *L'arte del periodo nelle opere volgari di Dante Alighieri e del secolo XIII*, Bologna, Zanichelli, 1902 (cf. PARODI, *Bullettino della Società dantesca italiana*, X (1902), pp. 57 *sq.*); BERTONI, 'La prosa della Vita Nuova', in *Poeti e poesie del medio evo*, Modena, Orlandini, 1922; SCHIAFFINI, 'Lo stil nuovo e la "Vita Nuova"', in *Tradizione e poesia*, Genoa, E. Degli Orfini, 1934, pp. 123–53 (2nd Ed., Rome, *Edizioni di Storia e Letteratura*, 1943).

On Dante's culture at the time when he wrote the *Vita Nuova* see P. CHISTONI, *La seconda fase del pensiero dantesco*, Leghorn, Giusti, 1903; but cf. BARBI, *Problemi*, I, pp. 87 *sq.*

V

PREPARING THE WAY FOR THE *DIVINE COMEDY*

DANTE's resolve to write of his lady 'what had never been said of any woman' required a preparation all the longer and more persistent in that, for the moment, he felt inadequate to obey his new intuition. He did not on that account despair of translating it into action; indeed, he made up his mind 'to study with all his might' in order to succeed. Now what form did his studies take? Or, in other words, along what road did Dante pass on his journey from the *Vita Nuova* to the *Comedy*? If we are to explain the workings of his mind it is clearly necessary for us to pass along that road in our turn.

Unfortunately the projected inventory of Dante's so-called library, i.e. of the books that he used for the formation of his culture, has not yet been compiled. Nevertheless, we can repeat nearly enough the procedure which he adopted. His studies were essentially of a philosophical and artistic order, and the second category naturally includes his efforts to acquire the technical skill which he felt he needed if he was to obey to the letter the intuition that had flashed before his mind.

So far as philosophy is concerned he himself informs us that he habitually attended 'the schools of the monks and the disputations of the philosophers', and he tells of the progress which, 'in perhaps thirty months', he made in these studies. The schools and the philosophical circles which he must have frequented were three in number: the academies of Santa Croce, Santa Maria Novella, and probably also Santo Spirito.

At Santa Croce he lived among the Franciscans. Pier Giovanni Olivi and Ubertino da Casale had recently given up teaching, but their names were on all men's lips. At Santa Maria the philosophy of St. Thomas was taught by the new star of the Dominican Order, Friar Remigio Girolami. The two philosophies differed, for while the one clung with particular tenacity to the word of Augustine and through him went back to Plato, the proudest boast of the other was to have christianized Aristotle and put him at the service of Catholic theology. Although while he lived among the friars of Santa Croce Dante became imbued with Franciscan sentiments, learning to regard St. Francis as the ideal saint of Christianity and to dream of the Church's return to the evangelic era, philosophically he was never a Franciscan. His was a systematic mind that sought lucidity in all things, and the intellectual vacillations of Bonaventure and Alexander of Hales could not entirely satisfy him. At the most he could derive from them, as he did, so much as he felt might prove helpful to his art and to the purpose by which he was guided. The development of his speculative faculty was influenced in a more positive way by the philosophy of St. Thomas, but he was not committed to it so inexorably as to be unable to tap other sources besides. The common element in the teachings of scholasticism passed into his understanding through the refining fires of Thomism, but he opened his mind to all the spiritual tendencies of his age and subordinated them all to the requirements of his art. A familiarity with these tendencies is thus absolutely indispensable to the Dantologist, and I can never urge the young student emphatically enough to acquire as complete a grasp of the poet's thought as he can. The history, the philosophy and the language of the period should be his three main subjects of study. The more thoroughly he understands these the more thoroughly will he succeed in understanding Dante.

When I speak of spiritual tendencies I naturally include in the term the trend of theology. Theology is the greatest achievement of the medieval mind, and is itself a philosophy of the soul. It is, if the expression may be allowed, the 'dialectization' of God, but God is found first and foremost in the soul. In Dante's thought philosophy, theology and religion are welded together in indissoluble unity. It may be that at this precise period he understood the first of the three elements better than the other two; but from philosophy he proceeded logically to theology, and from both to an unfailing comprehension of the value in life of the religious element. To this comprehension his contact, now and later, with the Franciscans must have contributed in no small measure. It is, however, impossible to indicate the different stages clearly. As we progress in our inquiry we may be led to distinguish between them, at any rate vaguely. At all events, if we wish to understand we shall do well from now on to study as exhaustively as possible all the prevalent philosophical, theological and religious tendencies of the century.

It is obvious that the critical expositions to be found in the best histories of philosophy largely serve this purpose. But it would be a mistake to think that they can suffice. All who wish to enter into the spirit of medieval speculation should study these expositions in conjunction with some of the supreme works of the great philosophers—St. Thomas and St. Bonaventure especially. If we rely, as some have done, on the analytical indexes to those works, and in particular to the *Summa Theologica* of Thomas Aquinas, with the object of singling out points of resemblance to the *Comedy*, we may fall into grave error. One could cite many cases in which even the foremost critics have been guilty in this respect. At the present stage the study of the *Convivio* may prove the best introduction to such an inquiry.

It was during this period that Dante wrote the so-called philosophical poems, the composition of which extended over several years. No edition with adequate notes is yet available. Barbi did not have the satisfaction of bringing his own commentary on the *Canzoniere* to completion. Contini's, though better than any other, is more particularly philological in character and —because they did not enter into the design of the work—omits the *canzoni* embodied in the *Convivio*. But it would be a mistake, in studying the philosophical poems, to confine oneself to their speculative content. For the understanding of the man their ethical value is even greater. So much is implicit in the subjects treated and in the poet's melancholy, not to say his grief, at the decay of those moral virtues which he regarded as the crown of life. Thus, with the glorification of these lofty moral values, the poet began that secular ministry which later was to become the supreme object of his art and of his life, and which was to attain the dignity of a true apostolate. Unless we bear all these facts and feelings in mind we cannot form a comprehensive picture of the man.

But Dante was above all a poet. It was therefore natural that he should concentrate even more on the study of his art, which he was for ever fashioning on the model of the classical and the Provençal poets, and on the artistic experiments which they suggested to his mind. Just as the *Convivio* is the key to his philosophical researches, so the study of the *De Vulgari Eloquentia* may provide a clue to his researches in the artistic field. The *De Vulgari* was, it is true, written at an age when the mellowing effect of the years and of exile was making itself felt on the spirit of the writer, but the study of the poets was his daily occupation from early youth, and during this period it was absorbing all his energies. First, naturally, came the Latin poets, with Virgil at their head, as being the unrivalled masters of their art. But among the Provençal troubadours whom he studied during this period Gerard de Bornello and Arnaud Daniel must have held an important place. He felt the need to adapt his art to the expression of everything, philosophical thought as well as shades of feeling, and above all to the representation of the most varied aspects of a given situation.

As a result he wrote the *canzoni* in honour of Madonna Pietra. Some have seen in them the eruption of a feeling that could not be held in check, of an overwhelming sensuality which merely confirms the poet's so-called aberration. With a total disregard for historical accuracy fables have been devised which have no substance outside the imagination of those who invented them. Scholars have attempted to trace the woman in whose honour the poems are supposed to have been written, and if they have overlooked Pietra degli Scrovegni or Dante's own sister-in-law they have unhappily chosen to identify her with the *donna gentile* and even, in open violation of chronology, with the lady of the so-called mountain *canzone*. Worse still, out of regard for a certain sense of propriety with which they have credited the poet, some have chosen to invest the *canzoni* with an allegorical significance. Such idle fancies have resulted from a lack of historical perspective. Set against their proper background, namely the period at which Dante was endeavouring through practice to acquire a more scrupulous proficiency in the art of self-expression, the poems at once look like an effort to portray a situation deliberately sought with the intellect, one that would lend itself to a series of variations on the same theme, so that the task of proving his proficiency would be rendered ever more difficult. Hence we cannot assume that they constitute a biographical document save with extreme reserve. A poet's experiences are often merely a figment of his imagination. Better still, if they may include a few biographical elements as a reminder of past enthusiasms, they are essentially a record of the efforts made by the poet to perfect his art. Literature rather than poetry, the *canzoni* require to be closely studied for their forcefulness of expression—the last of them, since it shows the author's imagination set in motion and excited by this same persistent striving, for the vividness of poetic imagery which it achieves in certain parts.

The same remark applies to the *rime* arbitrarily labelled 'to the *pargoletta*'. These *rime* have little artistic merit, even if there are not lacking occasional strophes in which poetry is achieved. Here one is at times left in doubt as to whether the meaning is literal or whether it is derived from the allegory which may lie beneath the surface. At all events these *rime* are of no importance for the reconstruction of Dante's life, and the fantasies which certain students of the poet have woven around them do not help us to get to know the man. It is even worse to seek a connection between these *rime* and the reproaches which Beatrice levels against the poet in the Earthly Paradise in view of the wholly objective fact that the word *pargoletta* recurs in Beatrice's speech (*Purg.*, XXXI, 58–60). *Pargoletta* is here a general term, a mere synonym for *fanciulla*—even if it has a touch of irony about it— and like *altra vanità* is a singular with a plural function. Rather should we consider the influence of Dante's philosophical studies on his mode of expression even in compositions which have, or seem to have, an amorous purport.

This, then, was for Dante a period of intensive study. It was a period of deliberate preparation for the lofty purpose which was ever before his mind. To speak of this period as though it were one of aberration is nonsense—or rather it is to be misled by what is implied in the fiction which the poet invented when, after the sorrows of his exile, the poem unfolded before his mind in all its grandeur. The action was set in Holy Week, 1300, and at a time when the spirits of so many were revived by the fact that, with the advent of the Jubilee, the waters of grace had been set free, it was logical that the poet should experience a similar feeling of exaltation. The time of the action being what it was, Dante's estrangement from Beatrice following her death, which in the fiction of the *Vita Nuova* had been limited to a few days, was necessarily lengthened into a separation lasting ten years, with a consequent moral aberration on the part of the poet. Conforming to the requirements of his art, Dante slurred over the fact that this period of imaginary aberration coincided with the very years in which by means of the most intensive study he was preparing for the glorification of Beatrice. Inasmuch as his mind was maturing all the while, this preparation continued even when his thoughts might have seemed furthest from her, or at any rate engaged in the glorification of values of a different kind. As for the common belief that there was indeed a period of aberration lasting ten years, this is due to the fact that Dante is a writer of such power that in the reader's mind his word becomes the truth. Indeed, his greatest triumph as an artist consists in the fact that his biographers, that is to say those who should have been able to distinguish the truth more clearly than others, have accepted his artistic invention as reality. Now is the time for the aberration myth to take its proper place as a mere poetic fiction.

The study of Dante's *Canzoniere* presents difficulties of no mean order, yet those who wish to comprehend his spiritual and artistic development should face them courageously in their every aspect. Nor should they confine their inquiry to the poems that are definitely authentic; they should, on the contrary, extend it to all those which Barbi in his edition included among the doubtful ones. Cautious though the distinguished scholar's choice was, we cannot rule out the possibility that further inquiry may establish that some of these were composed by Dante. In any event they all serve to increase our knowledge of the spiritual convictions of the age. And for this very reason the study of Dante's poems should be combined with the study of the poems written by his friends. The latter may indeed provide the information needed for a better understanding of the former. The student should bear in mind Dante's correspondence with Cino da Pistoia.

On Dante's relations with the Franciscans and the Dominicans by reason of his studies see COSMO, *L'ultima ascesa*, Bari, Laterza, 1936, IX, X, XI, and 'Le mistiche nozze di frate Francesco con Madonna Povertà', in *Giornale dantesco*, VI (1898), pp. 49–82, 97–118, *passim*. Also 'Noterelle francescane', in *Giornale dantesco*, VII (1899), pp. 63–70 and IX (1901), pp. 41–9.

For Santo Spirito see U. MARIANI, 'Il "De regimine christiano" di Giacomo da Viterbo', in *Giornale dantesco*, XXVII (1924), pp. 108–21.

For Dante and St. Thomas see P. H. WICKSTEED, *Dante and Aquinas*, London, 1913, and Busnelli's edition of the *Convivio*, which I shall cite in its place. For the reservations which should be made in interpreting Dante's Thomism see NARDI, *Dante e la cultura medievale*, Bari, Laterza, 1942, *passim*, and 'Dante e la filosofia', in *Studi danteschi*, XXV (1940), pp. 5–42; E. GILSON, *Dante the Philosopher* (tr. D. C. Moore), London, Sheed & Ward, 1948. Both critics, however, reveal a tendency to exaggerate.

In the light of the fantastic theories advanced by Imbriani regarding the *canzoni* in honour of Madonna Pietra (*Studi danteschi*, Florence, Sansoni, 1891) see G. DE LISA, *Madonna Pietra*, Pieve di Cadore, 1930; A. MOMIGLIANO, 'La prima delle canzoni pietrose', in *Bullettino della Società dantesca italiana*, XV (1908), pp. 119–32; F. NERI, 'Io son venuto al punto della rota', in *Bulletin italien*, XIV (1914), pp. 93 *sq.*; Sapegno's observations in the preface to his edition of the *Vita Nuova*. For the form of the sestina see G. MARI, *La sestina d'Arnaldo, la terzina di Dante*, Milan, Hoepli, 1899, from the *Rend. Ist. lomb.*, Second Series, Vol. XXXII (1899), pp. 953–85.

A. JEANROY, 'La "sestina doppia" de Dante et les origines de la sextine', in *Romania*, XLII (1913), pp. 481–9.

On the *pargoletta* see D'ANCONA, 'Della pargoletta e di altre donne nel poema di Dante', in *Scritti danteschi*, Florence, Sansoni, 1912; A. ZENATTI, 'Rime per la Pargoletta', 'Di nuovo della Pargoletta e di altre vanità', in *Intorno a Dante*, Palermo, Sandron, 1916; CONTINI, *Rime* (cited above), introduction to the ballad *I' mi son pargoletta*.

On Dante's so-called aberration see BARBI's remarks in *Problemi*, I, pp. 39 and 104; II, pp. 35–9 and 353.

VI

POLITICAL STRIFE

It was during these years of fruitful study, in the course of which his mind was transported to ever loftier planes, that Dante began to take part in the political life of his city, eventually being swallowed up in it completely. The date of his initiation cannot be affirmed with absolute certainty; but since those who did not actually carry on a profession were prohibited before 1295 from taking an active part in the life of the Commune, it is very probable that Dante's participation only began after this ban had been raised, or rather modified, by the extension of the privilege to include those who simply put down their names for a profession. This is all the more likely as we begin to find Dante's name mentioned in the councils of the Commune after that date, but not before it.

It is common knowledge that Dante was enrolled as a member of the guild of doctors and chemists, and in the attempt to discover the reason for this scholars have advanced all sorts of fantastic theories. Now it is agreed that because of the connection between natural and speculative philosophy the right of membership of the medical guild was also accorded to philosophers; and as such, or at least as a student of philosophy, Dante entered his name on the roll. He must also have been gratified by this concession inasmuch as it amounted to a recognition of his studies, and it probably served to justify him in the eyes of Guido, who as a member of the *Grandi* was debarred from joining any guild, and hence from taking any part in political activity.

It is thus necessary for us to trace in the *Codice* the whole story of the man's participation in the life of the Commune. Our evidence consists merely of bare reports of sessions, yet they enable us to see what opinions he expressed and how he voted, and hence to reconstruct in part his inner life. In a city that was divided, nay torn by factions, he too took sides; but the political history of Florence at this stage is so confused that, in the welter of self-interest and feeling that had divided the city's families, it is hard to determine, with any exactitude at least, why and how they formed their various groups. It is therefore anything but easy to account for what Dante thought and did, especially as, if he was moved by loftier motives as well as by economic conditions to side with those who later called themselves *Bianchi*, we should not confuse the high motives which spurred him on with the selfish interests which united the members of that party.

Belonging to the middle class, which had been ruined economically by the imperialistic policy of the powerful bankers and the wealthy merchants, and by the simultaneous growth of a capitalistic economy, he naturally allied himself to the 'worthy commoners', and as day by day he felt the people around him becoming more hostile towards the *nouveau riche* class with its sudden access of wealth, so his resentment and indignation mounted. And one has seen the signs of these feelings in the philosophical *canzoni*.

We must follow the course of events step by step in the writings of the chroniclers, co-ordinating our knowledge with the infinitely more exhaustive researches of modern historians. For us the fundamental point is Dante's priorate, which commenced on June 15th, 1300, because this contains two features which, if one understands history, illuminate the whole of his thought.

On April 18th of the year in question, following their denunciation by Ser Lapo Saltarelli, three citizens of Florence—Black Guelfs and bankers in the Court of Rome—had been sentenced for conspiring against the freedom of their city and against Tuscany. The sentence had aroused the violent anger of Pope Boniface VIII. Now the new *Signoria*, on assuming office, 'acknowledged and confirmed' the sentence. To understand Dante's mind, his conduct while he lived in Florence and his attitude towards the Pope in the *Comedy*, we must at this point examine the figure of Boniface VIII thoroughly, with scholarly rigour and with the balanced judgment of a historian. His is the complex figure of a great man—he was well called the 'noble-minded sinner'—to whom history now accords the deserts which he did not receive from his contemporaries. We must understand the antipathy and the anger with which he inspired the poet, tracing them back to the latter's Franciscan education, to his consequent aversion to theocracy, and to the wrongs that he suffered or thought he suffered at the Pope's hands. But the man's anti-theocratic ideas—from his acceptance of the sentence passed on the conspiring bankers to the whole attitude of hostility to Boniface which he subsequently revealed in Florence, together with the spirit that informs the *Monarchy* and the creation of the Veltro and the Dux, Scipio or whatever one chooses to call him— follow such a logical course of development that if we are to account for it completely we must at this point begin to examine it step by step.

And if we are actually to account for his conduct as a prior— since this was the year of the Jubilee, and there can be no doubt that Dante, like so many of his fellow-citizens, betook himself to Rome—we may logically suppose that his pilgrimage took place before he assumed office. His visit to Rome must have exerted a profound influence on his mind. The historic city was revealed to him in all the grandeur of its monuments and its memories, and it is very likely that this was the point at which he whose up- bringing had included so much philosophical research began his speculations about the history, the realization and the revelation of the thought of God. At the same time the worldly ambitions of Boniface, his posturings as a universal ruler and his crazy ambition must have aroused and fostered all Dante's antipathies to theocracy. And the whole of his work in this regard after his return to Florence is explained.

The study of Boniface's character is thus indispensable as a means to a thorough understanding of Dante's spiritual outlook. And with Boniface VIII we should couple Matteo d'Acquasparta, who was not only the papal envoy and intermediary in Florence, but the expositor and interpreter of his political thought. Dante must have been aware of the dominant role which the Franciscan cardinal played in 'determining the Pope's attitude in matters of doctrine'; and this knowledge likewise contributed to the severity of the judgment he later pronounced on the man who, after being head of the Franciscan Order, strayed so far in his political doctrines from the Franciscan creed.

E

The other fact which serves to reveal the character of the man is his attitude towards Guido Cavalcanti. Guido was his best friend, and it was to him that he had dedicated the *Vita Nuova*. But Guido was of a factious disposition, and when the priors had to pass judgment on those members of the *Grandi* who had attacked the Consuls of the Arts as they were on their way to San Giovanni to make their offerings, Dante felt that if peace was to be restored to the city it was necessary to punish all the rioters, no matter what faction they supported. And so the White Guido was exiled together with the Black Corso Donati. This is typical of Dante. Transcending friendship and party was the love of peace and justice. It was thus that he would one day be able without exaggeration, let alone misrepresentation, to proclaim himself the latter's 'faithful servant' (*Inf.*, II, 97–9).

Correlated along these lines the whole of Dante's activity in Florence and his protests during his exile become intelligible. The *Codice diplomatico* records all the occasions on which he intervened in the councils of the city; but the most important moment was when three times in a day he opposed the granting to Pope Boniface of the aid which he had requested for the prosecution of his war in the Campagna. *Quod de servitio faciendo domino pape nihil fiat*, to quote the unvarnished words of the secretary who recorded the minutes of the sessions. The opposition to the Pontiff's ambitious policy is undisguised: from now on Dante regarded him as the enemy who was disturbing the peace of the city and of the world.

This is not the place for a description of the events which led to the arrival in Florence of Charles of Valois—sent there by the Pontiff as a mediator—and to the resulting fall of the White faction. Did Dante foresee that the hesitant policy of the party, and more especially of the Cerchi, would lead to the city's ruin?

Probably he would have preferred a more resolute policy, particularly in Rome, where Black bankers were working to gain the Pontiff's support. It is common knowledge that at the last moment, when Charles of Valois was advancing on Tuscany, the Commune thought of sending a mission to the Pontiff. Among the three who made up the delegation was Dante. Doubts have been raised as to whether this mission was ever sent, and it has been the subject of much discussion. But Compagni's evidence, the allusion in the *Ottimo* and the account given by the well-informed Leonardo leave no room for doubt in the matter. For the present our best course seems to be to pin our faith on the latter's story.

It is common knowledge that after the first parleys the Pontiff allowed two of the envoys to go, but held Dante. The latter accordingly did not witness the revolution of the Neri, and learned of his sentence only when he was preparing to return to Florence. He must therefore have thought that he had been tricked by Pope Boniface. This conviction, combined with the other reasons, explains the poet's anger towards the Pope.

Having made themselves masters of the Commune the Black revolutionaries, after their first brutal displays of violence, resolved to establish themselves on a legal basis, and in violation of the Orders of justice the mayor was empowered to try the magistrates, who had already given an account of their actions.

The bands of White marauders which in the meantime were overrunning the neighbouring countryside forced the victors to adopt severe measures in order to secure their power. Thus Dante, together with Messer Palmieri Altoviti and two other citizens, was first officially tried in connection with the rumours of which he was the subject—*publica fama referente*—and then sentenced. The sentences published by the mayor should be read at first hand in the *Codice*, or at least in the version of an expert in the language of the period. It is well to study in this way the formalities of the trial, which must certainly have been observed, at least approximately, and the whole course of its development, because the study of the trial also helps us to establish whether or not Dante was in Florence when he was first summoned to appear before the mayor's tribunal. In this matter we should rely on Bruni's narrative, for he was in a better position than anyone else to see the official documents of the Commune and to know how matters went in reality.

According to Bruni, Dante learned of his condemnation at Siena, while he was on his way back from Rome, and the first meeting of the exiles took place in May at Gargonza, a stronghold of the Ubaldini. Early in June, on the 8th, the 'corporals of the party', among them Dante, assembled at San Godenzo in Val di Sieve with the object of inducing the Ubaldini to permit their powerful stronghold of Montaccenico to be used in the war on the Commune. The retaliation of the Neri was no less swift. After the meeting at Gargonza a magistrate was appointed for the specific purpose of trying and taking measures against the political criminals, it was forbidden to 'lend aid to the outlaws', who were guilty of 'fraud and treason', and provision was made for the confiscation of their possessions. Moreover, after San Godenzo they were condemned to death for breaking their bounds (July 21st). The exiles' war on the Commune had a sorry outcome, for in Mugello they were invariably defeated. But we must follow the war's progress in the pages of the chroniclers, and read Flavio Biondo's account of Dante's sojourn in Forlì, if we are to form an idea of the part that he played. In his endeavour to enlist help he visited Bartolomeo della Scala at Verona, and it was very probably the welcome he received at the hands of the Seigneur that induced him, after parting company with his companions, to seek refuge in Verona. There is accordingly no reason why we should not accept the evidence of so authoritative a historian.

For the rest, his frame of mind as he followed the progress of the war and the resulting merciless repression of the Bianchi and the Ghibellines who had remained in Florence, as well as of the prisoners, is revealed by the passage in the *Purgatorio* (XIV, 58–66) in which he brands for all eternity the ferocity of Fulcieri da Calboli, hunter of that 'living flesh'.

As is always the case, the defeats which they had sustained were the cause of bitter dissension among those concerned, and Dante himself tells us that he was forced to part company with his companions. But when did the rift take place? The documents published by Orioli led scholars to think for some time that it occurred at a very early stage. To be sure, Dante's name does not figure among those of the Bianchi who assembled at Bologna; and no account was taken of the fact that there were others who did not do so even though, like him, they were at San Godenzo. As a consequence of this parting it was also denied that Dante was the author of the letter which the University of the Bianchi addressed in 1304 to Cardinal da Prato in connection with his attempts to mediate between the two parties, and also of the one written about that time to Oberto and Guido da Romena on the subject of their uncle Alessandro's death. And it was a logical consequence. On the evidence which he himself provides, the poet's parting from his companions must have been violent: there were recriminations of a most serious kind, and probably swords were unsheathed. The idea that after such a rift Dante may have been charged by the party's University with the task of writing such an important letter on its behalf betokens ignorance of the psychology of these men, and is quite absurd.

We may accept the theory of Zenatti and Barbi that Dante changed in status from ambassador to guest, 'in other words that he returned to Verona after the defeat of Pulicciano, rejoining the other exiles before March, 1304', when the election of Benedict XI 'sufficed to revive the hopes of the Bianchi and the moderate party began to gain the upper hand'; but even this reconstruction of history rules out the theory that the rift had already occurred. It is, I think, more likely that after his mission to Verona Dante returned to Forlì, and that during the period 1303–4 he was in touch with his companions, living in Romagna and Tuscany. This explains his standing among them, and the fact that he was made a member of the Council of their University and was deputed to write the letter to Cardinal da Prato, who had been sent by the new Pontiff to Tuscany as a mediator. Dante had profited much by the lesson of events. After the ill success of the war the only hope lay in the authority of eminent men like the Pontiff and the Cardinal, and for a moment, indeed, it seemed that reconciliation was near. Certainly Dante in his letter poured out the whole of his great spirit. The sentiments that it expresses are so completely in accordance with his character that they are enough to prove its authenticity.

But the peace conflicted with too many feelings and interests, and it did not last. The unhappy outcome of the negotiations provoked fresh discussions; perhaps the idleness that lasted throughout their duration prevented the action which in the view of the more violent spirits would have been decisive. It is likely that Dante advised against it. Although the allusion to the episode in the *Ottimo* is obscure, it lifts the veil on a difference of opinion as regards procedure. The 'horrible disasters' had caused tempers to rise, and from the words of Ser Brunetto in the *Inferno* (XV, 70-5) and of Cacciaguida in the *Paradiso* (XVII, 61-8) we gather what must have been the nature of the rift. When the slaughter of the Lastra occurred Dante was already far from his companions in misfortune; and for a moment this may have afforded him a bitter satisfaction. Matters had gone as he had foreseen. This, I feel, is the reconstruction of events that is authorized by Bruni's narrative, by letters and by the *Ottimo* allusion, but the student should check it point by point. And he should first of all convince himself of the authenticity of the letters to the Romena brothers and the Cardinal, because they form the grounds on which the reconstruction is based. Nor should it be forgotten that in 1304 Francesco Alighieri was in Arezzo, where he was negotiating a loan, very probably in favour of his elder brother. Thus all the factors in the situation tend to support the reconstruction that I am recommending to the attention of the student.

I have used the data provided for the study of this period as material for part of Chap. IV and for Chaps. V, VI and VII of my *Vita di Dante*. I can therefore refer the reader to these passages for fuller explanations.

On the Reform of July 6th, which Dante cannot have suggested—as was supposed by GHERARDI, *Le Consulte della Repubblica fiorentina*, II, p. 470—see BARBI, *Problemi*, I, pp. 141 *sq*. As regards the part played by Dante in the Councils of the People from November, 1295, onwards, the sessions of the Councils and the meetings that he attended, see pp. 141-55 of the same work: Barbi has derived the part that bears more particularly on our researches from Gherardi's *Consulte*.

On Dante's enrolment as a member of the Guild of doctors and chemists see BARBI, *Problemi*, II, pp. 379-84, and SOLMI, *Il pensiero politico di Dante*, Florence, La Voce, 1922; R. CIASCA, 'Dante e l'arte dei medici e speziali', in *Arch. stor. it.*, Series VII, XV (1931), pp. 59-97, but cf. BARBI, *op. cit.*, p. 382, note. The relevant document is in the *Codice diplomatico* (No. 79).

For the documents recording the sessions of the Councils which

Dante attended see once again the *Codice diplomatico* (Nos. 53, 56, 81, 82, 83, 84, 86, 87, 88).

The books to which I drew attention in the first chapter apropos of the history of Florence are naturally of fundamental importance for this period. More especially I would recommend DAVIDSOHN, *Geschichte*, I, p. 254; CAGGESE, *Firenze* (cited above), II, Chap. I; DEL LUNGO, *I Bianchi e i Neri* (cited above); G. MASI, 'Il nome delle fazioni fiorentine de' Bianchi e de' Neri', in *Nuovi studi medievali*, III, undated [but actually published 1927], pp. 34-70; id., 'Sull'origine dei Bianchi e dei Neri', in *Giornale dantesco*, XXX (1927), pp. 124-32; id., 'La struttura sociale delle fazioni politiche fiorentine ai tempi di Dante', in *Giornale dantesco*, XXX (1930), pp. 3-28; id., 'I Banchieri fiorentini nella vita politica della città sulla fine del Dugento', in *Arch. giuridico*, CV (1931), pp. 57-89.

For a correct appraisal of Pope Boniface VIII see G. FALCO, *La Santa Romana Repubblica*, Naples, Ricciardi, 1945, Chap. XIII (which also contains a bibliography); P. FEDELE, 'I pontefici di Dante', in *Studi per Dante* (*Conferenze dantesche a cura del comitato milanese della Società dantesca*, Vol. III), Milan, Hoepli, 1935.

On the Jubilee see P. FEDELE, 'Il Giubileo del 1300', in *Gli anni santi*, lectures delivered at the Istituto di studi romani (1933), Turin, Società Editrice Italiana, 1934, pp. 7-25. On the imperial ambitions disclosed by the Pontiff during the period of the Jubilee see FINKE, *Acta Aragonensia*, Berlin und Leipzig, 1908, I, pp. 133-5, and cf. TORRACA, *Nuovi studi danteschi*, Naples, Federico e Ardia, 1921, pp. 188-90. As regards all the discussions and the various interpretations of the report made to King James of Aragon and the almost identical accounts given by Pipino and Ferreto see G. MARTINI, 'Per la storia dei pontificati di Niccolò IV e Bonifazio VIII', in *Rivista storica italiana*, LVIII (1941), pp. 3-41, and 'Regale Sacerdotium', in *Arch. R. Dep. rom. st. patr.*, LXI (1938-40). On the extremism of the Popes at the beginning of the fourteenth century see ERCOLE, *Dal Comune al Principato*, Florence, Vallecchi, 1929 (the chapter entitled 'Impero e Papato nel diritto pubblico italiano del Rinascimento'); F. RUFFINI, 'Dante e il protervo decretalista innominato', in *Mem. R. Acc. d. Sc. di Torino*, Second Series, LXVI (1926), pp. 1-69, now included in *Scritti giuridici minori*, Milan, 1936. As regards Acquasparta, the strong man of the Curia, see COSMO, *L'ultima ascesa*, pp. 141–7, and the bibliography, pp. 419–20; also my 'Rassegne francescane', in *Con Madonna Povertà*, especially pp. 301–3.

On the 'Controversie giurisdizionali di Firenze' see—in addition to the standard essay by G. LEVI, 'Bonifazio VIII e le sue relazioni col comune di Firenze,' in *Arch. Soc. rom. di st. patr.*, V (1882), pp. 365–474—the chapter so entitled in the essay by Ruffini cited above.

On Dante's initiation into the priorate and the notice given to the newly-appointed priors of the sentence imposed on the three criminal citizens in the Court of Rome, see the relevant document in the *Codice diplomatico* (No. 75).

On the political activity of G. Cavalcanti see BARBI, 'Guido Cavalcanti e Dante di fronte al governo popolare', in *Studi danteschi*, I (1920), pp. 101–11, now included in *Problemi*, II, pp. 371–8. On Dante's mission to San Gemignano see BARBI, *Bullettino della Società dantesca italiana*, VI (1899), pp. 95–7. The relevant document is in the *Codice diplomatico* (No. 73).

For the Guelf levy see NALDINI, 'La "tallia militum societatis tallie tuscie" nella seconda metà del secolo XIII', in *Arch. stor. it.*, LXXVIII, Vol. II (1920), pp. 75–113. On the modest appointment as superintendent of the straightening operations on the road to San Procolo, with which Dante was entrusted on April 28th, 1301, see BARBI, 'L'ufficio di Dante per i lavori di via San Procolo', in *Studi danteschi*, III (1921), pp. 89–128, now included in *Problemi*, II, pp. 385–413. The relevant document is in the *Codice diplomatico* (No. 80).

On 'La giornata parlamentare fiorentina del 19 giugno 1301' see Chap. XI of Ruffini's essay (cited above), which bears that title; BARBADORO, 'La condanna di Dante e le fazioni politiche del suo tempo', in *Studi danteschi*, II (1920), Chap. IV, pp. 33 *sq.* The relevant documents are in the *Codice diplomatico* (Nos. 83–4).

As regards the rise of the Caetani family and the policy of Pope Boniface in the Marittima see G. FALCO, 'Sulla formazione e la costituzione della signoria dei Caetani', in *Rivista storica italiana*, XLV (1928), pp. 225–78.

Dante's mission to Rome is generally accepted to-day as a

historical fact. The student would do well, however, to read
P. PAPA's essay, 'L'ambasceria di Dante Alighieri a Bonifacio
VIII', in BARTOLI, V, pp. 337–65, and DAVIDSOHN, *Geschichte*, III,
pp. 161 *sq.* and 199 *sq.* See also I. DEL LUNGO, *I Bianchi e i Neri*
(cited above), p. 168, note 2; O. ZENATTI, *Dante e Firenze*,
Florence, Sansoni, undated [1903], pp. 134 *sq.*; RUFFINI, *Dante
e il protervo decretalista innominato* (cited above), pp. 62 *sq.*

That the emissaries must have been received in the Lateran and
not at Anagni is to be inferred from the *Regesti* of Pope Boniface
(see COSMO, *Vita*, p. 298). The text of the charges preferred
against Dante and his fellow-exiles and of the sentences passed on
them is to be found in the *Codice diplomatico* (Nos. 90–1); there
is an elegant translation in DEL LUNGO, *Dell'esilio di Dante*,
Florence, Le Monnier, 1881, pp. 97 *sq.* For the course taken by
the trials see E. BARSANTI, *I processi di Dante*, Florence, Lumachi,
1908, and Barbadoro, *op. cit.*; the student should also consult
G. CUBONI, 'Le condanne di Dante', in *Convivium*, XI (1939),
pp. 1–45.

Regarding the extent to which Dante's part in the events at
Pistoia may have affected his sentence see L. CHIAPPELLI, 'Le
fazioni pistoiesi e Dante', in *Giornale dantesco*, XXV (1922), pp.
242–54.

The confiscation of the exiles' possessions raises a problem to
which a satisfactory solution is offered by P. GINORI CONTI in
Vita e opere di Pietro di Dante Alighieri, Florence, Fondazione
Ginori, 1939, Chap. V. On the bands of marauders and the
rebellions in the Arno Valley consult C. CIPOLLA, 'La Compagnia
malvagia e scempia', in *Gli studi danteschi*, Verona, 1921; also
BARBADORO, 'La condanna di Dante e la difesa di Firenze guelfa',
in *Studi danteschi*, VIII (1924), pp. 111–227.

The document relating to the meeting at San Godenzo is in
the *Codice diplomatico* (No. 92).

On Dante's stay at Forlì see BARBI, *Problemi*, I, pp. 189–95.

The wars in Mugello are described by DEL LUNGO in *I Bianchi
e i Neri* (cited above), pp. 375 *sq.* On the University of the
Bianchi at Arezzo and all the political activity which took place
there see the following essays in *Dante e Arezzo* (edited by G.
Fatini, Arezzo, 1922): 'Arezzo ai tempi di Dante', by A. BINI

(Chap. III), and 'Orme dantesche nell'Aretino', by G. Fatini (Chap. I). This book also deals with the debts contracted at Arezzo by certain of the exiles (pp. 50–1) and by Dante's brother (pp. 67–9). The relevant document is in the *Codice diplomatico* (No. 94). The genuineness of the letters to Niccolò Albertini da Prato, Bishop of Ostia, and to Oberto and Guido da Romena has been much questioned. On the whole, however, the criterion by which we should judge of the authenticity of Dante's letters is stated with admirable conciseness by Barbi in these terms: 'As to the authenticity of some of the letters that survive critics have been and still are doubtful, but valid reasons for denying that Dante was their author do not exist, save in the case of one addressed in the vulgar tongue to Guido da Polenta; the rest, though showing traces of the rhetorical style affected by the schoolmen, reveal the thought, outlook and manner of Dante' (*Dante*, Florence, Sansoni, 1940, p. 61). The authenticity of the letter to the Romena brothers was denied by Todeschini in *Scritti su Dante*, Vicenza, Buratto, 1872, I, p. 213, and by David-sohn, but was vehemently affirmed by O. Zenatti in *Dante e Firenze*, pp. 343 *sq.* For the letter to Cardinal da Prato see Appendix XIII to Del Lungo's Commentary on Dino's *Cronica*, where its authenticity is denied (subsequently the author was left in doubt: see *I Bianchi e i Neri*, p. 358). It is, on the contrary, affirmed by Zenatti, op. cit., p. 359. For the letters in general see Novati, 'Le epistole', in *Opere minori* (cited above), pp. 285–310; Torraca, 'Le lettere di Dante', in *Nuovi studi danteschi* (cited above), pp. 137 *sq.*

As regards the editions other than that of the Società dantesca see Toynbee's (Oxford, 1920), which contains the various manuscript readings, good notes and a translation. Also A. Monti's edition (Milan, Hoepli, 1921), with a translation and a commentary.

VII

IN THE WILDERNESS

DANTE himself tells us that his first refuge and sanctuary was 'the kindness of the great Lombard, whose stairway is adorned by the sacred bird' (*Par.*, XVII, 70-2). In the opinion of nearly all the ancient commentators the Lord of Verona who received him was Bartolomeo della Scala, who succeeded his father Alberto in 1301. But if Dante parted from his companions—probably at Arezzo— after writing the letter to Cardinal da Prato, by the time he reached Verona Bartolomeo had been dead for some while.[1]

Beyond doubt the exile preserved the memory of the latter's kindnesses to him when he had been his party's ambassador in Verona, and that memory, together with the promises which it is likely that he received, must have induced him to seek the protection of the Scaligers. Nobody who regards Dante as the author of the letter could think that his host was anyone but Alboino. It is true that Alboino does not show up well in the light of the verdict which Dante has recorded against him in the *Convivio* (IV, xvi, 6)—a verdict which cannot by any effort of interpretation be made to appear favourable. But Dante had a complex nature. Overwhelmingly conscious of his own greatness, he expected it to be recognized when it was still potential rather than actual; and there may have been some coolness between him and his host. The anecdotes attributed to him on the subject of his sojourn at the court of the Scaligers may be evidence of this, even if they are in part traditional and relate to Can Francesco, whose greatness was such that he easily eclipsed his brother. Petty slights, these, but they suffice to explain how, while they were still fresh in his mind, Dante allowed himself to indulge in the sharp-shooting that takes place in the *Convivio*.

But when the poet wrote his eulogy of the family in the *Paradiso* (XVII, 70-5) the splendour of Can Grande had driven every spark of ill-humour from his heart. What he had to say of

[1] He died on March 7th, 1304.

the Scaligers he had said freely in the *Convivio* and in the *Comedy* (*Purg.*, XVIII, 118–23; cf. *Inf.*, XVII, 68–9). Now it had been his desire to give special prominence to the fact that after parting from his companions he was first offered asylum in Verona, by one of the Scaligers. It was not the name but the fact that was important. He therefore did not mention the name of the individual, but designated him by an exalted title which befitted the entire house—namely 'the great Lombard'. The lofty character of the eulogy, which redounded to the whole family, was worth more than the name of the individual and, with the shrewd intuition of the artist, Dante succeeded in amending, without appearing to do so, his judgment of some fifteen years before, at the same time uttering a eulogy of the most unequivocal and solemn kind.

How long Dante remained at Verona cannot be definitely stated. As to his whereabouts following his departure from that city we can only be certain of one date—the October of 1306, when we find him staying at Sarzana with the Malaspina. His state of mind during this period may be reconstructed with the aid of Bruni's narrative, the indications provided in the first book of the *Convivio* and the *canzone* 'Tre donne'. These writings are all pervaded and inspired by the same sentiment, and it is precisely because they have not known how to integrate them that scholars have failed to throw as much light—of a relative kind, naturally—on this period as they might have done. Dante's party had been utterly defeated; he himself had parted from his companions, and was an object of calumny. As he reviewed his condition he must have yearned more keenly for his family and his native city. The letter which, according to Bruni (and we cannot doubt that it is authentic), he addressed to the people of Florence—*Popule mee, quid feci tibi?*—is conclusive. He became, says Bruni, all humility; but it was a humility typical of the man. Every charge that was laid against him in respect of his conduct in his native city he scornfully refuted; his desire that he should be permitted to return to Florence he proudly affirmed; but, as he stated in the loftiest of his *canzoni*, the fact that he had been exiled for his work of justice he accounted an honour. To one offence alone did he confess in the envoy of the *canzone*: that after his exile he had borne arms against his native city. But that he had been guilty of anything that merited his exile he utterly denied. He hoped by such loftiness of sentiment to obtain pardon, and he asked for it. This was an error, because it was not understood, and pardon was not forthcoming.

After he had left Verona the exile commenced his peregrinations among the courts of north Italy. It is not easy to give a precise account of them because every sojourn must have been of brief duration, and to attempt to deduce from the descriptions of places in the *Comedy* whether they are *de visu*, as the saying goes, or *de auditu* is dangerous, because Dante's imagination was so vivid that he succeeded in making all his descriptions live. Let the reader think of the tossing of the sea that 'hurls itself' against the Flemings between Wissant and Bruges. Dante certainly never visited that locality, yet he portrays the scene more effectively than he does the dykes along the Brenta which he saw dozens of times (*Inf.*, XV, 4–9). It may, however, prove as useful as it is pleasant to read the books which, so to speak, follow in the poet's footsteps. The problem is always to know how much reserve one should exercise in forming one's opinions.

In general it may be said of Dante's peregrinations in Lombardy —taking the word in the sense in which the poet uses it—that we should seek out the allusions in the *Purgatorio*, which is, as it were, his book of reminiscences. Yet it may be that not all his wanderings took place during this precise period. The kindly spirits who by giving him shelter mitigated his discomforts are duly celebrated in the *Purgatorio*; and in connection with the hospitality accorded to Dante during this period it is proper to mention his eulogies of the three old men who lived to censure the meanness of their contemporaries by the example which they themselves set of chivalry and kindliness. I refer to Currado da Palazzo, Guido da Castello, and above all Gherardo da Camino (*Purg.*, XVI, 121–6). The hospitality of the first two was probably of briefer duration than that provided by the 'good' Gherardo in Treviso. But the eulogies of Guido (IV, xvi, 6) and Gherardo (IV, xiv, 12) begin in the *Convivio*. In the case of Gherardo the eulogy is tempered by a sarcastic reference to his daughter Gaia (*Purg.*, XVI, 136–40) and open censure of his son Rizzardo (*Par.*,

IX, 49–51). In recent times, however, there has been a tendency to look upon Gherardo if not as an accomplice, at any rate as an accessory, in the murder of Jacopo del Cassero (*Purg.*, V, 73–8). We should therefore examine this personage more closely with the additional object of improving our knowledge of the poet's character and of explaining the attitudes that he adopted. Very probably not all that we know was known to him.

After his wanderings through Lombardy he must have proceeded to Lunigiana, and the nature of his reception at the hands of the Malaspina is indicated by his exaltation of the house in the *Purgatorio* (VIII, 121–32). Here too the fact of his sojourn is explicitly affirmed (ib., 133–9). But the best proof of the regard in which he must have been held by that noble family is afforded by the instrument of October 6th, 1306, whereby he was deputed to compose the differences existing between the Malaspina and Antonio, Bishop of Luni.

The member of the house of Malaspina who entrusted him with this task was the Marchese Franceschino, but Dante must have been, to a greater or lesser extent, the guest of all the families which made up that noble fraternity. It is probable that his principal hosts were Moroello, commander of the Guelf levy at the siege of Pistoia (*Inf.*, XXIV, 145–50), and his wife, the 'good Alagia' Fieschi, whose virtue he likewise extolled in the *Purgatorio* (XIX, 142–5). The length of his residence in Lunigiana cannot be stated with precision. He must, however, have remained there for a somewhat extended period, being encouraged to do so by the kindness of his noble friends, his preoccupation with the groundwork of the *Convivio* and the *De Vulgari Eloquentia*, and the presence of Cino da Pistoia. It is roughly to this period that we should likewise assign some of his poetical correspondence with Cino, inasmuch as he even wrote a sonnet in reply to him for the Marchese.

We cannot say for certain when Dante left the Malaspina to go back to Tuscany. He probably did so in 1307, prompted by the trend of events. That he first of all made his way in the direction of Casentino, where all the evidence suggests that he was the guest of the Conti Guidi in one or other of their castles, is shown by the letter which he himself wrote to Malaspina (IV), enclosing one of his *canzoni*, commonly called the 'mountain *canzone*', for the very reason that it was written in Casentino (*Rime*, CXVI). Many stories have been told of this poem by Boccaccio and subsequent writers, and it was even wrongly linked with the *canzoni* to Madonna Pietra, being regarded as a further manifestation of that fierce and violent passion which they were supposed to express. Probably written at the request of some noblewoman belonging to the house of Guido, it should, in my opinion, be related to the letter to Cino. Here the writer, by way of excusing his friend's levity in sexual matters, concedes that from the ashes of one love there might arise another. In the *canzone* Dante, having returned to the Arno Valley, the scene of his youthful loves, imagines that he has been struck by an amorous thunderbolt. Such flights of fancy tell us nothing of his life. Here too we should look rather for his irrepressible passion for the native city that 'shuts him without' its walls. Perhaps it was here, in the wilderness of Casentino, that he had the great inspiration which took his mind back to the 'wondrous vision' and grew into the *Comedy*. But of the poem's genesis I will speak in due course.

From Casentino the poet in all likelihood proceeded to Lucca. At Lucca Moroello's authority was great, and perhaps this was why Dante went there as the guest, or at any rate as the protégé, of that Gentucca Morla whom he extols for her kindness in the *Purgatorio* (XXIV, 37-8). And it was to Lucca that he probably brought his family, if—as is very likely—he was the father of the Giovanni whose name appears in a commercial deed of October 21st, 1308, and of whom subsequently we lose all trace. But not long afterwards (March 31st, 1309) the Commune issued an edict forbidding 'convicts and exiles from the city of Florence to reside in the city of Lucca and in the neighbouring district and countryside'. Before he proceeds further, however, the student will do well to assemble the information which the poet possessed about the city and its principal inhabitants. This task is greatly simplified by the indications at our disposal, and above all by those which Toynbee provides.

The poet was thus compelled to resume the life of an exile and a wanderer, and we lose track of his movements until the descent of Henry VII. But since Villani and Boccaccio assert that he went to Paris, and no apparent reason exists for disbelieving their word, it seems that there is no other period to which we may more fittingly ascribe his visit to that city. We may disregard the embroidery with which Boccaccio adorned his description of this visit: what is important is the fact. And the visit is explained by the poet's need—now that he had risen from the plane of the 'wondrous vision' to that of the *Comedy*—to enlarge his world and to sustain it with all the learning that the age could offer, and therefore in particular with theological learning. The reader should consider what the Sorbonne represented in the thirteenth and early fourteenth centuries: one of the three great institutions by which the human spirit was guided, the other two being the Papacy and the Empire.

This journey to Paris and the date of its occurrence have been the subject of much discussion. There are few episodes in Dante's life whose authenticity has been so heatedly denied. It is necessary to examine individually all the points raised in these discussions, carefully sifting them, if one desires to form an opinion of one's own on so important a matter. Such an examination may throw light on an entire epoch of history. The poet's journey to France explains his ever-growing interest in the policy of the country and the increasing severity of his judgment on that policy and on the Papal Curia's subjection to it. Above all it explains the broadening and crystallization of his cultural outlook.

Probably he would have stayed in Paris longer than he was able to do had not a great event, which was to exert a vast influence on his spiritual development, occurred to tear him away from his studies. And in so far as it affected the inspiration and composition of the *Comedy*—which is the most important thing —it was beneficial. From Paris he had followed with anxiety the progress of events—the nomination of the new Emperor and the first manifestations of his policy, which so faithfully expressed his own feelings. When, therefore, he learned that Henry VII was preparing to descend upon Italy, and that his plans had the Pontiff's approval, he immediately broke off the studies that he had undertaken and hastened to return. Nothing seems more in keeping with Dante's character, and nothing throws more light on the obscurities of this period than his journey and sudden return. If our reconstruction of his life has to be based on the fragmentary indications that have come down to us, we can only integrate them in the light of his essential logicality.

For Dante's visit to Verona see BIADEGO, 'Dante e gli Scaligeri', in *Discorsi e profili letterari*, Milan, 1903, and the commemorative work *Dante e Verona*, Verona, Tip. Cooperativa, 1921 (especially the unconventional but discerning essay by FAJANI). The student should constantly bear in mind and read what Del Lungo thought and wrote about Alboino, in his commentary on Canto XVII of the *Paradiso* (*Lectura Dantis*, Sansoni) as well as elsewhere. To form an idea of conditions at Verona it is always profitable to read C. CIPOLLA's *Compendio della storia politica di Verona* (Verona, Cabianca, 1899).

I should also refer the reader to Chaps. VII and VIII of my *Vita di Dante*. Here he will find a bibliography covering the relations that existed between Tuscany and Venice, which serve to explain more clearly why, after his separation from his companions, Dante made for those parts.

For the *canzone* 'Tre Donne' see CARDUCCI's essay in *Opere*, XVI, pp. 1–50; but chronological verification should be sought in LIVI, *Dante, suoi primi cultori, sua gente in Bologna*, Bologna, Cappelli, 1918, p. 24. As regards the interpretation of Dante's 'offence' and his 'repentance', which for his biographers is the most important question, see COSMO, *La Cultura*, New Series, X (1931), pp. 956–75, and for a contrary view BARBI, *Studi danteschi*, XVII (1933), pp. 97–103 and XX (1937), pp. 17–25, now included in *Problemi*, II, pp. 267–76; also COSMO, *La Cultura*, New Series, XII (1933), pp. 652–7. For Dante's peregrinations see especially A. BASSERMANN, *Orme di Dante in Italia* (Italian translation by E. Gorra, Bologna, Zanichelli, 1902).

For Dante's visit to Padua see A. BELLONI, 'Nuove osservazioni sulla dimora di Dante in Padova', in *N. Arch. ven.*, XLI (1921), pp. 40 *sq.*, and A. MOSCHETTI, 'Questioni cronologiche giottesche', in *Atti e Memorie della R. Acc. di sc. lett. e arti di Padova*, XXXVII (1921), pp. 181–201.

For Dante's visit to Treviso see A. SERENA, 'Dante a Treviso?' in *N. Arch. ven.*, XLI (1921), pp. 81 *sq.* For the Da Camino family see G. P. PICOTTI, *I Caminesi*, Leghorn, Giusti, 1905. For

F

Gherardo consult G. BISCARO, 'La correità di Gherardo e Rizzardo da Camino nell'uccisione di Jacopo del Cassero', in *Memorie stor. forogiul.*, XX (1923), and 'Dante e il buon Gherardo', in *Studi medievali*, New Series, I (1928), pp. 74 *sq.*

For Dante's stay in Lunigiana see L. STAFFETTI, *I Malaspina ricordati da Dante* (appendix to Vol. VI of Bartoli's *Storia della letteratura italiana*). But the student should above all consult *Dante e la Lunigiana*, by various authors, Milan, Hoepli, 1909, especially the essay with that title by Del Lungo, pp. 165 *sq.* The documentary evidence of his visit to Sarzana is included in the *Codice diplomatico* (No. 99).

With reference to the hospitality accorded to Cino da Pistoia by the Malaspina see ZACCAGNINI, *Cino da Pistoia*, Pistoia, Braccali, 1918, Chap. VIII and Chap. X ('Cino e Dante'); cf. CORBELLINI, *Giornale storico della letteratura italiana*, LXXVI (1920), p. 132, and BARBI, 'Cino fu di parte "bianca"?' (in *Studi danteschi*, VI (1923), pp. 113–30, and IX (1924), pp. 175–7, now included in *Problemi*, II, pp. 421–34).

On Dante's sojourn in Casentino see the chapter entitled 'Luci e ombre dantesche nel Casentino' in FATINI's *Dante e Arezzo* (cited above). It will also be profitable to consult BENI's *Guida illustrata del Casentino* (Florence, Bemporad, 1918); and even with all its exaggerations the chapter on 'L'Alpigiana' in Pascoli's *La mirabile visione* (Messina, Muglia, 1902) is always worth reading. As regards Dante's relations with women members of the Guido family whose relatives figure in the *Comedy* see TORRACA, *Nuovi Studi danteschi*, pp. 169 *sq.* There are some shrewd observations on the *canzone* 'Amor, da che convien' in F. FILIPPINI's *Dante scolaro e maestro*, Geneva, Olschki, 1929, pp. 122–5. For the interpretation of the *canzone* and of the letter (IV) that relates to it see COSMO, *Vita*, pp. 159–61. The allegorical interpretations I consider to be meaningless.

For the letter (IV: *Ne lateant*) to Moroello Malaspina, which is connected with the *canzone*, see F. NOVATI's essay in *Dante e la Lunigiana* (cited above), pp. 505 *sq.*, and G. VANDELLI, *Bullettino della Società dantesca italiana*, VII (1899), pp. 59–68.

For Dante's stay at Lucca and his relations with its citizens see LUISO, 'Dante e Lucca', in *Dante*, Milan, Treves, 1921; also

'L'anziano di Santa Zita', in *Miscellanea lucchese di studi storici e letterari in onore di S. Bongi*, Lucca, 1928. As regards Dante's son, see LUISO's *Un documento inedito lucchese che interessa la biografia di Dante*, Lucca, Tip. Cooperativa, 1921, and BARBI's article entitled 'Un altro figlio di Dante?' (*Studi danteschi*, V (1922), pp. 5–39) now reproduced in *Problemi*, II, pp. 347–70, in which the writings of Mancini and Zingarelli on the subject are also discussed. As to the likelihood that the poet resided at Lucca during this period see BARBI, art. cit. The proclamations announcing the exiles' banishment from Lucca are dealt with by BARBADORO in *Studi danteschi*, VI (1923), pp. 131–3.

All the possible objections to the theory that Dante went to Paris have been stated by A. FARINELLI in *Dante e la Francia*, Milan, Hoepli, 1908, I, pp. 91 *sq*. For Boccaccio's inconsistencies and contradictions apropos of the journey see TORRACA, *Nuovi Studi danteschi* (cited above), pp. 120–35. An essay containing general information has been written by H. HAUVETTE ('La France et la Provence dans l'œuvre de Dante', in *Revue des Cours et Conférences*, XXX, January 30th–March 30th, 1929). Next consult RAJNA, 'Per l'andata di Dante a Parigi', in *Studi danteschi*, II (1920), especially pp. 85–7.

At this point the reader would do well to study Friar Ilario's letter describing his meeting with the poet in the monastery of Monte Corvo. See RAJNA, 'La lettera di frate Ilario', in *Studj romanzi*, II (1914), pp. 133–4; id., 'Qual fede meriti la lettera di frate Ilario,' in *Da Dante al Leopardi*, by various authors, Milan, Hoepli, 1904, pp. 195–208.

The text of Friar Ilario's letter is reproduced in *Dante e la Lunigiana* (cited above), p. 233. As regards its authenticity see BIAGI, *Un episodio celebre della vita di Dante con documenti inediti*, Modena, Formiggini, 1910. This work contains a copious bibliography.

VIII

THE *CONVIVIO*

IT was during this period that Dante wrote the *Convivio* and the *De Vulgari Eloquentia*. The *Convivio* is an exacting book to read, and the problems arising out of it are many and difficult. To the intrinsic difficulties of the subject-matter must be added those inherent in the text, many parts of which have come down to us in such a mutilated condition that a satisfactory reading has only been arrived at in recent times. Yet it is a book that requires to be examined minutely in every part, and the satisfaction to be derived from the solution of these problems is great. Through it we come to know how Dante's cultural background was formed and we are enabled to discover the truth about some of the most critical moments of his life. It provides us with the means of gaining an insight into the moral fibre of the man who wrote it. And the man, like his work, is great.

Encyclopaedias, compendiums and thesauri—or whatever other title one chooses to bestow on such works—abounded in the Middle Ages. But Dante, however highly he regarded his teacher, was not capable of writing a work on the model of the *Trésor*. Even a learned work from his pen was bound to bear the stamp of his personality. Hence the particular form that the *Convivio* assumes and the passionate feeling with which some parts of it are imbued. Fancifully he imagines that he is offering his readers a kind of banquet, in which fourteen *canzoni*, concerned 'both with love and with practical virtues', will be, as it were, 'the meat', while the commentary with which he will illustrate them will be 'the bread'.

Doctrinally the subject-matter could not but be drawn from the storehouse of contemporary learning, but the passion that impelled the poet to write the work at that particular moment of history was his alone.

The first aim of our inquiry, then, is to establish the date of composition. Now all the indications that may be gathered from the work leave no doubt that it should be ascribed to the period between 1304 and, at the latest, 1308. Its origin is to be sought in Dante's spiritual condition during those first years of vaga- bondage, after his separation from his companions. It is a complex origin. He was far away from his native city and his family, and he had not the means that befitted his dignity as a gentleman. He was traduced by friend and foe alike, and the nobles who entertained him did not accord him the reception which he felt his genius entitled him to expect. Cheated of his fame, which was lessened by misfortune, and convinced that the scholar receives more consideration from common folk than the mere poet, he felt the need to elaborate his knowledge in a work that would announce his true worth to the society in the midst of which he lived. Artistically Dante does not pose as a scholar, but as a guest at the table of the learned who has gathered up the crumbs of their knowledge; yet even if he is too shrewd to consider himself an Aristotle or a St. Thomas he is obviously aware of the knowledge which during many years of study he has accumulated and of his superiority to the people among whom he lives. Indeed, it is his 'pity' for these people that moves him to write his treatise. They are 'very many': unrefined and illiterate people, 'princes, barons, knights and many other noble folk', who 'because of the pernicious negligence of the world' have 'abandoned literature' (*Conv.*, I, ix, 5). By imparting know- ledge to these people he was continuing to exercise his high office, which he had already assumed in his native city, of 'poet- preceptor'. This office affected on the one hand the language that he was to use in discharging it, and on the other his choice of the subjects that he was to treat of in the work.

Of the subjects it may be said, speaking generally, that they were to be essentially of an ethical order. Ethics constituted Dante's ruling passion, as is clearly demonstrated by the fourth book, which is concerned with nobility. As to the language, in view of the aims of the work and the people to whom it was addressed, it could only be the vernacular.

When he wrote the *Vita Nuova* Dante thought that the verna- cular was only suitable for the treatment of amorous subjects. With the development of his art his views had changed. As he wrote, and above all as he composed the philosophical *canzoni*, he had become convinced that the vernacular was a potential medium for all forms of expression. The fact that he adapted it to the interpretation of scientific thought, as though it were Latin, betokened intellectual power of a special kind and a superior brand of originality. In the poet's awareness of such values lies the reason for his lofty, impassioned defence and eulogy of the vernacular in the preamble to the work. If we set this eulogy against the reasons that had impelled Ser Brunetto to write the *Trésor* in French we can measure the progress which the Italian vernacular had made in the course of a few years, thanks most of all to the *stil novo* poets, chief among them Dante.

By now French was no longer the 'commonest and most pleasing' language: the Italian vernacular was about to take its place. Let the reader think of the high prophecy as to its future which the poet utters towards the end of the first book.

Besides these reasons, which constitute the theme of the entire work, Dante had a further motive in writing it—a motive of a more specific kind, but no less, perhaps indeed more, important for the understanding of the man. In the *Vita Nuova* he had suddenly interrupted the story of his love for the *donna gentile* with the allusion to 'a vivid fantasy' which had brought him back from the path of error to Beatrice. It had occurred unexpectedly 'some days' after his wooing of the lady. But the evidence of the little book was contradicted by the poems that he had written for the *donna gentile*, for these clearly implied that the intensity of his passion had been far greater than the story of it was meant to suggest. Dante sensed the contradiction between what he had so categorically asserted and the truth as it emerged from his poems, and he sensed the justice of the criticism which accordingly might be, and perhaps was, levelled against him, and of which, in his state of mind at the time, he was very prone to exaggerate the importance. 'I fear the infamy of a surrender to such a passion as that by which the reader of the above-mentioned *canzoni* will imagine that I was mastered.' And he considered that he must absolve himself from the charge of 'frivolity of mind' (*Conv.*, I, ii).

Hence the importance of the second book of the *Convivio*, in which, with the object of absolving himself from such a charge, he calls us to witness a most curious transformation of the facts, and at the same time enlightens us about an episode in his life which we should otherwise have had to reconstruct by a process of induction. Truth and fiction are intermingled and almost merge into one. These pages, then, require to be read with great circumspection. The truth of the matter is that Dante was seeking relief from the pain that racked him in the study of philosophy, and what he writes in this connection in Chapter XII of the *Second Treatise* is to us of capital importance. We learn of the first books of philosophy that he read, of the difficulties that he encountered, and of the passion that he felt surging within him as a result of his study. Dante is never so sincere as when he tells us of the ardent desire for knowledge with which his mind became inflamed and of the sleepless nights which he devoted to his quest for it. We can now understand how it was that, later on, so great a part of the *Comedy* was occupied with the question of knowledge.

But the very intensity of the yearning for knowledge which in fact possessed him suggested to his mind the form of his defence against the charge from which he desired to absolve himself. In order to justify the poems that he had written during his early youth for other ladies—true, they were written before he knew Beatrice, but they were at any rate inconsistent with the argument that she was the sole object of his love—he had resorted in the *Vita Nuova* to the fiction of the *donne dello schermo*; in the case of the love-poems written in praise of the *donna gentile* he resorted to the fiction of allegory. It was a fiction whose meaning was to be found in the mental habits of the time, just as the fiction of the *donne dello schermo* had had its meaning in the literature of Provence. And we find him asserting that in the first flush of his attachment he formed a mental picture of knowledge and sang of it as though it were a lovely woman. His song, then, was a song of love, but it was addressed to her on whom Pythagoras bestowed the name of philosophy. And since the two attachments —namely for the *donna gentile* and philosophy—in which he had sought relief from his pain at the death of Beatrice were contemporaneous he easily came to identify the one with the other.

The fact that he later wrote allegorical and doctrinal poems made his use of allegory in this case the more plausible. But it is indicative of the man's character that, finding himself obliged to prove his statement that he had only deserted Beatrice in favour of a loftier and worthier intellectual passion, he picked out from his *canzoni* as proof of his contention that which most clearly told against him. I refer to the *canzone* which signalizes the most conspicuous moment in his spiritual struggle, the portrayal of which he had begun and then so suddenly interrupted in the *Vita Nuova*. Thus the effort of adapting reality to the requirements of allegory is characteristic of the man. Dante does not blind himself to the difficulties, but deliberately faces them. The graver they are, the more apparent is the strength of his deliberate resolve to subordinate everything to the goal that he sets before him. We see him as he wished to appear in face of the malevolence of the envious, and as, in his last compositions, he had in fact appeared. 'Not passion but virtue had been the motive force' behind his poetry, and 'there was an ending of the infamy' which he feared would be the result of a popular belief in this passion.

He asserts that he does not wish in his new work to 'disavow' the *Vita Nuova*, but how this desire can be realized is past understanding, so glaring is the contradiction. And it is not so merely because a reality (the merciful lady) has been transformed into an allegorical phantasm, but because the love 'of the senses' which in the one book is termed 'evil desire and vain delight' and an incentive to licence is exalted in the other to the status of an emotion that gives rise to 'incessant, new and most lofty meditations'. In the *Vita Nuova* the abandonment of the misguided love for the merciful lady and the return to Beatrice are celebrated as a triumph of reason; in the *Convivio* the wooing of the *donna gentile* is the 'cultivation of an ideal friendship'. 'All other passions are dimmed and almost extinguished because the eternal object of this one surpasses and dominates other objects to an overwhelming degree' (III, xiv, 7).

Nor is the contradiction removed even if, as some have done, we look upon the merciful lady as the representation of an ideal. There still remains the contrast between the attitudes which Dante adopted towards the two women. Others, regarding the

two books as complete in themselves, each enshrining a truth of
its own, admit the reality of the merciful lady but ascribe an
allegorical significance to the *donna gentile*. In other words they
think that the allegorical poetry begins in effect with the *canzone*
'Voi che 'ntendendo'. But this interpretation does not explain
the state of Dante's feelings when he wrote the *Convivio*, nor does
it explain his character. Herein lies its essential weakness. To the
Dante of the *Convivio* the merciful lady of the *Vita Nuova* is also
a fiction, and the sonnets which refer to her require to be interpreted allegorically. The magnitude of such a task is obvious.

However, since this is one of the fundamental problems con-
fronting those who wish to understand Dante's life and works, it
must, whatever solution one chooses to offer, be carefully
considered from every angle. There are problems in Dante which
will always be the subject of controversy. To offer one's own
solution with an air of finality is presumptuous. The examination
of all the arguments for and against every solution, even if none
can be accepted as final, constitutes criticism.

As regards the structure of the new work which Dante proposed to compile, bearing in mind the biographical elements that
he intended to introduce, it did not differ to any great extent from
that of the *Vita Nuova*—in other words it was to be a mixture of
poetry and prose. But the prose of the *Vita Nuova* was, so to
speak, historical in content, because it announced the occasion of
each poem's composition. As to the *Convivio*, over and above the
historical element, an essential part of it would be concerned with
doctrine—that is to say, Dante would as he went along expound
the doctrinal problems arising out of his commentary on the
canzoni. The passionate element would therefore predominate
and would constitute the original feature of the work. Hence, to
the Dantologist the most important parts are those in which the
poet lives through his inmost passions and preoccupations, and
on which he leaves most clearly the imprint of his art.

He certainly envisaged, in outline at least, the structure of the
entire work, because from time to time he refers the reader to
the arguments of later books, as for example when he says that
in the 'fourteenth treatise', or book if one prefers, he will speak
of justice (I, xii, 12 and IV, xxvii, 11). But it is impossible,

except in so far as he tells us, to determine which *canzoni* he would have illustrated and what form the arguments would have assumed. None of the various conjectures on the matter stands up to criticism. As a creative artist Dante always surrenders to the enthusiasm of the moment; and fresh enthusiasms might supervene. The fact that he left the work incomplete after the fourth book, when he was to have written fifteen, was certainly due to his having been intoxicated by the great vision of the *Comedy* which had suddenly appeared before him, and to the imperious necessity of devoting his whole mind to that vision. But it is also true that in these four books the lofty impulse that had prompted him to take up his pen had spent its force—the impulse, that is, to defend and glorify his own character, to defend and glorify the vernacular, and to expound the new political thought which filled his soul with light and drew him on towards new and broader horizons.

Dante was certainly not a systematic philosopher, but he was a thinker who nurtured his intellect on all the resources of contemporary thought. He had too lofty a mind and was too much of a poet to be bound by the concepts of a rigid system. On the other hand, however, he was too serious a thinker not to worry about the coherence of his own theories or to cherish any theory which he saw to be at variance with the principles on which his own knowledge was based. Hence the study of his thought, as revealed in the work which was to have been a complete exposition of his knowledge, is for the Dantologist a necessity. During the century that has elapsed between the publication of Ozanam's book and the appearance in recent times of Gilson's, great progress has been made in this matter. Dante's sympathy with Aristotle, the pilot of human reason, and his adherence to the Philosopher's principles are evident; but few to-day would maintain that he was a strict Thomist, even though they acknowledged the great influence that St. Thomas exerted on him. A schoolman himself, he derived certain elements of his thought from other schoolmen, and latterly the extent to which his ideas were moulded by those of Albertus Magnus has been clearly revealed. But among the procedures and methods that he adapted to his art, and hence to his thought, were some derived from the Franciscan school, and he admired the Arabic commentators on Aristotle, above all that Averroes who wrote 'the great commentary'. He recognized their mistakes, but he felt their influence. He believed in the potency of human reason, but he never came to think that it could solve all the problems that confront the mind, and the view that the *Convivio* marks a spell of absolute rationalism, to which the return to mysticism in the *Comedy* affords a contrast, was an illusion shared by Witte and Scartazzini. This thesis found a new champion in Pietrobono, who did not, however, succeed in proving it. The *Comedy* may on occasion be less rational in tone than the *Convivio*, as when the poet bids mankind to rest content with facts (*Purg.*, III, 34–44), or when he says that there is no light but proceeds from the serene whose tranquillity is never disturbed (*Par.*, XIX, 64–6). But the limits of human reason are fully recognized in the one work as in the other, and if in the *Comedy* they are more strongly emphasized, such emphasis results from a lyrical and sentimental intonation that is a source of poetry. The clarification of this moment in Dante's intellectual life is of the utmost importance for the understanding of its history; and systematic study of the various opinions that have prevailed on the subject is the soundest method of arriving at the truth. For this reason young students can never be too strenuously urged to steer a prudent middle course between the various exaggerations in either direction. A complex nature like Dante's does not readily submit to the discipline of a system, and the more certain the critics feel that they have tied him down the more noticeably does some part of him assert its independence.

The same remarks are applicable to his political thought. I would say that the dissertation on Rome and the Empire is derived indirectly from the treatise on nobility. But it is precisely here that we are afforded the opportunity of learning about the man's *forma mentis*. When Dante warms a subject with the heat of his own passion and makes it his special preserve, nothing can keep him from revealing the fact. Thus, in the fourth book of the *Convivio* we detect his political thought in the first stage of its development, all alive with the enthusiasm he felt as it burst upon his mind. When later he faced this same problem of politics in the *Monarchy* and the *Comedy* he presented his ideas in a maturer, fuller form, but they were no longer imbued with the passionate feeling that had characterized them on the first occasion. Here we may surprise not only the thinker but the artist as he responds to the workings of his creative genius, and as we probe them we understand what he really meant by the famous reply to Bonagiunta's question (*Purg.*, XXIV, 52-4). In any event, all who desire to probe Dante's political thought should make this their starting-point.

The subjects examined in the *Convivio* broaden their scope as the author gets under way. Here we can to a large extent estimate the limits of his knowledge. It is probable that he owed his familiarity with a number of Greek and Arabic philosophers to Albertus Magnus; but all his citations of ancient and modern philosophers and of Latin writers such as Cicero and Boëthius require careful consideration if one proposes to fix the limits of Dante's culture. Only thus can we gain an insight into his mental processes and reconstruct them in their entirety. It is not our business to do this; our business is merely to indicate the road that those who wish to do it must travel.

But despite all these investigations the study of the *Convivio* remains incomplete. Since we are concerned with a poet, and a great poet, it is of even more interest to us to trace his artistic development. However we choose to interpret the poet's assertions (I, i, 17), it is indisputable that a number of years elapsed between the composition of the *Vita Nuova* and that of the *Convivio*; and they were the years during which he studied not merely philosophy but style, prompted by the final intuition that had flashed before his mind as he wrote the *Vita Nuova*. If in a certain respect the two works are comparable on the score of structure (poetry with prose illustrations), in style the difference between them is great. The prose of the *Vita Nuova* is still tenuous, while that of the *Convivio* is robust. We are made aware of the attention that Dante has devoted to style during the interval. Naturally, the studies that had led him to write the *canzoni* to Madonna Pietra also influenced the form of his prose. His training in the *cursus* cannot have influenced his Latin writing alone. He had too keen an intellect not to perceive that the vernacular lacked the flexibility of Latin, but on the other hand, since the *cursus* was an artistic model, it was proper that it should also be put into practice in the vernacular so far as the vernacular permitted. These efforts to make his readers aware of 'the great excellence of the vernacular' as revealed in the 'smoothness of its syllables', the 'distinctive qualities of its constructions' and the 'soft-sounding speeches that are created from it' seem obvious in view of the assertions made by the poet himself in Chapter X of the first book, where he extols the merits of the vernacular. Dante is not a primitive poet, but a clever artist. Accordingly, the logical way of completing the study of the work is to analyse its style. It is not the poet who triumphs over the artist; on the contrary, the reverse is often the case. Hence the painstaking nature of the work. At times, however, the fusion is perfect, and it is then that Dante reveals his greatness.

Comparisons between the *Vita Nuova* and the *Convivio* so far as regards style may therefore prove useful as a means to the understanding of the writer's artistic method. Also, we may well study the evolution of his thought. Ten or fifteen years had not passed in vain. But if it is always permissible for us to institute these comparisons, we must also constantly bear in mind that the two works were conceived at different stages of the poet's life and under different conditions. Each, therefore, should be interpreted in the light of the circumstances that gave it birth. The *donna gentile* of the *Convivio* furnishes no clue for the interpretation of the merciful lady of the *Vita Nuova*. They are two distinct individuals whom at a certain moment the poet, by reason of the fresh interests that clamoured for his attention, tried by his artistic method to merge in one, without, however, being able to fuse them into an artistic whole. Hence each must be examined in her due time and place.

The student should use the edition of the *Convivio* prepared by G. Busnelli and G. Vandelli and included in the collection of the *Opere di Dante* edited by M. Barbi (Vols. IV and V, Florence, Le Monnier, 1934–7). This edition is better even than that published in 1921 by the Società dantesca. It contains some 'important observations on a number of readings incorporated in the critical text' (A. PÉZARD, 'Le "Convivio" de Dante', in *Annales de l'Université de Lyon*, Third Series, *Lettres*, Part IX, Paris, Les

Belles Lettres, 1940; see NARDI, *Nuova Antologia*, February, 1946, pp. 221–6). The text is accompanied by an exhaustive and extremely learned commentary, which, though it perhaps draws too many parallels with Thomism, is by any standards of great value. As regards this over-emphasis on Thomism the student would do well to consider the modifications proposed by B. NARDI, who in his enthusiasm for his thesis perhaps goes too far in the opposite direction (*Dante e la cultura medievale*, Bari, Laterza, 1942, Essays V and VIII and *passim*). Chap. II ('Philosophy in the *Banquet*') of GILSON's *Dante the Philosopher* (already cited), which has a similar bias, should also be consulted. Apropos of this book see PIETROBONO, *Giornale dantesco*, XLI (1940), pp. 193–202, and NARDI, *Studi danteschi*, XXV (1940), pp. 5–42. Although Busnelli's essays are summarized in the notes appended to his commentary, it is always profitable, in view of the importance of the question, to get to know them at first hand ('Un famoso dubbio di Dante intorno alla materia prima' (*Studi danteschi*, XIII (1928), pp. 47–60)[1] and 'L'origine dell'anima razionale secondo Dante e Alberto Magno', in *Civiltà Cattolica*, LXXX (1929), Vol. II, pp. 289–300, and Vol. III, pp. 229–37 and 336–47). Busnelli's thesis is opposed by NARDI in his book *Dante e la cultura medievale* (cited above) ('Sull'origine dell'anima umana', pp. 187 *sq.* and 'L'immortalità dell'anima', pp. 210 *sq.*). Still with an eye to this over-emphasis on Thomism the student would do well to consult NARDI, *Studi danteschi*, XXVI (1942), pp. 148–60; also *Giornale storico della letteratura italiana*, LXXXI (1923), pp. 307–34, and *Giornale dantesco*, XXII (1938), pp. 83 *sq.* For a full illustration of Dante's thought in the *Convivio* he should next consult NARDI's *Saggi di filosofia dantesca* (Milan, Società Dante Alighieri, 1930) and the long article in the *Giornale storico della letteratura italiana*, XCV (1930), pp. 73–114, entitled 'Alla illustrazione del Convivio dantesco'. In addition there is always something to be learned from the nineteenth-century scholar OZANAM (*Dante et la philosophie catholique*, Paris, 1839). For another point of view see G. GENTILE, *Storia della filosofia in Italia*, Milan, Vallardi, 1905, Book I, Chap. IV, pp. 105 *sq.*

---

[1] But cf. the essay by Nardi (op. cit., pp. 176 *sq.*), 'Se la materia prima de li elementi era da Dio intesa'.

Next, for a discussion of all the aspects of the problem by scholars of opposing tendencies the student should consult PIETROBONO, 'Il prologo della Divina Commedia', in *Giornale dantesco*, XXVI (1923), pp. 323 *sq.*, and BARBI, 'Razionalismo e misticismo in Dante', in *Studi danteschi*, XVII (1933), pp. 6–44 and XXI (1937), pp. 5–91, now included in *Problemi*, II, pp. 1–86.

PIETROBONO: 'Il rifacimento della Vita Nuova e le due fasi del pensiero dantesco', in *Giornale dantesco*, XXXV (1934), pp. 3–82; 'Prefazione alla nuova edizione della Vita Nuova del Casini', in *Giornale dantesco*, XXXIV (1933), pp. 113–37; and 'Filosofia e teologia nel Convivio e nella Divina Commedia', in *Giornale dantesco*, XLI (1940), pp. 13–71.

W. H. V. READE, 'Intellectual Toleration in Dante', in the *Journal of Theological Studies*, XXVII (1925), pp. 1–19; see BUSNELLI, *Studi danteschi*, XIII (1928), pp. 82 *sq.*

As a means of learning what important critics have thought in the past about Dante's alleged intellectual aberration it is advisable to consult P. A. MENZIO, *Il traviamento intellettuale di Dante Alighieri secondo il Witte, lo Scartazzini, ed altri critici e commentatori del secolo XIX*, Leghorn, Giusti, 1903. Of WITTE's writings see *Dante Alighieris lyrische Gedichte*, Leipzig, 1827 and 1842. A. SCROCCA, *Il peccato di Dante*, Rome, Loescher, 1900 (but cf. BARBI, *Problemi*, I, pp. 134–9); J. KLACZKO, *Causeries florentines*, Paris, Plon, 1880, pp. 157 *sq.* See also G. ZUCCANTE, 'La donna gentile e la filosofia nel Convivio di Dante', in *Fra il pensiero antico e il moderno*, Milan, Hoepli, 1905; and U. FRESCO, 'Il "Convivio" e le canzoni "sì d'amore come di vertù materiate" ', in *Giornale dantesco*, XXVIII (1925), pp. 13–27.

As regards the date of the book's composition the student should see the list of the most reliable indications afforded by the actual text which Barbi has drawn up in the *Introduction* to Busnelli's edition. The entire introduction should moreover be carefully read as being an excellent preparation for the study of the work. N. ANGELETTI's book on the subject (*La cronologia delle opere minori di Dante*, Città di Castello, Lapi, 1886) may also be consulted. On the genesis of the work and the poet's feelings as he wrote it see COSMO, *Vita*, VIII.

As a means of forming an idea of the nature of contemporary

learning the young student will find it very profitable to read two characteristic works, viz. Ser Brunetto's *Trésor*[1] and the *Composizione del mondo*, edited by Narducci, Rome, 1859. (For the editions see D'ANCONA, *Manuale*, I, p. 198.) Also useful as complementary reading are DUHEM's *Le système du monde*, Paris, 1919, and C. H. HASKINS's *Studies in the History of Medieval Science*, Cambridge, 1927. For the medieval encyclopaedias see V. CIAN, 'Vivaldo Belcalzer e l'enciclopedismo italiano delle origini', in *Giornale storico della letteratura italiana*, Suppl. V (1902).

A. MARIGO, 'Cultura letteraria e preumanistica nelle maggiori enciclopedie del Dugento', in *Giornale storico della letteratura italiana*, LXVII (1916), pp. 1–42 and LXVIII (1916), pp. 289–326.

There is a good commentary on Book III, Chap. V in ANGE-LETTI, *Sito, forma e dimensioni del Purgatorio dantesco*, Palermo, 1906, pp. 24–31.

See also PROTO's 'Note al Convivio dantesco', in *Giornale storico della letteratura italiana*, LXV (1915), pp. 199–262; also LV (1910), pp. 57–66.

As regards Dante's scientific acquirements see the indications given in the chapter on the *Comedy* concerning the role of science in the poem (pp. 164–5).

In addition to the notes of Busnelli and Vandelli and the century-old essay by MAZZUCCHELLI, *Luoghi degli autori citati da Dante nel Convivio* (at the end of the Education Department's Paduan edition, 1827, pp. 361–450), MOORE's essay, 'Scripture and Classical Authors in Dante' (in the first volume of the *Studies*, Oxford, 1896), is still of fundamental importance as a guide to the authors whom Dante constantly cites as sources of his knowledge. See also the references to the *Convivio* in TOYN-BEE's dictionary (under the appropriate headings) and in *Dante Studies and Researches*, London, Methuen & Co., 1902, and *Dante Studies*, Oxford, Clarendon Press, 1921.

SCHERILLO, 'Dante e Tito Livio', in *Rend. Ist. lomb.*, Second Series, Vol. 30, Part 5; cf. *Bullettino della Società dantesca italiana*, IV (1897), pp. 202–3.

---

[1] Although not free from error, Gaiter's edition (Bologna, 1878-83) may prove adequate.

P. CHISTONI, *L'etica nicomachea nel Convivio*, Pisa, 1897.

In so far as it actually refers to the subject see also P. CHISTONI's book, *La seconda fase del pensiero dantesco: periodo degli studi sui classici e filosofi antichi e sugli espositori medievali*, Leghorn, Giusti, 1903. But see BARBI, *Problemi*, I, pp. 87–97.

On the conception of history and politics first formulated by Dante in Book IV, Chap. IV, see especially ERCOLE, 'Le tre fasi del pensiero politico di Dante', Chaps. I–IV, in *Il pensiero politico di Dante*, Milan, Alpes, 1927–8, II, pp. 271–310. For a fuller bibliography see the chapter on the *Monarchy*.

As regards the manner in which the form of Dante's art was affected by the first impact on his mind of this conception of history and politics, by its development in the form of a treatise in the *Monarchy*, and by his lyrical return to it in the *Comedy* (*Par.*, VI), see COSMO, *L'ultima ascesa*, Bari, Laterza (Chap. VI).

A complete study of the form of the *Convivio* is lacking. The student should, however, consult Lisio's book, *L'arte del periodo* (cited above), in conjunction with Parodi's review, and SCHIAFFINI's essay, 'Il "Convivio"', in *Tradizione e poesia* (cited above), pp. 157–81. The essay written many years ago by VITO FORNARI, 'Del Convito di Dante' (in *Dante e il suo secolo*, Florence, Cellini, 1865, pp. 443–59) should also be read.

G

IX

THE *DE VULGARI ELOQUENTIA*

THE first book of the *Convivio* is to a great extent a lofty, passionate defence of the vulgar tongue—'this precious vulgar tongue, which, if it is contemptible at all, is only so in so far as it is heard upon the uncouth lips' of the 'detestable, wretched Italians who treat it with contempt' (*Conv.*, I, xi). And in this very treatise the author announces that 'he intends, God willing, to write a little book on the subject of *vulgar* speech' (*ib.*, v). It was accordingly written at the same time as, or a little later than, the early books of the *Convivio*.

As the poet progressed in his task, and hence in the study of thought-expression, he grew more and more convinced of the 'great excellence' of the vernacular, due to its capacity for 'representing the loftiest and most abstruse ideas in a seemly, adequate and dignified manner' (*ib.*, x). To praise the vernacular was to praise his own work, to re-establish his prestige among the 'many' who, because of the misfortune which had stricken him, had come to regard every work from his pen as 'of minor worth'. And a similar fate was in store for those 'that he was intending to write' (*ib.*, iii). Since vernacular writings were held in little regard, if they were not positively despised, by scholars, the treatise had to be written in their language. Latin would also serve to lend it authority. Hence the work was composed under the stress of a lively emotion, which explains the haste in which the part of it that has come down to us must have been written, and the fact that after the author's fervour had died away he abandoned it half-way (Chap. XIV) through the second of the four treatises of which it was to have consisted.

The fundamental problem was to find the language that was a suitable medium for lofty poetry, and that would be to Italians what Latin had been and still was. Dante makes a clear distinction between the native idiom—the vernacular—which is determined by usage and may therefore change, and the language evolved by scholars—Latin—which is determined by artistic principles and is therefore not subject to change. The problem was simply to raise the first to the dignity of the second and, in the poet's phrase, to convert a vernacular into the language of literature.

Having defined the problem so clearly, Dante could very well have kept within the limits that it prescribed. But he was too deeply imbued with philosophic culture, too obedient to the speculative inclinations of his own mind, not to go back from the specific problem to its origins. His monograph was not liable to be confused with the ordinary practical treatises written for ignorant learners, and furthermore it was because he went back and surveyed the problem in all its breadth that his work was original. Hence these early chapters should be considered carefully, because, while they reveal the temper of the author's mind, they also serve to clarify the parts that follow.

Dante begins, then, by asserting that speech is the property of man and of man alone, and wonders what was the first human word and how Adam spoke immediately after his creation, in the place in which he was created. The first word was 'God', or rather 'El', and the language of the Earthly Paradise was Hebrew. The Hebrew language was spoken by Adam's descendants until the confusion of Babel, and it would have continued to be the language of all mankind if the latter had not been dispersed in consequence of its arrogant rebellion. The confusion was due to forgetfulness of the single language which had been used up to that point, and the languages that were derived from this one were equal in number to the groups of artisans engaged in the construction of the tower. Hebrew, however, continued to be spoken by those who did not take part in the work, or rather who discouraged it. Christ when He came down to earth could speak not 'the language of confusion but the language of grace'.

Of all this great variety of languages Dante only stops to consider those that had been imported into Europe, and here he sees three original groups of languages. 'There remains as a sign of the common origin' of those that constituted the first group 'the fact that almost all men when making affirmation answer *jo*'. 'Those whom we now call Greeks occupied part of Europe and part of Asia.' 'Throughout that part of Europe which remains outside the sphere of these idioms a third idiom gained currency, although it now appears to have three forms. Some, indeed, say by way of affirmation *oc*, others *oil*, and others yet *sì*, as, for example, the Spanish, the French and the Italians.' But the primeval unity of language 'is evident from the fact that in the case of many words we all use the same form' (I, ix).

At this point Dante reaches the heart of the matter. The subject of his inquiry is the 'illustrious vernacular' of Italy. What is this in reality, and where is it to be found? Or (what is at bottom almost the same thing) which of the dialects of the peninsula most closely resembles it? The 'illustrious vernacular' is not a dialect, but a literary elaboration, first attempted by the Sicilian poets at the Court of the Emperor Frederick, continued by the Bolognese writers of whom Guido Guinizelli—'the greatest'—was the prototype, and carried on by the Florentine poets of the *stil novo* school. As such, then, it 'is capable of diffusing its perfume through one dialect rather than another, but not of being identified with any one in particular'. Hence the dialects are condemned *a priori*, but Dante confirms his judgment by following them under his microscope along the line of the Apennines. His examination is rapid; from each dialect he selects some peculiarity that suffices to condemn it and finally justifies the conclusion that even if each reveals some trace of what he is seeking, none can aspire to the honour of proclaiming itself to be 'illustrious'.

We need not record his separate judgments here. The dialect which more than any other resembles the sought-after model is that of Bologna, because it is 'modulated to a praiseworthy softness'—but not in such a high degree that 'it is to be preferred without qualification'. In any event the student should ponder these judgments carefully, both because they serve to give us an idea of the state of the Italian dialects at the beginning of the fourteenth century and because each judgment is formulated in accordance with an aesthetic criterion which enables us to gain an insight into the taste of the man who pronounced it. Dante does not perceive that the standard of comparison on which his judgments are based is the harmony of that Florentine dialect— albeit purged of all coarsenesses—which he and his friends have employed in their poems. He does not perceive that he reads the verses of the Sicilian poets not in their original text but after they have been subjected to a polishing process in the transcriptions of Tuscan amanuenses. Since much of this language has become his own, since he and his friends are for ever bringing it to a higher pitch of refinement, and since he has constantly before him the model of Latin, on which this work of polishing is based, he becomes more and more convinced that this ideal language is a literary elaboration that has already to a great extent become a reality.

Thus the first part proves to be a logical preparation for the second, in which he begins to expound that rhetorical doctrine which he more particularly had in mind. He begins—since, whatever may have been the reason, he suddenly interrupts his dissertation mid-way through the fourteenth chapter. The series of questions that he confronts himself with and answers is a new one. This 'illustrious vernacular' that he has so ingeniously discovered—who are best fitted to employ it? And what should be their theme? For assuredly it does not befit all writers, nor is it suited to every theme. It befits, then, only men of 'talent and learning', *in quibus ingenium et scientia est*, and it is only suited to three themes, *Salus videlicet, Venus et Virtus*. 'These themes, therefore, namely safety, amorous delight and virtue, appear to be the things of wondrous grandeur that should be treated of in the grandest manner, or rather those things which conduce to them in the highest degree, such as armed prowess, ardent love and uprightness of will' (II, ii). Dante asks himself which 'doctors' have sung of *ista magnalia* in France, Provence and Italy. For himself he reserved the honour of being the poet of virtue. This is the first step in the direction of the *Comedy*.

Of all the forms of lyrical writing the most excellent is the *canzone*, and on this Dante holds forth to the extent of seven chapters. But however important a place these may hold in the history of Romance versification, especially if we compare them with treatises whose theme is similar—however important they may be, they are to the student of Dante less so than the four preceding ones, in which he discourses upon the fundamentals of the art of poetry, the lofty verses demanded by the *canzone*, composition in the tragic style and the magnificent words which the latter requires. Here we have the poet's theories of style, derived from the study of other writers' verses and of similar treatises, but also from his own artistic experience—theories which in their turn influenced his art. How is this influence revealed in his most artistic poems, and how is it revealed in the _Comedy_, in particular where the poem rises from the comic to the tragic style, as it does more especially in the _Paradiso_? These are questions to which those who desire to fathom the inmost secrets of Dante's art must seek an answer.

The _De Vulgari Eloquentia_ is a difficult book. Written by a poet who was acquainted with all the elegant refinements of his art, it also needs to be carefully studied for its Latin. Marigo's edition, with its appendixes and glossary, furnishes all the necessary means to this end. Familiarity with the Latin is an effective preparation for the understanding of the _Epistles_ and the _Monarchy_.

For the editions, the student should above all consult the critical edition, prepared for the Società dantesca by P. RAJNA, _Il trattato De Vulgari Eloquentia (Opere minori di Dante Alighieri,_ critical edition), Florence, Le Monnier, 1896, and the smaller edition, with new emendations and remarks, Florence, Le Monnier, 1897. For the text see also the same author's essays in the _Bullettino della Società dantesca italiana,_ XXV (1918), pp. 136 _sq.,_ and _Studi danteschi,_ XIV (1930), pp. 5–78. The discovery of the Berlin codex was followed by the publication of L. BERTALOT's _Dante Alighieris De Vulgari Eloquentia,_ Friedrichsdorf apud Francofurtum ad M., 1917. And now there is an especially important addition to Barbi's collection (Vol. VI), _De Vulgari Eloquentia ridotto a miglior lezione e commentato da_ A. MARIGO, with an introduction, a metrical analysis of the _canzone,_ a study of the language and a glossary, Florence, Le Monnier, 1938. Apropos of this book see G. CONTINI, _Giornale storico della letteratura italiana,_ CXIII (1939), pp. 283 _sq.,_ and also, with reference to the harmony and structure of the stanza, U. SESINI, _Convivium,_ XI (1939), pp. 463–72.

A rendering of the first chapter has been furnished by P. RAJNA, who promised a complete translation of the work ('Il primo capitolo del trattato De Vulgari Eloquentia tradotto e com-

mentato', in *Miscellanea Hortis*, Trieste, 1910, I, pp. 128 *sq.*).
Marigo has provided a full rendering side by side with his text,
and this is the only version that it is safe to use. By reason of its
exhaustive, though perhaps over-long, commentary and the
wealth of erudition that it contains the book is altogether most
useful.

The student will always do well to read Manzoni's letter to
Bonghi (1868). As we study it we begin to see what was the
guiding principle of the work. Useful sources of information as
to the medieval outlook on the problem of language are ROTTA's
La filosofia del linguaggio nella Patristica e nella Scolastica, Turin,
Bocca, 1909; NARDI's 'Il linguaggio in Dante e la cultura medie-
vale', in *Dante e la cultura medievale* (cited above), pp. 148 *sq.*;
D'OVIDIO's 'Dante e la filosofia del linguaggio', in *Studi sulla
Divina Commedia*, Palermo, Sandron, 1901.

Critical studies:

F. D'OVIDIO, 'Sul trattato De Vulgari Eloquentia', in *Archivio
glott. it.*, II (1873), pp. 59 *sq.*; a second edition appears in *Versificazione italiana e arte poetica medievale*, Milan, Hoepli, 1910, now
included also (under the new title *Versificazione romanza. Poetica
e poesia medievale*) in *Opere*, IX. This volume contains in addition
the essay entitled 'La metrica della canzone secondo Dante'.

It will also be profitable to read D'OVIDIO's volume on *Le
correzioni ai Promessi Sposi e la questione della lingua* (Naples,
Pierro, 1895; now included in *Opere*, VIII) for its rapid but lucid
historical survey of linguistic questions.

P. RAJNA, 'Il trattato De Vulgari Eloquentia', in 'Lectura
Dantis', *Le opere minori di Dante*, Florence, Sansoni, 1906, pp.
193–221. A familiarity with RAJNA's 'La lingua cortigiana' may
also prove useful (in the *Miscellanea linguistica in onore di G. I.
Ascoli*, Turin, Loescher, 1901).

On the *De Vulgari Eloquentia* see in addition CASELLA's study in
Giornale della coltura italiana, I, No. 3, and BERTONI, *Archivum
Romanicum*, XX (1936), pp. 91 *sq.* On the style of the Latin
employed in the treatise consult Marigo's appendix. On the
cursus see TOYNBEE's notes in *The British Academy*, XI (1923) and
XXII (1927); also MARIGO's ('Il cursus nella prosa latina dalle
origini cristiane ai tempi di Dante', in *Atti e mem. d. R. Acc. di*

scienze lett. e arti in Padova, 1931, New Series, LXVII, pp. 41 *sq.*)
and E. TESTA's ('Il cursus medievale', in *Rivista di sintesi letteraria*,
III (1937), pp. 5–30).

RAJNA's study, 'Per il "cursus" medievale e per Dante' (in *Studi
di filologia italiana*, III (1932), pp. 7–86) remains uncompleted.

X

THE DESCENT OF HENRY VII

WE are now entering upon one of the most important periods of Dante's life. It is important for the immediate part which he played in events, and it is vitally so for the development of his political thought which, following the general vision adumbrated in the *Convivio*, becomes ever more clearly defined in the *Epistles* and is crystallized in the *Monarchy*.

This is not the place to describe the progress of events. We are concerned with a period of history that should be studied attentively by the Dantologist both in the works of the modern writers who have examined it most closely and in those of contemporary authors. Indeed, it is only through the latter that we can fully appreciate the repercussion of events on the poet's mind, which for us is the most important thing. The Dantologist does not apply his mind to history in order to verify an objective reality (if the term is permissible), but to establish the truth of some fact connected with Dante. For example, the final chapters of Dino's *Cronica* throw more light on the attitudes which Dante adopts in the *Epistles* than does the most circumspect modern historian.

It is essential that we should trace the progress of events from the very beginning. We must reflect upon the hopes of the King of France, upon his efforts to conquer the Empire, if not for himself, for some member of his house—and we must remember that he was that landless Charles who 'with the lance with which Judas fought his joust . . . split the paunch' of Florence (*Purg.*, XX, 73–5). On the other hand we should recall the subterfuges to which the Pontiff resorted in order to free himself from a yoke that grew daily more oppressive. The conflict between these two potentates resulted in the election of Henry of Luxembourg. From France Dante must have followed the negotiations between the new sovereign and the Pontiff with watchful attention. Henry was a cavalier and a dreamer with a consciousness of the high office that had been entrusted to him. For this reason all eyes were turned in his direction.

The months during which these events took place were months of strain, hope and trepidation. This state of mind explains the fact that, as soon as the new sovereign's plan to descend upon the peninsula as a peacemaker declared itself, Dante cut short without ado the studies on which he had embarked in Paris and betook himself to Italy, his destination being Forlì. The information supplied by Flavio Biondo is so precise, and proceeds from such an immediate source, that no doubt can remain as to its substantial accuracy. Nor can we doubt the authenticity of the letter which the poet, in the name of the other exiles as well as of himself, wrote to Can Grande, who, in company with his brother, had lately risen to power. From that time forth Dante saw from which quarter opposition to Henry's enterprise would be forthcoming; hence he followed every move that Florence made with rapt attention. I can never emphasize enough that in considering Dante's life we must, if we wish to understand it, distinguish between the man as he was in historical reality and the image with which he was pleased to identify himself—an image symbolical of the ideal to which he aspired and which after much labour he realized. One of the principal distinctions that we must draw is indicated by the fact that he had ceased to have any dealings with the exiles, having become, immediately after the rift, the champion of his own cause.

The impending advent of the new sovereign was announced to the Italian people in a letter from the Pontiff and an *encyclica Italicis missa* from the Emperor. Now we cannot fully understand the letter which Dante wrote 'to the kings and senators of Rome the bounteous, to the dukes, marquises, counts and all the peoples, *universis et singulis*', unless we are familiar with the letters issued by the two supreme authorities. But how did he who called himself the *humilis italus* achieve such a consciousness of his own grandeur that he addressed himself to the entire Italian people, urging them to listen to the words of the two supreme potentates? It is one of the most ticklish psychological problems that the Dantologist has to face. Nor can we explain it except by supposing that Dante had for some time past been engaged in the great work to which henceforth he was to devote his entire life, and that from the heights to which the act of describing his vision had exalted him he had become prophetically aware of his own grandeur. The controversy regarding the date of the poem's composition must end in favour of the years 1308-9 or there-abouts for the simple reason that only the composition of so great and original a work can explain this sudden prophetic intuition.

We must, however, beware of exaggerating, as too many have done, the letter's significance as a political document. Dante's political thought had not yet taken definite shape in his mind. There are manifest inconsistencies between the assertions in the *Monarchy* that the two powers are of equal standing and the declaration in the letter regarding the inferiority of the 'lesser light'. We must note these inconsistencies if we wish to under-stand how Dante's mind developed.

So that he might follow the progress of events Dante moved from Romagna to Tuscany. His precise destination was Casen-tino, where in all probability he was the guest of the Conti Guidi. He had seen clearly that the main bulwark of resistance to the Emperor was Florence; accordingly, writing from the source of the Arno, he addressed a vehement letter to the 'iniquitous Florentines within the city', threatening them with every sort of punishment if they did not open their gates to the Emperor.

Having read this heated letter, the student should at once turn his attention to the other one, addressed to the Emperor. The course of events, Henry's procrastinations and his undue delay in Lombardy, while Florence prepared ever more energetically to resist, had a profoundly disheartening effect on Dante and precipitated a crisis in his soul. Henry could only succeed in his enterprise if he gained the victory over Florence. It was now that Dante decided to write the letter to the Emperor urging him to march on his native city forthwith.

Never had Dante abandoned himself to such vehemence of expression. More than from their political significance—of which we must repeat what we said in reference to the first letter—these two derive their importance from the fact that they not only throw light on his state of mind at this juncture, but explain certain of the attitudes that he adopts in his greatest work. To know the man is to understand the poet better. He had threatened his city with a tremendous outburst of divine wrath, but when the Emperor finally encamped at San Salvi and laid siege to Florence Dante did not, like the other exiles, hasten to wreak his revenge. 'He did not choose to be there', writes Bruni; and this decision expresses the whole spirit of the man who created the figure of Farinata.

An attitude of such resolute hostility to the Black Commune could not fail to rouse the latter to retaliation. Accordingly, with the object of ensuring 'that the Guelf element in the people and Commune of Florence should be strong, robust and at peace with itself' the Commune granted a general amnesty to those who had been sentenced on political grounds, but among the large number mentioned as being excluded from the pardon was 'Dante Allegherii'. This was the so-called Reform of September 2nd, 1311, sponsored by Messer Baldo d'Aguglione. It is a document that we must read in its entirety if we are to understand the spiritual condition of Florence in this extremity and the savagery of Dante's feelings so many years later, when he was still conscious of the stench with which the boor of Aguglione filled the city (*Par.*, XVI, 55–6).

Henry's undertaking was doomed to failure. The resistance of the Florentines became ever more resolute and tenacious, and the relations of the Emperor with the Pontiff grew increasingly strained. The two potentates had founded their idyll on a miscalculation, and hence it could not last. The miscalculation consisted in the belief that the Empire and the Kingdom of Naples, which was a fief of the Church, were capable of living in harmony. When the Pontiff saw that Henry meant to play the role of Emperor in earnest he could not refrain from taking up the cudgels on his vassal's behalf. The change of policy was made inevitable by circumstances, but this Dante failed to comprehend. What was a political necessity looked to him like a betrayal. But it is precisely on that account that this period of history must be closely studied in its every aspect by all who would appreciate its repercussions on the poet's mind and the attitudes that it led him to adopt in his poetry. The investigation of history is the surest means of understanding poetry, if to understand poetry is by definition not merely to appreciate its formal qualities but to search the poet's mind for an explanation of all the refinements of his spirit. Thus, here too, history proves to be the surest foundation of criticism.

The failure of the venture after all the excitement and all the hopes that had been entertained of its success, coupled with the unexpected death of the Emperor, produced in Dante a fresh mood, first of discouragement, then of resurgent, irrepressible hope, and contributed to his idealization both of the enterprise and of the man who had sponsored it. The triumph of the inept Robert increased the scorn, not to say the hatred, with which he filled Dante, as well as the poet's feeling of admiration for the opponents of his policy. All these emotional attitudes are reflected in the *Comedy*.

Much has been written in recent years about Henry VII and his expedition. Of fundamental importance are the relevant pages in DAVIDSOHN, *Geschichte*, III, Chap. III (pp. 345 *sq.*). See also F. SCHNEIDER, *Kaiser Heinrich VII*, Greiz i. V. und Leipzig, 1924–8; there is an exhaustive bibliography in each of the three parts, of which the second and third are of especial interest to us. Of the older authorities consult P. VILLARI, *I primi due secoli ...* (cited above), II, pp. 145 *sq.*; DEL LUNGO, *I Bianchi e i Neri* (cited above), pp. 398–435; and CAGGESE, *Firenze* (cited above), II, Chap. II. There are full accounts in CAGGESE, *Duecento-Trecento* (cited above), which includes a bibliography of the immediate sources (pp. 424 *sq.*), and in SALVATORELLI, *L'Italia comunale* (cited above), pp. 755 *sq.*

With reference to KERN's *Acta Imperii Angliae et Franciae ab anno 1267 ad annum 1313* (Tübingen, Mohr, 1911), see SOLMI, *Bullettino della Società dantesca italiana*, XVIII (1911), pp. 241 *sq.*

Of the chroniclers the student should read Compagni (final pages of the *Cronica*), Villani (Books VIII and IX), Ferreto da Vicenza, Giovanni da Cermenate, Niccola di Butrinto ('Relatio', in *Rerum Italicarum Scriptores*, IX) and A. Mussato ('Historia Augusta', in *Rerum Italicarum Scripta*, X).

For Dante's letter to Can Grande and the relevant passage in Biondo see the edition published by the Società dantesca (pp. 449–50) and BARBI, *Problemi*, I, pp. 193–5.

The Pontiff's letters and the Emperor's encyclical are reproduced in SCHWALM, 'Constitutiones et Acta publica', in *Mon. Germ. hist.*, Vol. IV, Part 1, Nos. 435–41 and 444.

Dante's letters referred to above are those numbered V, VI and VII. Parodi's reflections upon them are worth reading, although he exaggerates their political significance. The arguments regarding the authenticity of these letters have by now ceased to have any meaning.

The three short notes written on behalf of the Countess of Battifolle to Marie of Brabant are merely of a complimentary nature. Yet it is advisable to read them because they too help to give a clearer picture of Dante's feelings. Apropos of them see MOORE, *Studies*, IV, pp. 256 *sq.*, and RICCI, *L'ultimo rifugio di Dante*, Milan, Hoepli, 2nd Edition, 1921, pp. 16 *sq.*

On Dante's stay in Casentino it is both profitable and pleasant to consult C. BENI's *Guida illustrata del Casentino*, Florence, Bemporad, 1918.

On Dante's meeting with Petrarch's father at Pisa see the *Bullettino della Società dantesca italiana*, XII (1905), p. 26 and XIII (1906), p. 202. The article by A. FORESTI, 'Sull'incontro di Dante col Petrarca in Genova nel 1311', in *Giornale dantesco*, XXVI (1923), pp. 270–1 (reprinted in *Aneddoti della vita di Francesco Petrarca*) does not carry conviction.

For the text of Messer Baldo d'Aguglione's so-called Reform see the *Codice diplomatico* (No. 106).

The decree whereby Clement V rescinded the sentence passed by Henry VII on King Robert is reproduced in *Clementinae*, Vol. IX, Book II.

XI

THE *MONARCHY*

ACCORDING to the most widely held opinion, it was precisely during this period that Dante wrote the treatise *De Monarchia*. We must, however, be cautious: it is a belief, not a certainty. To form our own opinion we are therefore bound to conduct a systematic inquiry, which must be based on a close and thoughtful study of the treatise.

It is a difficult book to read. Conforming to the scholastic convention of the time, it proceeds by syllogisms, and its arduousness is increased by the stylistic refinements of the *cursus*. At the beginning, therefore, the help of a good translation is absolutely essential. All Dante's Latin writings are difficult, but here we have to master the intricacies of his method. To this end it is a good thing to be familiar with the dialectical methods of the schoolmen, just as it will be very helpful to examine in detail each of the three books and the syllogisms of which they are compounded.

Since the treatise is an *inquisitio* Dante takes as his starting-point a principle that is universally recognized and accepted as such, one to which he recurs in order to verify the propositions that he subsequently takes for granted: *Et quia praesens tractatus est inquisitio quedam, ante omnia de principio scrutandum esse videtur, in cuius virtute inferiora consistant* (I, 2). First of all, then, we must establish what this principle is in the case of each of the three books, and then carefully observe how the author derives from it the syllogisms on the basis of which he proceeds to his proof. This process demands care and vigilance.

The first two books (I: *An ad bene esse mundi* [*Monarchia*] *necessaria sit*; II: *An Romanus populus de iure Monarche officium sibi adsciverit*) are at bottom an elaboration and a logical proof of the theses upheld in Chapters 4 and 5 of the fourth book of the *Convivio*. But since the purpose is different, so too is the treatment. Now there is no better way of acquiring a knowledge of

Dante's mental processes than to compare the two forms of treatment—in the one case the immediate expression of a thought that has flashed before his mind for the first time, in the other the logical demonstration of the truth of that thought. There are, moreover, the passages in which the man triumphs over the austere political theorist and gives free rein to his feelings. Here we see Dante in his role of poet, and for the understanding of his character and his art these passages prove to be the most interesting of all.

The hypothesis that these two books were aimed especially at the French Guelfs, who rejected the two theses, need not be strictly adhered to, because in the mind of the writer the first two books are an essential preparation for the third, the theme of which is that civil power is independent of ecclesiastical power and that it is derived immediately from God (*An auctoritas Monarche dependeat a Deo immediate vel ab aliquo Dei ministro seu vicario*). The final thesis arises logically out of the first two, which are put forward as a divine truth—as the realization in the moral world of the order imposed by God on the universe. Here already we see, clearly formulated, the concept that is destined to become the main prop of the *Comedy*: order as the principle on which the universe is founded.

Having thus stated the concept that informs the treatise, together with its analytical proof, we are entitled to speculate as to the nature of Dante's political ideal. In order to comprehend this ideal in its entirety we must seek its origin first in the pages of the *Convivio*, then in the *Epistles*, in the *Monarchy*, and finally in the *Comedy*, which it pervades and in which it shines forth in all its glory. The *Monarchy* thus proves to be one of the keys to the understanding of Dante's greatest work.

A knowledge of the political thought, and hence of the history, of the Middle Ages presupposes a knowledge of the *Monarchy*. It is therefore impossible to estimate the importance of the book and the greatness of the man who wrote it without reference to the other political writings of the time. Dante asserted that he proposed *intentatas ab aliis ostendere veritates* (I, 1). Now in what way are we to ascertain the nature of these truths if we are not acquainted with the other political theorists—

resolute champions of Imperial and Papal privilege, essayists who try to enter the thick of the great struggle and who attempt to reconcile the two powers? In addition to the essayists proper we ought to be familiar with the writings that issued forth from the various chancelleries—Imperial, Papal, French and Angevin—in support of the theses that suited their respective causes. In the same way useful aid towards the full understanding of the book is provided by the confutations written about the same time, e.g. Friar Guido Vernani's *Reprobatio*. This friar, who was an expert in all the philosophy of his age, saw, for example, where the treatise was vulnerable, and unhesitatingly accused its author of Averroistic tendencies. Indications of such traces of Averroism as are to be found in the work are now provided in recent studies.

Having examined the formation of Dante's political thought with an eye to its origin and related it to writings of a similar kind, one may tackle the problem as to when the treatise was written. It is impossible to study this problem without at the same time studying the whole question of the relations that existed between State and Church at the end of the thirteenth and the beginning of the fourteenth centuries. Indeed, the only way to reach a conclusion that enables one to fix, with the probability, if not the certainty, of accuracy, a date approximating to the true one is to fit the treatise into its historical setting.

The opinions as to the date may be reduced to three. It is a good thing to consider them all, both because those who advocate them are authorities in the matter and because the dates in question cover the whole of the period—1300 to 1317 or 1318—during which Dante's thought and work matured. To-day it is no longer held that the treatise should be ascribed to the years of the poet's residence in Florence, on the assumption that it was written in consequence of Pope Boniface's claims to rule Tuscany and in reply to the bulls in which the Pontiff proclaimed his ideas on theocracy. At variance with this opinion—apart from all other considerations—is the actual course of development of Dante's political thought, in so far as it may be gathered from the *Convivio* and the *Epistles* and from an assertion in the *Monarchy* itself (II, 1); and this argument would alone suffice, if there were no others,

H

to destroy such a hypothesis. This was noticed by those who actually supported it, and they were reduced to the expedient of making a new approach to the treatise and assuming that only the first two books were written in Florence, the third being composed later. But all appreciate how the understanding of the problem is simplified by reference to the Papal bulls and in particular to *Unam sanctam*, which must certainly have made a deep impression on the poet's mind.

The usual tendency is to ascribe the composition of the treatise to the moment when Clement V openly took the part of King Robert—a view based essentially on the fact that this episode provided historical conditions that favoured the book's composition. As to the truth of this there can be no argument, just as there can be none regarding the fact that the thought and sometimes even the phraseology of the treatise coincide with those of the political writings published by the chancelleries for the occasion. But this coincidence of historical conditions and political writings is also found a few years later, when the Pontiff's nomination of King Robert as Imperial vicar led to a new flare-up in the controversy between the champions of Angevin privilege and the defenders of the Imperial right. I think the book was begun in 1312 or 1313 as a defence of the ideals dearest to the poet's heart and of the man whom most of all he venerated, and that it was completed in a calmer frame of mind after the Emperor's death. But only by scrupulously examining and comparing the various writings of various periods can one arrive at a conclusion which, if not final, is at any rate very plausible. We must also note that in so short a space of time the problem had not greatly altered, and hence the poet's writings are based on the same arguments.

As regards the significance of the treatise, a number of critics have exaggerated the importance of the third book as an anti-ecclesiastical document. In reality Dante loses himself in the process of confuting certain arguments which, given the chance, he deemed it necessary to confute, but which, unlike the argument about the two luminaries, in themselves lack coherence. And the final chapters, the very chapters that proclaim the independence of civil power, are wanting in the logical perspicuity which characterizes so many of the others. Again, we must consider carefully the way in which, at the end of the treatise, he qualifies the most categorical of his earlier assertions. I would say that in the *Comedy* he shows greater firmness in this respect—but it is a firmness which may owe something to the fact that his poetry has greater potency of form than his prose. At all events these differences are illuminating when we come to study the individuality of the poet. If on the one hand it is true that the analysis of political ideas cannot be separated from the study of the great men who have made an original contribution to thought, it is also true that an effective contribution to the full understanding of such men is made by the study of their political thought. The Dante of the *Monarchy* appears more cautious, as though the act of drafting a scientific treatise has the effect of cramping his style. Dante the poet seems freer and less restrained, as though in his great moments of inspiration he obeys only the prophetic genius that leads him on.

The last chapter of the treatise, in which, as he thinks, Dante demonstrates conclusively that civil power is independent of ecclesiastical power and that it is derived directly from God, is therefore of capital importance as a means of determining the allegorical significance of the *Comedy*, and particularly of the two characters that more especially typify it, namely Virgil and Beatrice. There is no need to summarize here the contents of the chapter or to show how in the poem the two characters discharge the function that Dante attributes to the two powers. For us it is enough to show that by making this chapter the starting-point of our efforts to understand their significance we are building on a solid foundation, and so rejecting all the fantastic notions which they have inspired. If it is always necessary to compare the two works where they deal with the same subject—and we must never forget that the treatise was written at a time when the poet's mind was wholly bent on the greater work—it is all the more necessary to do so in order to establish with certainty the symbolic value of the two characters that express the dominating idea of the work. Only if we make this idea our starting-point will close examination subsequently enable us to grasp the finer points of their complex make-up. Even if our object is simply to form an aesthetic judgment, it is essential, unless we wish to descend to a mere battle of words, that we should know what were the general ideas by which Dante was guided.

Clearly, then, the *Monarchy* is important as a standard by which the figure of Dante may be appraised. It is, to be sure, a utopia, but it is the utopia of a great spirit, who believed that through it he was influencing the trend of history. Dante did not understand the historical trend of his own times, but his failure to do so enabled him to invest this utopia with all his ideals and to wander freely in the realms of universality. And it is precisely in this that his greatness lies.

Hence, in order that our understanding of the book may be complete it is appropriate that we should also follow its fortunes. If we know how it was regarded through the ages—with malevolence or with fear by fanatical papists, with respect by great Catholic spirits, as a weapon of battle by Protestants or fanatical enemies of the papacy, with understanding by free-thinkers—we can estimate its worth ever more accurately.

The student should, as a matter of course, avail himself of the edition sponsored by the Società dantesca, the text of which has by now been adopted by all publishers. Also BERTALOT's edition (*Dantis Alagherii De Monarchia*, libri III, Friedrichsdorf in monte Tauno apud Francofurtum, 1918).

A useful Italian translation is that made by N. VIANELLO, *Il trattato della Monarchia di Dante Alighieri*, Genoa, Stab. Graf. Edit., 1921. Chap. II of the preface ('Struttura e metodo del trattato') will prove an extremely valuable aid to the understanding of Dante's syllogistic method.

As regards the date of composition it has been maintained that Dante wrote the treatise while he was still living in his native city at the end of the thirteenth century (Witte, followed by Boehmer), or in the middle of the year 1300 (Grauert).

See Witte's *Prolegomena* to his edition of the *Monarchy* (Halle, 1863–71 and Vienna, 1874) and *Dante-Forschungen*, I, p. 79; BOEHMER, *Ueber Dantes Monarchie*, Halle, 1866; GRAUERT, 'Zur Dante-Forschung', in *Historisches Jahrbuch*, XVI, Munich, 1895, and *Dante und die Idee des Weltfriedens*, Munich, 1909; cf. PARODI, *Bullettino della Società dantesca italiana*, XVI (1909), pp. 285 *sq.*

Also STEINER, *Per la data del De Monarchia*, Novara, 1892; cf.
ROSSI, *Bullettino della Società dantesca italiana*, IX (1902), pp.
279 *sq.*

For the years 1317–8 see especially SCHEFFER-BOICHORST, *Aus
Dantes Verbannung*, Strasbourg, 1882, pp. 103–38; KRAUS, *Dantes
Leben*, pp. 271 *sq.* (cf. *Bullettino della Società dantesca italiana*, V
(1898), pp. 156 *sq.*); ZINGARELLI, II, Chap. 25. For the date see
also CHIAPPELLI, 'Sulla età del "De Monarchia" ', in *Arch. stor. it.*,
XLIII (1909), pp. 237–56.

The writings published at the time of the dispute between
Boniface VIII and Philip the Fair have been assembled by F.
SCHOLZ in *Die Publizistik zur Zeit Philipps des Schönen und
Bonifaz' VIII*, Stuttgart, Enke, 1903; cf. TOCCO, *Bullettino della
Società dantesca italiana*, XIII (1906), pp. 100 *sq.* For the relation-
ship of Dante's thought to the French anti-curialist movement
consult C. CIPOLLA, 'Il trattato De Monarchia di Dante Alighieri
e l'opuscolo De potestate regia et papali di Giovanni da Parigi',
in his publication *Gli studi danteschi*, Verona, 1921; F. ERCOLE,
'Impero e papato nel diritto pubblico italiano del Rinascimento',
in *Dal Comune al Principato*, Florence, Vallecchi, 1929, pp. 118 *sq.*;
J. RIVIÈRE, 'Le problème de l'Église et de l'État au temps de
Philippe le Bel' (*Spicilegium sacrum lovaniense*, Part 8), Louvain,
1926. For Dante's attitude in face of the various trends of opinion
see also:

DE WULF, 'Les théories politiques du moyen âge', in *Revue
néo-scolastique de philosophie*, XXVI; U. MARIANI, 'La posizione
di Dante fra i teologi dell'imperialismo ghibellino', in *Giornale
dantesco*, XXX (1927), pp. 111–7; R. W. and A. I. CARLYLE, *A
History of Mediaeval Political Theory in the West*, Edinburgh,
1927–8, Vol. V.

The writings published in the time of Henry VII are to be seen
in SCHWALM's *Constitutiones et Acta publica*, Mon. Germ. hist., Vol.
IV, Part 2, *Memoralia et disquisitiones Imperatori vel Papae tradita*,
Appendix VII, pp. 1308–98. There is a bibliography of other
writings of the time in ERCOLE's *Dal Comune* (cited above), p. 157,
note 1. For the treatise written by Friar Guglielmo di Sarzana in
support of King Robert see P. FEDELE, 'Per la storia del De

Monarchia', in *Giornale storico della letteratura italiana*, LVI (1910), pp. 271–2.

The literature dealing with the *Monarchy* and with Dante's political thought is enormous. For this reason I am only indicating a few writings which for one reason or another merit the attention of those who wish to form an adequate idea of the subject, viz. F. LANZANI, *La Monarchia di Dante, studi storici*, Milan, 1864; G. CARMIGNANI, *La Monarchia di Dante, considerazioni*, Pisa, 1865; A. D'ANCONA, 'Il De Monarchia', in *Scritti danteschi*, Florence, Sansoni, 1912–3, pp. 315–76; P. VILLARI, 'Il De Monarchia', in *Scritti vari*, Bologna, Zanichelli, 1912, pp. 349 *sq.*; F. TOCCO, 'Polemiche dantesche', in *Rivista d'Italia*, IV (1901), pp. 417–40; id., *Bullettino della Società dantesca italiana*, VIII (1901), pp. 240–6 and XIII (1906), pp. 111–3; JORDAN, 'Dante et la théorie romaine de l'Empire', in *Nouvelle revue historique de droit français et étranger*, XLV (1921), pp. 353–96 and Series IV, 1st year (1922), pp. 191 *sq.* and 333 *sq.*

G. SOLARI, 'Il pensiero politico di Dante,' in *Riv. stor. ital.*, XL (1923), pp. 373–455; SOLMI's extremely sane essays, 'Il pensiero politico di Dante' and 'Stato e Chiesa nel pensiero di Dante', in *Studi su Dante*, Florence, 1922; F. ERCOLE's essays assembled in the two volumes entitled *Il pensiero politico di Dante*, Milan, Alpes, 1927–8. Of paramount importance, even if they harm his case, are Ercole's lawyer-like tendency to over-systematize and the fact that he has not re-arranged his subject-matter in such a way as to avoid numerous repetitions. The work includes a very copious bibliography.

E. G. PARODI, 'L'Ideale politico di Dante', in *Dante e l'Italia*, Rome, Fondazione M. Besso, 1921, pp. 75–135; M. BARBI, 'Impero e Chiesa', in *Studi danteschi*, XXVI (1942), pp. 9 *sq.*; B. NARDI, *Saggi di filosofia dantesca*, Milan and Rome, Soc. ed. Dante Alighieri, 1930 (Essay No. X); id., 'La donatio Constantini e Dante', in *Studi danteschi*, XXVI (1942), pp. 47 *sq.*; id., *Note alla Monarchia*, ib., pp. 97 *sq.*; G. LIZERAND, 'Les constitutions "Romani principes" et "Pastoralis cura" et leurs sources', in *Nouvelle revue historique de droit français et étranger*, XXXVII (1913), pp. 725–57.

F. KERN's *Humana civilitas* and *Staat, Kirche und Kultur. Eine Dante-Untersuchung* (Leipzig, Kohler, 1913), despite their exaggerations, are well worth reading.

A. DEMPF, *Sacrum Imperium* (Italian rendering by C. Antoni, Messina, Principato, 1933).

XII

AFTER HENRY

As regards Dante's life following Henry's expedition there are only a few dates which we can fix with certainty. Hence the task of reconstruction becomes very difficult. Where was he at the time of the Emperor's death? Very probably in Tuscany. All the facts suggest that he was still living with the Conti Guidi. But how long did he remain with them? Of the Guidi, unfortunately, we know very little. They, or at any rate a number of them, are violently attacked by Dante in the episode of Master Adam (*Inf.*, XXX, 49–90) and in the course of a savage allusion in the *Purgatorio* (XIV, 43–5). This is strong evidence against the hypothesis that at this stage the final draft of the *Inferno* had already been made. It is hard, indeed, to accept the view that the canto was written when the poet was still the guest, if not actually of the nobles whom he assails, at least of some member of their clique. As regards the *brutti porci* ('filthy swine') mentioned in the *Purgatorio*, the poet's allusions in the canto in question all have a political motive, and political affairs in Casentino were conducted by the nobles of the district. If we water down the allusion by making it refer to all the inhabitants, eliminating the thrust at the Counts of Porciano, we deprive the irony of all its sting. It is therefore logical to imagine that at a certain point—we do not quite know why, but it was very probably for political reasons— a serious rift developed between the poet and one of his hosts, with the result that he left Casentino.

Thus his restless pilgrimage began anew. Many critics, indeed the majority, maintain that he left Tuscany to seek refuge at the Court of Can Grande della Scala, but against such a theory is Boccaccio's assertion that from Tuscany he went to Romagna, and from there to Ravenna. Now if Boccaccio knows little of the early years of Dante's exile, his information about the last part of the poet's life was gathered directly from the latter's friends at Ravenna. In this matter, then, his authority is of the highest order, and it is unsound criticism to dispute it. Add to this that it is illogical to imagine Dante's wanderings took him very far from Tuscany when all his associations and interests served to keep him closely identified with that region. And all the facts imply that he continued to have dealings with people in Florence who took an interest in his fortunes.

A third argument against the theory that at this juncture the poet went to Verona is furnished by the actual letter which he wrote to Can Grande. But since the authenticity of this letter has been and still is called in question by numerous shrewd critics, it is appropriate, before drawing any conclusion from it, to make sure that it is genuine. Much has been written on the subject, but when all is said and done the critics merely repeat one another's arguments. We may therefore confine ourselves to essentials, and these will be indicated in the bibliography. My opinion is that if we relate the letter to the culture of the period we are bound to conclude that it is authentic. If Dante had written a commentary on the whole of the *Paradiso* he would have continued in similar vein, and would not have written anything substantially different.

But if the letter is authentic it is permissible to draw the conclusions which follow from what Dante writes at the beginning, which is, after all, the only part written strictly in the form of a letter (1–4). Now if we read it without prejudice we see from the opening lines that it was written not long after Dante had left Verona, when he still had a clear impression of what he had seen there and of the welcome that had been accorded him. He had seen Can Grande as a boy at the Court of Alboino and had been led to expect much of him; nor had he been mistaken, for he had found him now at the very height of his glory. This is tantamount to saying that he saw him again in 1317 or 1318, so that he did not come from Tuscany immediately after the death of Henry. Hence, all the evidence encourages us to side with Boccaccio and for the moment to try to pick up the poet's trail in Romagna.

But a word of caution is necessary. In writing the *Vita di Dante* I had to take up a definite position, otherwise I should not have been able to reconstruct the episode of history which I was examining. As one whose task it is to recommend a line of study I do not feel so positive. I cannot, in fact, forget how critics of repute have maintained that immediately after Henry's death Dante went to Verona, remaining there for some years. From there they suppose that he subsequently proceeded to Ravenna— some would have it that he did so after a great lapse of time. Now one cannot dismiss established theories without a careful examination of all the data on the basis of which they are con- structed. I have therefore indicated all the sources for such an examination in the bibliography. The important thing is to seek. By seeking one may always find something better.

In going to Romagna Dante was returning to a locality in which he had established numerous contacts, and with a view to finding out details of the hospitality that he may have enjoyed there it is a good thing at this point to assemble everything that he wrote about the region and to list the cases in which it provided inspiration for his poetry. But these early years must have con- stituted a period of exile, in the course of which he wandered about central Italy. And since for many reasons we cannot doubt that he paid at least one visit to Assisi and Fonte Avellana, I think it should be ascribed to this period, whether it was that he went there directly from Casentino *before* going down to Romagna, as seems to me probable, or that he went up again from there. In any case the whole of the period was spent in central Italy. With an eye to his studies, and in view of the independence of his nature, Dante must have sought and accepted without hesitation the hospitality afforded by convents and monasteries. As to his description of Assisi, his sympathy with the great saint and the reasons why he was attracted to the monastery hallowed by Pier Damiano's penance, I need only refer the student to my *Vita di Dante* and *L'ultima ascesa*.

From Romagna Dante could keep a watchful eye on the progress of events in Tuscany and north Italy, nor did important happenings in Europe escape his attention. If a knowledge of history forms an indispensable background for as full an under- standing of the man and his art as circumstances permit, even more essential is a knowledge of these years during which he established his greatness and drew ever closer to that ideal type with which he identified himself in his poetry. All we need do here is to recall the sequence of events: the Curia's affirmation of the absolute power of the Pope; King Robert's nomination as Imperial vicar; the revolt of the Ghibellines; the deaths of the two great political malefactors, Clement V and Philip of France; the conclave; the Battle of Montecatini. And in the midst of this spate of events Dante wrote his two great letters to the cardinals and his friend in Florence.

There is no longer any reason to question the authenticity of these letters, yet the discussions that have centred around the second of them will help us to understand it better. These discussions, which have dispelled so many doubts, shed light on so many facts, and afforded so clear an insight into Dante's soul, are one of the proudest boasts of the historical school.

The letter to the cardinals is the loftiest and most inspired of Dante's epistles. The man who called himself 'the last among the lambs that feed on the pastures of Christ' possessed the culture of the most learned ecclesiastics and bethought himself of the Church's interests far more than did her highest dignitaries. He addresses the cardinals, but the audience he has in mind is the whole of Christendom. 'All the feelings and attitudes that are most characteristic of the *Comedy* here find expression. Canto XIX of the *Inferno* and Canto XVI of the *Purgatorio*, which are so intimately religious and so intensely political, find an echo here, as if they still dominated the writer's soul.' Now we must note all these echoes from the *Comedy* and the *Monarchy* if we really desire to understand Dante and to form an adequate idea of his thought and his moral stature. 'The politician who only a short while ago composed the *Monarchy*,' I wrote, 'no longer has any doubts. The hierarchical conception of the two luminaries, which is reflected in some of the letters written at the time of Henry's invasion, has vanished. Now the two powers are two suns of equal brilliance; and, as in the *Comedy*, Dante weeps for Rome *utroque lumine destituta*. The writer's feeling for Rome completely dominates his soul. . . . Rome is the *caput latiale* which all Italians should dutifully venerate as the universal fountain-head of their civil life. Her abandonment arouses the pity "not only of men in general but of Hannibal himself". More than this, her wretchedness is the bane of Italy, and the ruin of the Church.

'To Dante's way of thinking Rome, Italy, the Church and the world are welded together in indissoluble unity. The life of one is the life of all. And "on behalf of the bride of Christ, the bride's abode, which is Rome, our beloved Italy—indeed, to speak in more general terms, on behalf of the whole city which they who travel on the face of the earth inhabit" he finally calls upon the cardinals to save "the glory of the Latins" from the supreme disgrace—*Vasconum obprobrium*. It is a crescendo of emotion which grips the writer's entire being, and the passion with which he is imbued and his consciousness of the mission with which he has been entrusted lead him to raise the tone of his letter and to attack both Pontiff and cardinals.... All the misery of the partisan, all the narrowness of a specific emotion have vanished. The Empire is there, but not the Ghibellines; the Church, but not the Guelfs. There is the Italian too, but as the ills of Italy are one with the destruction of the Church the idea of the nation has broadened for him into that of the whole of Christendom.... The writer has attained the height of his power, the man the fullness of his moral force.'

After reading this letter we may turn our attention to the one addressed to Dante's friend in Florence. The subject-matter is different, but the moral tone is equally exalted. Dante has built up his individuality, his ideal and real selves are identical. Those who thought that because the epistle appears in a Boccaccio manuscript the latter may have been its author knew neither Boccaccio nor Dante. The poet's dream is still the same—that he may return to his native city—but his innocence, *quibuslibet manifesta*, nearly fifteen years of suffering and the labours endured in the course of study no longer permit him those small concessions he had been prepared to make for his recall in earlier years. By this time he feels that he is speaking to the world. The letter, then, must be examined from end to end; it is necessary to find out the circumstances that gave rise to the talk of an impending amnesty, the terms in which it was formulated, and the names of the individuals who may have given Dante notice of it and of those who busied themselves on his behalf in Florence. All the relevant details will be found in the *Bullettino della Società dantesca* and the *Studi danteschi*. Here it must suffice to mention in particular the inquiries which Della Torre and Barbi have conducted on the subject.

Not long after (August 29th, 1315) was fought the Battle of Montecatini. On Dante's relations with Uguccione della Faggiuola and the hopes which he placed in him much was written during the last century; but to-day the researches of Troya, Balbo and their followers are more important for what they tell us of the history of the poet's fortunes during the nineteenth century than for anything else. It is, however, a good thing to be familiar with them, and since we are concerned with men of lofty intellect and character such a familiarity must in the long run always be useful.

Now it was Florence that, following her defeat, modified her stern attitude. Even Dante's name was included by the *ad hoc* Commission in the list of those sentenced for political crimes whose punishment might be commuted. But they had to appear before the court presided over by King Robert's delegate and provide a guarantee that they would submit to temporary banishment and that they would observe its terms. In conformity with his letter to his friend in Florence Dante naturally did not appear: he could not admit that the faintest shadow of guilt attached to himself. And on November 15th, 1315, sentence was passed on him and on his children: *Caput a scapulis amputetur ita quod penitus moriantur.* Anyone, then, can see the importance of this period of history from the point of view both of Dante's life and of his spiritual development. The student may with justice suppose that in all probability he re-opened his *Inferno* after the death of Clement V with the object of finding a place in its pages for the simoniacal Pontiff. Furthermore and better still: every page which he still intended to write was destined to reflect the haughtiness of his spirit.

For this period in general see COSMO, *Vita*, Chap. XIII, and *L'ultima ascesa*, Chap. XIII.

As regards the Conti Guidi and Casentino consult C. BENI, *Guida illustrata del Casentino*, Florence, Bemporad, 1918, and FATINI, 'Luci e ombre dantesche nel Casentino', in *Dante e Arezzo* (cited above), pp. 89 *sq.*

C. Verani, 'I conti Guidi', in *Atti e memorie della R. Accad. Petrarca*, Arezzo, 1938, New Series, XXV.

Regarding Assisi and the differences in spiritual outlook between the poet and St. Francis see Cosmo, *Le mistiche nozze*, *passim*; 'Il canto di santo Francesco', in *Giornale dantesco*, XXI (1913), pp. 137–51; *L'ultima ascesa*, Chap. X. Apropos of Fonte Avellana see, in addition to the older studies, F. Tarducci, *Dante e la Badia di Fonte Avellana*, Perugia, Tip. Umbra, 1921; G. Vitaletti, *Giornale dantesco*, XXIV (1921), pp. 23–31, XXV (1922), pp. 261–5, and XXVI (1923), pp. 52–67. For the letter to Can Grande see F. D'Ovidio, 'L'epistola a Can Grande', in *Rivista d'Italia*, Sept., 1899 (now reproduced in *Studii sulla Divina Commedia*, Palermo, Sandron, 1911, and in F. D'Ovidio's *Opere*, I, Caserta, Casa editrice Moderna, 1931); Torraca's article in *Rivista d'Italia*, Dec., 1899 (now included in *Studi danteschi*, Naples, Perrella, 1912); F. P. Luiso, 'L'epistola a Can Grande non è opera dell'Alighieri', in *Giornale dantesco*, X (1902), pp. 83–97, and XI (1903), pp. 60–9; Moore, *Studies*, III, 1903; G. Boffito, 'L'Epistola di Dante Alighieri a Can Grande della Scala', an attempt at a critical edition with a commentary, in *Memorie R. Acc. delle Scienze di Torino*, Series II, LVII (1907), *Cl. di sc. mor. stor. e filol.*, pp. 1–39 (cf. V. Biagi, *Bullettino della Società dantesca italiana*, XVI (1909), pp. 21–37); G. Vandelli, *Bullettino della Società dantesca italiana*, VIII (1901), pp. 137–64, IX (1902), pp. 273–9, and XII (1905), pp. 193–200; L. Pietrobono, 'L'Epistola a Can Grande', in *Giornale dantesco*, XL (1939), pp. 1–51. As regards the interpretation of the first part of the letter, which for the biographer of Dante is the most important part, see A. Fajani, *Dante e Verona* (Part III, *Verona nella vita di Dante*, Chaps. 3 and 4), Verona, Tip. Coop., 1921.

For the letter to the cardinals see G. Crocioni, *L'epistola di Dante ai cardinali italiani*, Perugia, 1901, and F. Di Capua, *Note all'epistola di Dante ai cardinali italiani*, Castellammare di Stabia, 1919. The student will also do well to read Cardinal Orsini's letter to Philip the Fair in S. Baluzius, *Vitae paparum avenion.*, Paris, 1693, II, No. XLIII (and in the new edition of G. Mollat, Paris, Letouzey, 1916–28, III, pp. 237–41).

As regards the letter *amico fiorentino* it is essential to consult A. DELLA TORRE, *Bullettino della Società dantesca italiana*, XII (1905), pp. 121–74, and BARBI's article in *Studi danteschi*, II (1920), pp. 115–48 (now reproduced in *Problemi*, II, pp. 305 *sq.*). The sentences of October 15th and November 6th, 1315, are in the *Codice diplomatico* (Nos. 114 and 115).

XIII

RAVENNA AND VERONA

ACCORDING to our interpretation Dante spent the whole of this period in Romagna. His reputation must have been great in those parts, and so far as it was known his artistic achievement must have been admired. The passages in his works which concerned Romagna were very probably known already. It was actually during his residence here, while he was perhaps leading an insecure existence as a guest in one household after another, that he was invited to Ravenna by Guido da Polenta, into whose hands the mayoralty of that city had fallen after the death of Lamberto (June 22nd, 1316). So much is asserted by Boccaccio, and all the evidence tempts us to believe him. Guido, who encouraged poetry, was aware of the glory that would accrue to him from such a visit, while everything tempted Dante to accept the invitation—the assurance of a home at long last, the suitability of Ravenna as a place from which to observe the political movements of Tuscany, Venice and Naples, the city's great memories, both Roman and Christian, and finally—and perhaps more than anything else—the peace he needed to complete his work. He was probably about to start work on the closing scenes of the *Purgatorio* and to prepare for the last exalted phase of the *Paradiso*. And it was to Ravenna that he brought at any rate part of his family. In virtue of the comforts it offered him, the inspiration with which it provided him, and the friendships that he formed while it was his home, Ravenna constitutes a vitally important chapter in Dante's life. It is therefore an absolute necessity for the student to examine every aspect of the city's life at this moment of history. At the Mayor's expense one of the poet's daughters had come to furnish him with the amenities of home life—that same daughter who afterwards retired to the monastery of Santo Stefano dell'Oliva. (Probably the Mayor himself made strenuous efforts to ensure that she should be admitted without financial provision.) In addition, his son was accorded a benefice.

122

Some have maintained also that the poet taught rhetoric in the city's university, but this does not seem likely. To be sure, he was regarded as a high authority in literature, and more especially in poetry, by his friends and by all who cultivated the humanities in the city. Those who made out that while at Ravenna he resumed the *De Vulgari Eloquentia* and wrote his dissertation on the *canzone*, the work being interrupted by his death, were not very far from the truth, not because he there resumed the treatise, which he had discontinued after writing the first book, but in the broader sense that technical discussions on poetry must have been frequent in that *milieu*. Certainly all listened reverently to the opinions and suggestions of so great a teacher.

His poetical inspiration was to a large extent derived from his strong political feelings. Meditating on the causes of Henry's failure, Dante had grown convinced that the formation of a powerful Ghibelline State in north Italy was essential if the venture was to succeed when a new Emperor chose to renew it. Hence the interest with which he followed the policy of the Ghibelline lords of Lombardy, their resistance to the pretensions of the new Pontiff, who wished to undo all the work accomplished by the great Henry, and above all his sympathy with the young Can Grande, who more than any other seemed imbued with the desire to execute the plan that was so near the poet's heart. In writing the *Paradiso* he had ascended into the realms of the ideal; yet, although this constituted the essential part of his life, it did not distract his attention from politics. Indeed, the latter was a source of inspiration for his poetry. It is this combination of feelings which at a certain stage must have decided Dante to visit Verona, and from there perhaps to proceed to other cities of Lombardy. I therefore think we should look upon the poet's visit to Verona as having taken place at this juncture, in accordance both with his own letter and with the logic of the facts. Probably Can Grande himself had given him to understand that he desired his presence. With the lord of Verona Dante had always had dealings, and he was now no longer the man he had been so many years before when, rejected and slandered, he had presented himself to Alboino. His reputation as a great poet was now established; as a political writer he was without a peer.

I

Accordingly his name lent rare strength and authority to the policy pursued by the lord of Verona, and it brought glory to his court. In certain respects Can Grande foreshadowed the noblemen of the *Quattrocento*, and these cultural and political conditions explain the welcome that the poet received. Perhaps Can Grande exploited him for the furtherance of his policy. The fact that we find Dante at Mantua, coupled with Galeazzo Visconti's mysterious allusion, tempts one to think so.

This was, maybe, the happiest moment in Dante's vagabond life, and all who wish to account for the eulogy of the Scaliger in Canto XVII of the *Paradiso* and for the political allusions in the same *cantica* must acquire a complete knowledge of Can Grande's work and of the policy pursued by the lords of Lombardy in their dealings with Pope John XXII and King Robert. Dante watched that policy with lively attention compounded of hopes and fears and, in so far as the subject of the *Paradiso* permitted, by a magnificent paradox imbued several parts of the *cantica* with the sentiments of which it was the expression. Had he so desired, he could certainly have continued to reside at Verona. But however much his attention may have been distracted by politics he was less a politician than a poet, and his first thought was for the completion of his great work, which was to create the historical conditions necessary for the political revival. Now Verona, however much comfort and satisfaction it might afford, was not a suitable place for concentrated thought. To convince oneself of this it is only necessary to read the *Bisbidis*. And so Dante returned to Ravenna. This does not rule out the possibility that he went back to Verona on some other occasion. Indeed, he was at Verona in January, 1320, when, in the presence of the clergy and the most eminent figures of the 'renowned city' he 'settled' the question of the depth of water in relation to land, a question which he had heard debated at Mantua. What I think must be ruled out is the theory that his stay was a long one, and in my opinion the stories of years of residence originate from a legend that sprang up later when scholars confused the poet's sojourns in the city and lumped them together, thus increasing their apparent duration.

The *Questio* is of no great importance in itself; yet, having convinced oneself that it is authentic, one should study it, not in the hope of learning anything new, but in order to get to know the character of the man better. While staying at Mantua he heard discussed a problem which was directly concerned with the world that he had created. He at once perceived the disputants' mistake, and having 'grown up from childhood', as he wrote, 'with a love of truth' and with a 'hatred' of all that was 'false', and since, albeit 'the least among philosophers', he was in his passion for truth second to none, he felt bound to shed the light which he had seen upon those who walked in darkness. He had probably intervened in the discussion while he was actually at Mantua, and the news had reached Verona. It is possible that he was credited with the expression of some opinions that were at variance with his scientific theories, and his reputation may have been damaged as a result. It must be remembered that in only a few months the last *cantica* of his great work, which was to be the climax of his long years of travail, was actually due to be published in Verona. Boccaccio's assertion that he used from time to time to send a few cantos to the lord of the city, coupled with Quirini's sonnet, leaves no room for doubt in the matter. Hence the determination with which he conducted his public readership and those sturdy declarations that were so characteristic of him.

Meanwhile the poet's reputation was growing. The publication of the *Inferno* and the *Purgatorio* established him as incomparably the greatest Italian poet. And it is precisely this growth in his reputation that explains the letter in verse addressed to him by Giovanni del Virgilio. The latter was a modest teacher of rhetoric in the University of Bologna who out of his devotion to the greatest of poets had appended the mighty name of Virgil to his own. He had read Dante's two *cantiche* and had perceived their beauty. But why did such a great new poet waste his talent by writing in the language of the mob? Let him write Latin and he, Giovanni, would present him for recognition by his peers. And he sent him an ode that began with a recognition of his greatness: *Pyeridum vox alma.*

Even if the ode had evoked no reply it would always remain important as evidence of the growth of Dante's reputation among men of learning. But Dante, moved by this recognition and invitation, replied; he replied by refashioning the Virgilian eclogue for the admirer of Virgil. This in its turn elicited a reply from the Bolognese teacher to which Dante again replied with another eclogue. This was perhaps the last of his poetic labours or was at least written at the time when the poet was putting the finishing touches to the *Paradiso*.

Thus light is thrown on Dante's stay at Ravenna and on his last years by these compositions, which need to be studied closely. Especially is this true of the first eclogue, which reveals in its entirety the feeling of the man: his contentment at the recognition and the invitation that had been accorded him, his desire to be crowned with the poet's laurel—a desire which he had already expressed at the commencement of the *Paradiso* and which he was about to formulate once more in the loftiest terms at the beginning of Canto XXV. He did indeed wish to be crowned, but it must be at Florence, among his own people, and at his baptismal font, in his own beautiful San Giovanni. And therefore it must be a religious ceremony.

'*Clerus vulgaria temnit*,' the teacher at the University had told him; and in exhorting him to write a poem he had indicated a number of themes from contemporary history which lent themselves to poetic treatment, *carmine vatisono*. But history was the very material from which Dante had woven the fabric of his own poem. Not that he had unfolded a continuous narrative, as del Virgilio suggested, but as a poet he had derived lofty inspiration from history. And the *Paradiso* was not written for laymen, but for those few who had raised 'their heads in good time to receive the bread of the angels'. With the specific object of showing the teacher how he, albeit in the despised vernacular—which, however, thanks to him was destined to become the language of literature—had carried into effect all that he, Giovanni, desired of him, and how by virtue of this truly 'prophetic ode' he very rightly aspired to the poet's laurel, Dante sent him the first ten cantos of the *Paradiso*. But the poet wrote an eclogue and, in accordance with the convention of the time, spoke in allegorical terms. The ten cantos of the *Paradiso* accordingly became, in the language of bucolic poetry, 'ten little buckets of milk' drawn from an *ovis gratissima* (vernacular poetry, according to our interpretation), whose udder was so swollen that all it asked for was to be milked.

These *decem vascula*, like the *ovis gratissima*, have been much discussed. Some have chosen to see in them the promise of nothing more or less than ten eclogues, which Dante proposed to write after he had finished the *Paradiso*. This is absurd, because one whose thoughts had recently been fixed on God would find it impossible to write anything more. Others insist that they symbolize the actual eclogue which he sent to del Virgilio; but in that case it is incomprehensible that there should be ten *vascula*, and not one. At all events, in view of the importance of the question and its direct bearing on the poet's last years the student should acquaint himself with the numerous and in some cases truly learned discussions of which it has been the theme, and should give them his careful consideration.

Dante hesitated to accept Master Giovanni's invitation to go to Bologna because it was a Guelf city and full of snares—*rura ignara deorum*. Giovanni by way of reply persisted in his invitations: *Huc ades, et nostros timeas neque, Titire, saltus.* Yet Dante would not be persuaded. Giovanni's assertions were a temptation, teachers and pupils desired to see him and to listen to his words, but at Bologna Polyphemus had his cave *assuetum rictus humano sanguine tingui.* But whom did he mean to designate by such a name? Anyone can see what an advantage it would be if we could solve this problem in a way that left no room for doubt. The key can only lie in the history of Bologna and Lombardy; but opinions are many and varied. For myself I think that what must have impressed Dante most of all, in view of the conditions that obtained in Bologna, was the appeal to act as leader in the Guelf war, with full powers, issued to Fulcieri da Calboli, who entered the city in great haste on July 20th. This was the 'old' wild beast' who had decimated the population of Florence, and who, lusting for revenge and slaughter, was now preparing to lay Bologna waste. But it is well to study the question thoroughly. What is even more important is the fact that at Ravenna Dante must have found himself comfortably situated.

He had several dear friends who encouraged him to remain—first and foremost Guido.

Had he during this period entered the Order of Penitent Friars or, to put it more simply, become a Franciscan tertiary? I think I have proved as much; and the evidence of Friar Mariano seems to me incontrovertible. Buti's assertion to the effect that he was enrolled in the Order of Minor Friars during his early manhood is certainly a gross error, due in all probability to a confusion of facts and to a misinterpretation of a passage in the *Comedy*. It is astonishing that it should have been taken seriously by serious scholars—scholars who, however, have been inclined to exaggerate the mystical tone of the *Vita Nuova*. It is another matter so far as the last stage of the poet's life is concerned. He was sustained by his effort to ascend into the presence of God and by his poetry, the tone of which he raised more and more so that it should match its sublime theme. His poetical and spiritual exaltation melted into one. Nothing could be more natural than that, in thus elevating his human self to the plane of his poetic self, he should have drawn even closer to the friars of an Order which he held so dear, and that he should have joined its ranks.

We have by now reached the end. How it came about we know from the writings of Villani and Boccaccio. Relations between Ravenna and Venice having become embittered, Dante was sent by Guido on an embassy to the Venetian senate, but he achieved nothing. During the journey back along the coast, probably in the heat of early September, he contracted a malignant form of malaria. A few days later (during the night of September 14th-15th), worn out by his labours, he surrendered his great spirit to God at Ravenna.

As regards Dante's stay in Ravenna, *L'ultimo rifugio di Dante*, by C. RICCI (Milan, Hoepli, 2nd ed., 1921), is still of fundamental importance. See also the same author's 'I rifugi dell'esule', in *Ore ed ombre dantesche*, Florence, Le Monnier, 1921, pp. 43–67; BISCARO, 'Dante a Ravenna', in *Bull. ist. stor. it.*, No. 41 (1921), pp. 1–42 (but the writer's theses are disputed by G. GUERRIERI-CROCETTI, 'Negli ultimi anni di Dante', in *Giornale dantesco*, XXVI (1923), pp. 27–32 and 142–6). With special reference to the poetic inspiration which Dante derived from places the student should also read the chapter entitled 'In Ravenna' in Pascoli's *La mirabile visione*. For a full description of the city in the time of Dante see also *Ricordi di Ravenna medioevale per il VI centenario della morte di Dante*, published privately by the Cassa di Risparmio di Ravenna, 1921, and A. ANNONI, 'Ravenna monumentale per il centenario di Dante', in *Emporium*, LIV (1921), pp. 46–138. As regards the University and the schools of Ravenna and the possibility that Dante taught in them see, in addition to Ricci, O. ZENATTI, *Dante e Firenze* (cited above), pp. 79 *sq.* and 462 *sq.*; P. AMADUCCI, 'Dante e lo studio di Ravenna', in *Bullettino della Società dantesca italiana*, XV (1908), pp. 132–42; S. BERNICOLI, 'Maestri e scuole letterarie in Ravenna nel secolo XIV', in *Felix Ravenna*, Part XXXII (Dec., 1927), pp. 61–9.

As regards Dante's teaching, the various attestations of Boccaccio are listed in Appendix IV of ZENATTI's work cited above. There is a bibliography of the subject in FILIPPINI, 'L'insegnamento di Dante in Ravenna' (in *Documenti e Studi pubblicati per cura della R. Dep. di storia patria per le prov. di Romagna*, Vol. IV, Bologna, Zanichelli, 1922), and in the same author's *Dante scolaro e maestro*, Geneva, Olschki, 1929 (*Biblioteca dell'Archivium romanicum*, Series I, Vol. XII).

Against the thesis: NOVATI, 'Se Dante abbia mai pubblicamente insegnato', in *Indagini e postille dantesche*, Series I, Bologna, Zanichelli, 1899, pp. 5–35; TORRACA, 'Dante maestro di scuola?' in *Atti d. R. Acc. di archeol. lett. e belle arti*, Naples, New Series, IX (1926), pp. 47–73. Filippini replies to Torraca in *Dante scolaro*, etc. (cited above), pp. 186 *sq.*

As regards Can Grande, in addition to SPANGENBERG's book, *Can Grande I della Scala* (Berlin, Heyfelder, 1892–5), the student should consult C. CIPOLLA, *Compendio della storia politica di Verona*, Verona, Cabianca, 1899, and A. SCOLARI, *Il Messia dantesco*, Bologna, Zanichelli, 1913 (like all natives of Verona, this writer identifies the greyhound with his own city's hero). The *Bisbidis* may conveniently be read in C. CIPOLLA and F. PELLEGRINI, 'Poesie minori riguardanti gli Scaligeri' (in *Bull. ist. stor. it.*, No. 24 (1902), pp. 50–5) and in V. DE BARTHOLOMAEIS, *Rime giullaresche e popolari d'Italia*, Bologna, Zanichelli, undated [1926], pp. 68–71.

Apropos of the exiles' residence at the Court of the Scaligers see CIPOLLA, *Antiche cronache veronesi*, pp. 227 *sq.*; id., 'Le fazioni politiche di Bologna e i Signori di Lombardia', in *Memorie R. Acc. delle Scienze di Torino*, Series II, LXII (1912), *Cl. sc. mor. stor. e filol.*, pp. 1–21; LIVI, *Dante, suoi primi cultori, sua gente in Bologna*, Bologna, Cappelli, 1918.

For the famous hospitality of the Scaligers see MAGISTRI MARZAGAIAE, 'De modernis gestis', in CIPOLLA, *Antiche cronache veronesi* (*Mon. stor. pubbl. dalla R. Dep. veneta di st. patr.*), Venice, Visentini, 1890, I, pp. 343 and 405.

As regards Dante's attitude in face of the excommunication of Can Grande and ll. 127–9 of *Paradiso*, XVIII, see PARODI's review (*Bullettino della Società dantesca italiana*, XVIII (1911), pp. 72–3) of the *Lettere di Giovanni XXII riguardanti Verona e gli Scaligeri (1319–1334)*, published by CIPOLLA (Verona, Franchini, 1909). Also Chap. I of BISCARO's *Dante a Ravenna* (cited above).

On the *Questio* consult E. MOORE, *L'autenticità della Questio de aqua et terra*, Bologna, Zanichelli, 1899 (*Bibl. Critica* Passerini Papa, No. 12); id., *Studies*, II, pp. 303 *sq.*; see ANGELITTI, *Bullettino della Società dantesca italiana*, VIII (1900–1), pp. 52–71.

V. RUSSO, *Per l'autenticità della quaestio de aqua et terra*, Catania, 1901 (see ANGELITTI, *Bullettino della Società dantesca italiana*, VIII (1901), pp. 290–9); G. BOFFITO, 'Intorno alla quaestio de aqua et terra', in *Memorie R. Acc. delle Scienze di Torino*, Series II, LI (1902), Cl. sc. mor., pp. 73–159, and LII (1903), pp. 257–342. Cf. *Bullettino della Società dantesca italiana*, X (1903), pp. 388–400.

V. BIAGI, *La quaestio de aqua et terra di Dante, bibliografia, dissertazione critica sull'autenticità, testo e commento, lessigrafia, facsimili*, Modena, Vincenzi, 1907. Cf. ANGELITTI, *Bullettino della Società dantesca italiana*, XV (1908), pp. 161–82.

F. ANGELITTI, 'La Questio de aqua et terra di Dante Alighieri ridotta alla più probabile lezione, nuovamente tradotta e commentata', in *Pubblicazioni del R. Osservatorio Astronomico*, No. 35, pp. 1–256, Palermo, 1915 (published posthumously in 1932). The Società dantesca's critical text of the *Eclogae* was edited by Mancini. See also: P. H. WICKSTEED and E. G. GARDNER, *Dante and Giovanni del Virgilio, including a Critical Edition of the Text of*

Dante's Eclogae Latinae and of the Poetic Remains of Giovanni del Virgilio, Westminster, A. Constable & Co., 1902; and cf. PARODI, *Giornale dantesco*, X (1902), pp. 51–63; G. ALBINI, *Dantis eclogae, Joannis de Virgilio carmen et ecloga responsiva*, text, commentary and translation, Florence, Sansoni, 1903.

On Giovanni del Virgilio see G. ALBINI, 'Giovanni del Virgilio', in *Dante e Bologna*, lectures, Bologna, 1922; C. MARCHESI, 'Le allegorie ovidiane di Giovanni del Virgilio', in *Studj romanzi*, VI (1909), pp. 85–135; E. CARRARA, *Il Diaffonus*, Bologna, 1925. On the bucolic literature of the fourteenth century consult F. MACRÌ LEONE, *La Bucolica latina nella letteratura italiana del secolo XIV*, Turin, Loescher, 1889; E. CARRARA, *La poesia pastorale*, Milan, Vallardi, undated (*Storia dei gen. letter.*), pp. 68 *sq.*

There is a bibliography (up to 1913) on the correspondence between the two poets in LIDONNICI, *Giornale dantesco*, XXI (1913), pp. 205–43; see in addition the articles by the same author, ib., XXVII (1924), pp. 79–90; XXVIII (1925), pp. 324–35; XXIX (1926), pp. 141–58. Here I will only mention ALBINI, 'Le ecloghe', in 'Lectura Dantis', *Le opere minori* (cited above), pp. 259–82, and in *Dante*, Milan, Treves, 1921, pp. 171 *sq.*; PARODI, 'La prima ecloga di Dante e l'ovis gratissima,' in *Atene e Roma*, XIV (1911), pp. 193–213; and PASCOLI, *La mirabile visione* (cited above).

Apropos of the poetic laurel which Dante desired so keenly, the student should never fail to read—even if he does not subscribe to the theses propounded—TODESCHINI, *Studi*, II, p. 316, and NOVATI, *Indagini e postille* (cited above), pp. 73 *sq.* But cf. D'OVIDIO, *Studii* (cited above), pp. 437 *sq.* (see *Bullettino della Società dantesca italiana*, IX (1901–2), p. 76).

As regards the identity of the personage whom Dante designated by the name of Polyphemus, this is a question on which every annotator of the eclogues has naturally tried to throw light. With considerable skill Lidonnici has demonstrated that he should be connected with events in Bologna ('Polifemo', in *Bullettino della Società dantesca italiana*, XVIII (1911), pp. 189–205), but his thesis, even though accepted by Albini and Filippini, is not convincing. BISCARO, in *Dante a Ravenna* (cited above), p. 76, believes as I do that the reference is to Fulcieri da Calboli. But see G. MAZZONI, 'Dante e il Polifemo bolognese', in *Arch. stor. it.*, I (1938), reprinted in *Almae luces* (cited above), pp. 349–72, and Mancini's recension in *Studi danteschi*, XXIV (1939), pp. 139–43.

On the struggle between Ravenna and Venice, Dante's journey and mission, and his death, the leading authority is Ricci.

XIV

THE *COMEDY*—I

General Remarks

The *Comedy* is above all a great poetic creation—perhaps the greatest the human mind has ever conceived. In studying it, therefore, we must regard it essentially as a work of poetry. But since both its inspiration and its material are drawn from history it can only be understood in the light of history. As Ugo Foscolo rightly said in his own day, 'The more Dante is looked upon as a historian, the greater the illusion he creates and the more wonderful he appears as a poet.' Foscolo was the precursor of the great historical school; hence the importance of his part in the development of Dante studies is great. After him came De Sanctis, who clarified a number of episodes from the *Inferno* in a way that has never been surpassed, and shed light on parts of the entire work; but in virtue of the suggestions which he offered to young students in his Essay on Francesca he would seem to have founded a school of *dilettanti*, who were content to understand those passages in the work which present fewest difficulties and are therefore most easily appreciated as poetry. The *Comedy* is not merely, as Croce insisted, 'a series of lyrical compositions of varying tone' set within the framework of a theological romance; it is a vast and compact poetic organism, formulating in concrete terms the solution which an exalted religious system, in accordance with the aspirations of millions and millions of men, has for countless centuries offered to the problem of human destiny. We cannot wholly understand the *raison d'être* of this organism and so appreciate to the full the poetry that pervades and animates it unless we examine, individually and collectively, all its constituent elements.

Hence, the first thing the young student should do is to read carefully the entire work. He should not skate over any difficulties. Indeed, the graver they appear, the more resolutely should he face them. Critical studies and explanations of particular passages will come later. One cannot judge the effective value of a critical study unless one is familiar with the whole work. For the first examination all that is necessary is a good commentary. But not just one commentary. All have their merits, but none solves all the vast and complex problems inherent in the work. The rigorously scientific commentary, the dream and for a long time the refrain of Michele Barbi, is unfortunately still to be written. For the illustration of any given passage such a commentary would employ all the resources of historical, philological and philosophic learning; where points of controversy existed it would relate their history; it would enable the reader to decide in favour of one or another interpretation, so that there would arise 'an exegetical tradition with a sufficiently firm and secure basis, whether for literal or merely philological interpretation, or for the explanation of symbols, or even for the acquisition of a deeper insight into every inspiration and manifestation of the poet's sentiment' (Barbi). For the present, the surest way of discerning mistakes, avoiding them and forming a less incomplete picture of the work and one that is more clearly defined in its details is to compare the views of the various expositors on the disputed passages and to correlate their respective shortcomings.

Happily, there is an abundance of good academic commentaries, and a bibliography will indicate them all. I shall confine myself to singling out just a few of the most notable ones. The young student should, however, realize that when he has followed up all the indications he will only be starting to learn. Thorough understanding is arrived at by personal effort, and is the outcome of patient research, and of serious reflection on such research and on the results obtained.

As regards the title of the work, which provoked so many heated discussions during the sixteenth and seventeenth centuries, and which holds such an important place in the story of Dante's fortunes, the student should read P. RAJNA, 'Il titolo del poema dantesco', in *Studi danteschi*, IV (1921), pp. 5–37.

From Bambaglioli's, which was the first, down to the most recent ones, commentaries on the *Comedy* have been very plentiful, and one need only glance at the *Tavola* of bibliographical references at the end of Scartazzini and Vandelli's edition in order to form an idea of their number. Without having recourse to the great bibliographies, the reader will find a list of the principal commentaries published up to 1900 in Scartazzini's *Dantologia*. But at the start the young student will derive more profit from the modern commentaries, the word 'modern' being used in a very broad sense. The ancient commentaries should be referred to, particularly for the language (though unfortunately good modern editions are lacking). The two most important ones are the *Ottimo* and Benvenuto's, and considering the extent of our present knowledge of the various editions the expense of reprinting them in a critical edition would be amply justified. The ordinary needs of those who wish to delve into the past may be met by *La Divina Commedia nella figurazione artistica e nel secolare commento*, published by Utet under the editorship of Biagi, Passerini, Rostagno and Cosmo (Turin, Utet, 1921–40, three large volumes). This contains the finest work of twenty-three commentators, from Dante's children to Tommaseo and Andreoli, and in order to form an idea of their merits and of their possible usefulness the student should see my *Licenza* at the end of the third volume.

For more detailed information regarding the first commentators see L. ROCCA, *Di alcuni commenti della Divina Commedia composti nei primi venti anni dopo la morte di Dante*, Florence, Sansoni, 1891. Cf. ROEDIGER's article in *Riv. crit. d. lett. it.*, Florence, III (1886), No. 6, and see BARBI, *Problemi*, I (the heading 'Commedia: Commenti' in the index).

For Landino and the sixteenth-century commentators see BARBI, *La fortuna di Dante nel secolo XVI*, Pisa, Nistri, 1890.

There are already glimpses of what might be termed a historical commentary in Lombardi. It is still presentiment rather than the thing itself, but it is the presentiment of a man of learning and keen acumen. The new edition of his commentary from the Education Department's presses (Padua, 1822), with the additions of recent editors, seemed to Cesari to mark the point that Dante studies had reached by the early nineteenth century. Five years later Torri's edition of the *Ottimo* was printed at Pisa, while in 1837 Tommaseo published the first edition of his commentary at Venice. Tommaseo saw at once how much of value could be gleaned from the *Ottimo* and from the ancient expositors in general, and he made good use of it. By now Romantic criticism was yielding its fruits. In order to comprehend a poet the reader must transport himself into his environment, studying him through the medium of all his works and focussing the light that they diffuse on the point which it is desired to clarify. He must illuminate the poet's language by means of the language used in the poet's lifetime, and throw light on his art and thought by reference to the art and thought of the poets and philosophers whom he took as his models.

How Tommaseo discharged his task and what are his merits and defects I have endeavoured to show in the Introduction to the edition of his commentary which I prepared for Gustavo Balsamo Crivelli's Library of Italian classics (Turin, Utet, 1920). This is the only edition that comes readily to hand. However, Antonelli's astronomical illustrations are not included. Just as the Education Department's edition does in the case of the early eighteen-hundreds, so Scartazzini's commentary, published in four volumes[1] by Brockhaus (Leipzig) between 1870 and 1890, may give an idea of the progress made in the interpretation of Dante's works up to the end of last century. This commentary is still useful, especially that part of it which deals with the *Purgatorio* and the *Paradiso*, because it relates the history of the most important problems, and quotes or summarizes the various interpretations of the disputed passages. If death had not prevented Vandelli from reaping the fruits of his prolonged labours by publishing his critical text, all the arguments about the various readings would automatically have come to an end. In its absence they may still prove a useful aid to the formation of an opinion.

Giacomo Poletto's commentary (Rome, 1894, three volumes, large octavo) may also be found useful on account of its many references to scholasticism, especially to Thomism. But see Torraca's long review (*Di un commento nuovo alla Divina Commedia*, Bologna, Zanichelli, 1899).

Scartazzini later condensed his commentary into a smaller edition (Milan, Hoepli, 1893). In successive editions, revised by

[1] The first volume, the *Inferno*, was republished in 1900 in an entirely new form.

Vandelli, this has undergone many changes, and the last (the tenth) contains the most accurate rendering of the text. From the point of view of philological interpretation this commentary is perhaps the most reliable. Casini's (Florence, Sansoni) may justly be regarded as its equal, especially in its treatment of history; an improved version of it has since been published by A. S. Barbi in his edition. More original are the commentaries of Torraca (Milan, Albrighi e Segati) and Pietrobono (Turin, Seit). But as to Passerini's (Florence, Sansoni), Scartazzini and Vandelli's, and Torraca's, the student should consult BARBI, *Problemi*, I, pp. 197–303. For Steiner's (Turin, Paravia), Scarano's (Palermo, Sandron), Flamini and Pompeati's (Milan, Vallardi), Pietrobono's, and Grabher's (Florence, Nuova Italia), which is more particularly aesthetic in its approach, see BARBI, *Con Dante e coi suoi interpreti*, Florence, Le Monnier, 1941, pp. 1–116. In view of the sober and definite interpretations which they offer Del Lungo's (Florence, Le Monnier) and Venturi's (Milan, Signorelli) are also worthy of mention. The last-named is excellent from the academic standpoint.

Two volumes have been published of Rossi's commentary (Albrighi e Segati), which is chiefly notable for the introductions to the individual cantos. As regards the second volume, which was completed by S. Frascino, see COSMO's article in *Studi danteschi*, XXVI (1942), pp. 161–74. Then we must not forget the various *Lecturae Dantis*, the merits of which naturally differ greatly. The commentaries on some of the cantos, for example those by Romani, Del Lungo, Parodi and Bertoldi, to mention a few names, are well worth studying.

Origin and Composition of the Work

In order to comprehend a work one must face the problems that arise out of it and attempt to solve them. The first problem is that of its origin. When and how did the first intuition of a journey to the realms beyond the grave flash before Dante's mind, and how did it grow until it became the *Comedy*? Some have chosen to see the poem's inspiration in the *canzone* 'Donne ch'avete'—to be precise, in the second stanza, where God, in reply to the angels and saints who have entreated Him to summon

Beatrice back to heaven, says that she must remain yet awhile on
earth—

> Where dwelleth one who pines for loss of her,
> And who shall say to those in hell: 'O ye that were born
>   in an evil day,
> I have seen the hope of the blessed.'

I do not believe that the allusion here is to any *detto*—I do not
use the word poem[1]—which Dante at that time intended to write
on the subject of hell, and I have already shown how these lines
should be interpreted. Yet for the understanding of the first
orientation of Dante's spiritual life it is important to note how
from the time of his first youthful essays he was transported in
imagination to the world beyond and laid the scene of the
conversations between his characters in paradise and hell. Without his knowing it these conversations constituted the bonds that
united the world in which he passed his temporal life with the
world that was one day to be his home.

Next comes the allusion at the end of the *Vita Nuova* to the
'wondrous vision' that he had after he had written the sonnet
'Oltre la spera'. No one will ever be able to say with certainty
what form that vision took. Some have seen in it a development
of the sonnet, and have therefore sought its scene in the Empyrean. Others have identified it with the appearance of Beatrice
in the Earthly Paradise. Many excellent pages have been written
on the subject—pages which may be read with pleasure, and also
with profit, because they enable us to get closer to the heart of the
matter. But any attempt to be definite is labour wasted. Certainly the poet envisaged a eulogy of Beatrice that would trans-
cend in its conception the narrow limits of the world in which
he lived, and therefore something which, in view of its scope,
could only be achieved after long preparation. Undoubtedly, as
we have seen, Dante prepared his mind by means of long and
patient study. But what did he write? He must at any rate have
attempted some sort of rough draft, and Boccaccio's account of
the discovery of the first seven cantos of the *Inferno*, even when
it has been stripped of all embroidery, must contain an element

---

[1] i.e. because *poema* referred exclusively to Latin verse. (Translator's note.)

of truth. These must have been the notes which were entrusted to the watchful care of Gemma by her husband when he was in Lunigiana. But more than this one cannot say.

As to the view that the *Comedy* was begun in 1300, there is no need even to discuss it. It is due to a naïve confusion of the year in which Dante completed his imaginary journey with the year in which he began to describe it. At all events this view, even allowing for its naïvety, is yet another indication of the poet's power of suggestion, as a result of which his narrative is mistaken for reality.

In point of fact, even if the *Comedy* had its origin in the old project—to which the poet alludes in the last chapter of the *Vita Nuova*—of glorifying Beatrice, and even if, so to speak, it was grafted on to that project, it springs from a vision of life that is immeasurably vaster, one that is in the widest sense of the term universal. Such a vision could only take shape in the poet's mind after the lugubrious experiences that came his way when he participated in the political life of Florence and in the various attempts made to re-enter the city by force of arms. He had not yet experienced the sorrows and the humiliations of exile; he had not yet seen at first hand the ruin which had spread throughout the whole of Italy in consequence of the wickedness of her rulers and the turmoil created by the warring factions. The injustice of which he had been a victim was merely the common lot of countless innocent men in all the cities of Italy. The baneful effects of a simoniacal Pontiff's mad pride and of the clergy's consuming greed for worldly goods spread from Florence to the whole of Christendom. Only amid all this misery and ruin could Dante's new political consciousness reach maturity. It was this consciousness that enabled him to abandon his narrow parochial outlook and to conceive the loftier idea of a universal monarchy, as being alone capable of guaranteeing peace and justice to all men. This idea is first expressed in the fourth book of the *Convivio*.

In the present state of Dante studies there are only two hypotheses regarding the origin of the *Comedy* and the date of its commencement which seem to me to deserve the student's careful consideration. I associate the two questions because, as

K

was well said by Gorra, the problem of the date of composition is intimately connected with the fundamental study of the work —with the study of its origin, its purpose, its historical and aesthetic *raison d'être*. Of the hypotheses in question one ascribes the commencement of the work to roughly 1307 or 1308, after the completion of Book IV of the *Convivio*, while the other puts it as late as the period following the death of Henry VII.

Each hypothesis has valid arguments in its favour, and each has the support of able scholars. I confess that for a long time I myself hesitated between them. Only when I studied Dante's mental development as a prelude to writing his life, and had to account for his attitude in face of the announcement of Henry's descent upon Italy, did I decide in favour of the first. It is the attitude of a man inspired—a man who believes that he has a mission, like the great ones of the earth. The Pontiff and the Emperor had written their encyclical letters giving the great news to the peoples of Italy, and Dante likewise, as though he were of their company, wrote his encyclical 'to the lords of Italy, to the kings and senators of Rome the bounteous, to the counts and all the peoples, *universis et singulis*'. This attitude and the tone of the letter cannot be explained merely by the natural sense of exaltation with which he, like all the other unfortunates, had been filled by the news of the descent. We feel instinctively that his mind is dominated by the consciousness that he has been entrusted with a unique mission. This consciousness could only have been inspired by the grandeur of the new work which he had conceived and begun and which, he felt, gave him a place among those great spirits whose right and duty it is to speak in the name of something that transcends the common run of things. *Humilis italus* he was indeed, but, in virtue of the mission that he had undertaken, worthy to stand beside St. Paul and Aeneas.

If we accept this hypothesis everything becomes clear and logical. About 1308 Dante had returned from Lucca to Casentino. The *Convivio* and the *De Vulgari Eloquentia* had represented the writer's experience of the lugubrious political conditions prevalent in Italy as one of ever-growing intensity. It had manifested itself in cries of grief that lay bare his soul. In the fourth book of the *Convivio* the theory of the necessity of the

Empire is expounded in a style eloquent of the emotion of one whose mind is excited by the discovery of a great truth. Again, the two works are suddenly broken off in the middle as though the writer's thoughts are directed to something far more important which completely monopolizes his attention. His return to Casentino enabled him to read an apocalyptic book written by a Franciscan friar, Ubertino da Casale—a book studded with dreams and hopes of regeneration. It was very probably in this environment that the old idea of glorifying the woman who had long been loved and of spiritualizing her poet expanded into a vision in which Beatrice remains, indeed, the central figure of the work, but the first intuition broadens into a religious and political conception of the regeneration of society through the portrayal of the writer's own regeneration. This idea is developed in the course of a journey through the realms beyond the grave. The privilege of undertaking such a journey is accorded to him in the same way as it was accorded to Aeneas and St. Paul in days gone by, and his good fortune is due to the intercession of the Virgin. As a result, the consciousness of a mission entrusted to him by the Almighty for the benefit of a corrupt world is crystallized in his mind and becomes the driving force of his whole life. Since the work embraces all the history and science of his time, the need to clarify and to solve the many problems that arose out of it explains his visit between 1308 and 1310 to the Sorbonne, the fountain-head of contemporary learning, just as the announcement that the Emperor had descended upon Italy on an errand of peace explains his sudden return.

I think, however, that it is a mistake to believe that the *Inferno* and the *Purgatorio* were completed before 1313, and that the poet did not return to them at a later date. The unhappy outcome of the expedition and the death of the Emperor, coupled with the deaths in swift succession of the two great political malefactors, Clement V and Philip of France—a dual event which, in view of the happenings that accompanied it, seemed like a punishment from heaven—cannot have failed to exert a powerful influence on the poet's mind, inducing him to amend a number of passages and to introduce new material. To think that Dante wrote Canto XIX of the *Inferno* in 1308 or 1309, or at any rate before

1313, and that, prompted by the Pope's uncertain health, he prophesied his impending death with such exactness of detail, is to credit him with an irresponsibility that is out of keeping with his character. And further evidence could be adduced if this were the proper place. Here I am merely pointing out the line of approach which may lead the student to contemplate the facts and to estimate their importance, guided by those who have investigated the problem most thoroughly.

It must not be thought, however, that weighty arguments in support of their own hypothesis are not also brought forward by those who maintain that the work was written as late as the period following the death of the Emperor. They stress the profound impression that the event must have made on the poet's mind, first causing disappointment and loss of heart, and immediately afterwards intellectual revolt, and the courageous project of preparing men's minds for the great Coming, if it should be repeated by a new Emperor—as it certainly would be, since order is the keynote of the universe and God could not remove His hands from the reins of history. The poet's manner of writing, his speed, the certainty that the *Paradiso* was written during his last years and the last cantos during his last days, the rediscovery of the latter by his son Jacopo—a fact which, when stripped of all irrelevancies, cannot be doubted—these circumstances, coupled with all the other indications, lend weight to the conjecture.

Anyone can see, then, how numerous and grave are the problems implicit in the study of the origin and composition of the *Comedy*. The subject therefore requires attentive and profound thought, and the student, instead of adopting the easy course of acquiescence, will do well to return to the problem again and again as he progresses in his examination, and deepens his understanding, of the other problems that arise from the study of the work as a whole.

The origin of the *Comedy* has naturally been the subject of much discussion. As regards the school of thought which tried to discover the first rudimentary germ of the poem in the second stanza of 'Donne ch'avete', see the chapter entitled 'I primi germi della Divina Commedia nella Vita Nuova' in G. FEDERZONI's *Studi e diporti danteschi*, Bologna, Zanichelli, 1902 (definitive edition, 1935). The writer's argument is opposed by BARBI, 'La data della Vita Nuova e i primi germi della Commedia', in *Problemi*, I, pp. 99 *sq.*, and by G. MAZZONI, 'Il primo accenno alla "Comedia"', in *Miscellanea nuziale Rossi-Teiss*, Bergamo, Arti Graf., 1897, pp. 129–38, now reproduced in *Almae luces* (cited above), pp. 157–66. See also the note summarizing the various opinions held in the *Appendice* which Melodia added at the end of his commentary on the *canzone* in his *Vita Nuova*, pp. 140–6, and the *Indice decennale* (1893–1903) to the *Bullettino della Società dantesca italiana*, p. 143.

E. GORRA, 'Per la genesi della Divina Commedia', in *Fra drammi e poemi*, Milan, Hoepli, 1900, pp. 109 *sq.* See Melodia's references in the note on the last chapter of the *Vita Nuova*.

E. COLI, *Il paradiso terrestre dantesco*, Florence, Carnesecchi, 1897, pp. 208 *sq.*; G. SALVADORI, *La mirabile visione di Dante nel Paradiso terrestre*, Turin, Libr. ed. int., 1915.

PASCOLI, *Sotto il velame*, Messina, 1900, pp. 593 *sq.*

P. RAJNA, 'La genesi della Divina Commedia', in *La vita italiana nel Trecento*, Milan, Treves, 1902.

G. FERRETTI has re-opened the question as to whether Dante began the *Divine Comedy* in Florence and indeed wrote the first seven cantos there in *I due tempi della composizione della Divina Commedia*, Bari, Laterza, 1935. His treatment is shrewd and extremely detailed, and he fully upholds the truth of Boccaccio's narrative. The book contains a complete bibliography of past works. But cf. PORENA's article in *La Rassegna*, XLIV (1936), pp. 3–8. The reader may also consult on the subject HAUVETTE, *Études sur la Divine Comédie*, Paris, Champion, 1922.

The later date of composition was supported with great vigour by PARODI, 'La data della composizione e le teorie politiche dell'Inferno e del Purgatorio', in *Poesia e storia nella Divina Commedia*, Naples, Perrella, 1921, pp. 365–509. This work also contains a record of the author's various disputations with Gorra, who upheld the contrary thesis. Parodi is supported by BARBI, subject to a number of modifications, especially as regards the year of commencement,[1] in *Problemi*, I, pp. 69 *sq.*, and by ERCOLE

---

[1] In fact Barbi maintains that Dante only began the *Comedy* after he had ceased work on the *Convivio*.

(*Il pensiero politico*, cited above, I, pp. 108 *sq.* and *passim*), ROSSI, etc.

F. D'OVIDIO, 'La data della composizione e divulgazione della Commedia', in *Studii sulla Divina Commedia* (Opere, I, Vol. II, Caserta, Casa ed. mod., 1931, pp. 191–202); id., *Il guelfismo di Dante nel II canto dell'Inferno e la cronologia delle tre cantiche, Nuovo volume di studii danteschi* (Opere, IV, Caserta and Rome, 1926).

F. EGIDI, 'L'argomento barberiniano per la datazione della Divina Commedia', in *Studi romanzi*, XIX (1928), pp. 135–62. But see G. VANDELLI, 'Per la datazione della Commedia', in *Studi danteschi*, XIII (1928), pp. 5–29 and COSMO's article in *Riv. stor. it.*, XLVI (1929), pp. 110–1. Also L. PIETROBONO, 'L'argomento barberiniano e la data della Divina Commedia', in *Giornale dantesco*, XXXII (1931), pp. 133–46.

For the contrary thesis, according to which the work was written as late as the period following the death of Henry VII, see TRENTA, *L'esilio di Dante nella Divina Commedia*, Pisa, 1892, Appendix III.

L. LEYNARDI, *La psicologia dell'arte nella Divina Commedia*, Turin, Loescher, 1894, Part I, Chaps. 3 and 4. Cf. COSMO's article in *Giornale dantesco*, II (1894), pp. 214–9.

PASCOLI, *La mirabile visione* (cited above); COSMO, *Vita di Dante* (chapter entitled 'La grande luce'); E. GORRA, 'Quando Dante scrisse la Divina Commedia', in *Rend. del R. ist. lomb.*, Series II, XXXIX (1906) and XL (1907), notes I, II, III; id., 'I nove passi di Beatrice', in *Mélanges Chabaneau*, 'Romanische Forschungen', XXIII (1907), pp. 585–90; id., 'Dante e Clemente V', in *Giornale storico della letteratura italiana*, LXIX (1917), pp. 193–216.

KRAUS, *Dantes Leben* (cited above), pp. 394 *sq.*

VOSSLER, *La Divina Commedia studiata nella sua genesi e interpretata*, Bari, Laterza, 2nd ed., 1927, Vol. I, Part 2, pp. 289 *sq.*, and Vol. II, Part I, pp. 320 *sq.*

ZINGARELLI, *Dante* (cited above), II, Chap. 28.

The student must not confuse, as so many have naïvely done, the date of the work's composition with the year in which Dante imagined that his journey took place. It is almost universally agreed that this was 1300, the year of the Jubilee; but there has been no lack of able opponents of this thesis—first among them

Angelitti—who for reasons connected with astronomy have maintained that the year in question was 1301. See the brief exposition of the problem, described by D'Ovidio as 'learned and well-balanced', in SOLERTI's article entitled 'Per la data della visione dantesca', in *Giornale dantesco*, VI (1898), pp. 289–309.

D'OVIDIO, 'L'anno della visione', in *Studii sulla Divina Commedia* (*Opere*, cited above, I, Vol. II, pp. 385–404).

Sources

Intimately bound up with the problem of the origin of the *Comedy* is that of the sources of the poem. It may be that when historical studies were in their heyday too much importance was attached to this problem; on the other hand, scholars of to-day pretend to belittle it. Either school of thought is guilty of an error of perspective.

The *Comedy* is assuredly a creation of such powerful originality that no resemblance to it is to be found in any previous work. It is a drama for which Dante is entirely responsible, because, thanks to the wonderful force of his imagination and the intensity of his consuming passion, he fused the elements—legendary, historical, political and doctrinal—of which his world consisted into a compact and entirely new organism. But when we have said all this and think we have thus solved the problem, we have in reality said less than nothing. It is true that Dante derived the elements of his drama from every conceivable source—from sacred books, from religious beliefs, from his reading of the poets, from his contemplation of the philosophers, from the heterogeneous learning which he had accumulated during all his years of study, from the history of the past and from that which unfolded before his very eyes. As a result even he himself would often not have known the source to which he was indebted for such and such an element. The sum of these elements constituted the spiritual reality of his time. His religion assured him of the existence of this world, scholars argued about its location and its form, popular imagination found an outlet in describing it and told of the journeys which adventurous and devout pilgrims had undertaken with the object of discovering it. Pictorial representations of this world appeared even on the windows and frescoes of churches. What is the relationship of these figurations to Dante's? It cannot be denied that the answer to this question will enable us to understand better and to gain a deeper insight into all the vagaries of the poet's imagination.

Our investigation of the sources cannot, then, be restricted to the elements which, for the sake of clearness, we will term legendary and imaginary, while realizing that before they can be transformed into poetry all the elements that go to make up the poet's world must merge to form his intuition. In other words, they must lose their material identity before they can be transformed into an organism. But we must also realize that if we are to gain an insight into the nature of this organism we must trace the entire process by which it was evolved.

A host of analogies taken from the Bible, Virgil, the Latin poets, Boëthius and medieval texts with both legendary and doctrinal themes was assembled by Tommaseo in his commentary. In many cases the number of parallels cited was excessive, and too often the analogy was forced. Many later commentators have made the same mistake. But the odd scraps of information that may be gleaned from the commentaries are not sufficient to enable us to form an exact idea of the poet's world. We must refer directly to the texts and to critical works with a special bearing on the subject.

Dante confessed that for the beautiful style which brought honour to his name he was indebted to Virgil. But, in the words of a nimble-witted critic, his beautiful style was not the only thing for which he had to thank the Roman poet. No one, then, will wish to deny that by re-reading the *Aeneid*, and in particular the sixth book, one is enabled not only to appreciate the refinements of Dante's style but to compare the novelties of expression which that poem may have inspired with their prototypes, and in so doing to understand both poets better. And as with the *Aeneid*, so with the most important and best-known medieval legends— they merely provide raw material and fleeting, indefinite images. It is common knowledge that the material is *res nullius* until the poet has set his own authentic seal upon it; and Dante described his world in such concrete terms that it was even possible to map it in accurate outline. Now even comparisons help one to know and measure the force and grandeur of a man's imagination. At all events comparison facilitates the study of the creative processes of the imagination.

The images conjured up by the poet's fancy are so rigidly concrete that sometimes even a simple metaphor is enough to suggest the idea of a punishment. Let the reader consider the wind of passion that blows in the circle of the carnal sinners or the smoke of anger in the nostrils of those wrathful souls who frequent the Styx (they are also mentioned in the *Purgatorio*). We may go further: even etymology can suggest a new image to Dante. Having read in the *Magnae derivationes* of Uguccione da Pisa that the word *hypocrite* is derived *ab 'yper' quod est super, et 'crisis', quod est aurum, quasi 'superauratus'*, he gives the idea concrete expression in the gilded cloaks in which he dresses the lost souls whom he encounters in the sixth pit. But these are merely indications.

If it were possible to reconstruct Dante's library—so to term it—in its entirety, we should gain a clear insight into many facets of the man the significance of which escapes us. No one who wishes to study Dante in earnest can afford not to include in his library at any rate the *Summa Theologica* of St. Thomas; yet it would be a mistake to think that this work enshrines the whole of Dante's world, and consequently the thought of the man who created it. The grand and sublime qualities which we find in the *Comedy* also characterize school-theology, and more especially thirteenth-century theodicy. The true forerunners of Dante are not the recorders of visions; they are the doctors of the schools, above all St. Thomas. But for the conceptual achievements of scholasticism Dante's world could not have been anything more than the pale, evanescent world of the visionaries. To make anything out of that chaos it was necessary to find the regulative idea; and this idea could only be suggested by theology.

In this way investigation of the sources—whether imaginary, doctrinal, literary or historical—proves to be essential as a background to the full understanding of the work, and only a superficial philosophy—which by virtue of its superficiality would cease to be a philosophy—could lead us to ignore the necessity of such an investigation.

For a start it is advisable to study some of these medieval

visions or legends. With this end in view see P. Villari, *Antiche leggende e tradizioni che illustrano la Divina Commedia*, Pisa, Nistri, 1865 (*Annali delle Università toscane*, VIII). Rather than read the *Visio Alberici* in the translations the student may conveniently do so in the Education Department's edition of the *Divine Comedy* (Padua, 1822). Here he will also find the writings which relate to the controversy provoked by the discovery of the legend. Consult on the subject Cosmo, 'Le prime ricerche intorno all'originalità dantesca', in *Primi saggi*, Padua, Tip. dell'Università, 1891.

For the journey of the three monks to the Earthly Paradise see D'Ancona, *Manuale*, I, pp. 437–42. For the Earthly Paradise see Graf, *Miti, leggende e superstizioni del medio evo*, Turin, Loescher, 1892 (2nd ed., 1925), and E. Coli, *Il Paradiso terrestre dantesco*, Florence, Carnesecchi, 1897; cf. in this connection Cosmo's article in *Giornale storico della letteratura italiana*, XXXII (1898), pp. 176–8.

The 'Visio Monachi de Eynsham' is included in *Analecta Bollandiana*, XXII (1903), pp. 225 *sq.* Apropos of this vision see Cosmo, 'Una nuova fonte dantesca?' (in *Studi medievali*, I (1904), pp. 77–93).

The 'De Jerusalem celesti' and the 'De Babilonia infernali' of Friar Giacomino da Verona are included in E. I. May's *The 'De Jerusalem celesti' and the 'De Babilonia infernali,'* Florence, Le Monnier, 1930.

Friar Bonvesin's 'Le tre Scritture' is included in *Le opere volgari di Bonvesin da la Riva*, edited by G. Contini, Rome, Soc. Filol. romana, 1941, I, pp. 101 *sq.* The visions are listed and summarized in C. Fritzsche's 'Die lateinischen Visionen des Mittelalters bis zur Mitte des XII Jahrhunderts' (in *Romanische Forschungen*, II (1885), pp. 247–79, and III (1886), pp. 337–68).

Consult also C. Pascal, in *Le credenze d'oltre tomba*, 2nd ed., Turin, Paravia, 1924, II, pp. 45–9, and W. Zabughin, 'Quattro "geroglifici" danteschi', in *Giornale storico della letteratura italiana*, Suppl. 19–21 (1921), pp. 505–63.

The following studies of the subject may be read with advantage: Labitte, 'La Divine Comédie avant Dante', in *Revue des deux mondes*, Series IV, XXXI (1842), pp. 704–42; Ampère, 'Les visions ont préparé la Divine Comédie', in *Histoire littéraire de la France avant le XII siècle*, Paris, 1833; OZANAM, 'Des sources poétiques de la Divine Comédie', in *Dante et la philosophie catholique*, Paris, 1845, pp. 324–424; A. D'ANCONA, *I precursori di Dante*, Florence, Sansoni, 1874 (also in *Scritti dantesch*, ib., 1912–3, pp. 3–108); P. RAJNA, *La genesi della Divina Commedia* (cited above); D'OVIDIO, 'Dante e San Paolo' and 'Dante e Gregorio VII', in *Studii sulla Divina Commedia* (cited above) (*Opere*, I, Vol. II, pp. 41–156); F. TORRACA, 'I precursori della Divina Commedia', in *Lectura Dantis*, *Opere minori* (cited above); V. CAPETTI, 'Dante e le leggende di S. Pier Damiani', in *Studi sul Paradiso dantesco*, Bologna, Zanichelli, 1906; id., 'L'oltre tomba iranico e la Divina Commedia', in *L'anima e l'arte di Dante*, Leghorn, Giusti, 1907, pp. 1–73. Apropos of the last-named essay and of other books on the subject see COSMO's article in *Giornale storico della letteratura italiana*, LII (1908), pp. 211–8.

For the 'Purgatorio' (*Nuovi studii danteschi*) see the book with that title by D'OVIDIO, Milan, Hoepli, 1906 (now reprinted in *Opere*, II, Vol. III, Naples, Guida, undated).

W. ZABUGHIN, *L'oltre tomba classico medievale dantesco nel Rinascimento*, Florence, Olschki, 1922.

On P. AMADUCCI's book, *La fonte della Divina Commedia scoperta e descritta* (Bologna, Libreria L. Beltrami, 1911) see COSMO's article in *Giornale storico della letteratura italiana*, LIX (1912), pp. 422–5.

Finally I would call attention to the work by M. ASÍN PALACIOS, *La escatología musulmana en la Divina Comedia* (Madrid, 1919), which created such a sensation. A complete detailed exposition of the book was immediately undertaken by G. GABRIELI, *Intorno alle fonti orientali della Divina Commedia*, Rome, Poliglotta, 1919 (excerpt from *Arcadia*, III).

Gabrieli himself indicates the most substantial reviews (of which I will confine myself to mentioning PARODI's in the *Bullettino della Società dantesca italiana*, XXVI (1919), pp. 163–81) in his essay 'Dante e l'Islam', included in *Scritti vari pubblicati in occasione del VI centenario della morte di Dante Alighieri*, Milan, Soc. ed. Vita e Pensiero, 1921, pp. 97–139. See also his 'Dante e il musulmanismo', in *Studi su Dante*, Vol. V of the *Conferenze a cura del Comitato milanese della Società dantesca* (Milan, Hoepli, 1940).

K. VOSSLER examines the origins—religious, philosophical, ethical, political and literary—of Dante's thought and culture in the first three parts of *La Divina Commedia studiata nella sua genesi e interpretata* (I cite the Italian version, Bari, Laterza, 2nd ed., 1927). This work, which is of a general character, was on its first publication (Heidelberg, 1907–10) commended more highly than its effective value for the purposes of our investigations warranted. However, it helps one to form an idea of the vastness of Dante's world.

MOORE's essay, 'Scripture and Classical Authors in Dante' (*Studies in Dante*, I) is still a fundamental source of information on Dante's quotations and derivations from the Bible and the classics. See also TOYNBEE's *Dictionary* (under the appropriate headings) and C. CAVEDONI, *Raffronti tra gli autori biblici e sacri e la Divina Commedia*, Città di Castello, Lapi, 1896 (*Coll. op. dant.* Passerini, Nos. 29–30).

E. PROTO, *L'apocalissi nella Divina Commedia*, Naples, Pierro, 1905.

M. SCHERILLO, 'Dante e lo studio della poesia classica', in *Arte, Scienza e Fede ai giorni di Dante*, Milan, Hoepli, 1901, pp. 219 *sq.*

G. FRACCAROLI, 'Dante e i classici', in *Miscellanea Graf*, Bergamo, Arti Graf., 1913, pp. 143 *sq.*

E. PROTO, *Dante e i poeti latini*, Florence, 1910 (excerpt from *Atene e Roma*, XI (1908), pp. 23 *sq.* and 221 *sq.*; XII (1909), pp. 7 *sq.* and 277 *sq.*; XIII (1910), pp. 79 *sq.* and 149 *sq.*).

G. FERRETTI, *I due tempi della composizione della Divina Commedia* (cited above), Part II, Chap. IV ('Il valore della cultura antica per Dante').

D. COMPARETTI, *Virgilio nel medio evo*, new edition prepared by G. Pasquali, Florence, Nuova Italia, 1937–41.

D. COMPARETTI, 'Dante e Virgilio', in *Atene e Roma*, New Series, V (1924), pp. 149–64.

F. D'OVIDIO, 'Non soltanto lo bello stile tolse da lui', *Studii sulla Divina Commedia* (cited above), (*Opere*, I, Vol. I, pp. 353–77); PASCOLI, *La mirabile visione* (cited above), pp. 406 *sq.*; PARODI, *Poesia e storia* (cited above), pp. 248–52; G. SZOMBATHELY,

Dante e Ovidio, Trieste, Tip. del Lloyd, 1888; V. Ussani, *Dante e Lucano*, Florence, Sansoni, 1917; M. Scherillo, 'Stazio nella Divina Commedia', in *Studi di filologia, filosofia e storia (pubbl. della R. Acc. scient. lett. di Milano*, Vol. I), Milan, Hoepli, 1913.

G. Albini, 'Stazio nella Divina Commedia', in *Atene e Roma,* V (1902), pp. 561-7.

G. Landi, 'Sulla leggenda del cristianesimo di Stazio', in *Atti e memorie della R. Acc. di Padova*, XXIX, Part III, Padua, 1913.

R. Sabbadini, 'Dante e l'Achilleide', in *Atene e Roma*, XII (1909), pp. 265-70.

P. Mustard, 'Dante and Statius', in *Modern Language Notes*, XXXIX, No. 2 (Feb., 1924).

R. Murari, *Dante e Boezio*, Bologna, Zanichelli, 1905.

M. Da Carbonara, *Dante e Pier Lombardo*, Città di Castello, Lapi, 1897 (*Coll. op. dant.* Passerini, Nos. 44-5).

I. Oeschger, 'Antikes und Mittelalterliches bei Dante', in *Zeitschrift f. rom. Phil.*, LXIV (1944), pp. 1-87.

For St. Thomas see Chap. VIII, in which part of the bibliography may also be used for the *Comedy*.

For the material derived from the *Trésor* see Chap. III, pp. 27-9.

As regards Dante's indebtedness to Ubertino da Casale, if the student desires to get some idea of the latter's *Arbor vite crucifixe*, which is very rare as well as being difficult reading, he is advised to consult the useful rendering of part of the book by Fausta Casolini (*Arbor vitae crucifixae Jesu*, by Ubertino da Casale, Lanciano, Carabba).

For the material which Dante derived from the mystics see Kraus, *Dante* (cited above), pp. 738 *sq.*; Cosmo, *Le misticeh nozze* (cited above), pp. 61 *sq.*; id., 'Noterelle Francescane,' in *Giornale dantesco*, VII (1899), pp. 63-70; E. G. Gardner, *Dante and the Mystics*, London, Dent, 1913, pp. 343-8; P. A. Martini, *Ubertino da Casale alla Verna*, La Verna, Arezzo, 1913, pp. 193 *sq.*

Allegory

The essential task that confronts the student is to delve as deeply as he can into the poet's mind. It was concerned amongst other things with allegory, and indeed, as in all medieval works, allegory and doctrine play a notable part in the *Comedy*. But the fact that they play a part does not mean, as many—indeed, too many—have been led to believe, that they inform the entire work. Allegory of a general kind is clearly visible in the first two cantos, and specific instances of the use of allegory are apparent here and there, as in the description of the noble fortress that guards the city of Dis; the old man of Crete; the groups of four and three stars which light up the southern sky; the pleasant valley before the gate of Purgatory; in Dante's dreams and, in a broader sense, tying up with the general allegory, in the portrayal of the scene in the Earthly Paradise. Little or no allegory is employed in the description of the Heavenly Paradise. But there is a great difference between the allegory envisaged in the *Convivio* and the allegory that we find in the *Comedy*. The author regards the literal meaning of the *canzoni* on which he comments in the *Convivio* as nothing more than a beautiful deception, a rhetorical *fictio* which hints at the underlying truth. And the truth, he declares, is embodied in the exposition that he gives in the commentary. It is not so in the *Comedy*. Certainly, the journey is a fiction, but a fiction which from the poet's point of view it is both desirable and necessary that his readers should accept as the truth. Otherwise there would be no meaning in the injunction which he receives from Beatrice, Cacciaguida and St. Peter to recount what he has seen for the benefit of a corrupt world. Nor would there be any meaning in the ethical, political and religious goal which the poet sets before him and which derives its suggestive power from the reality that is portrayed. Those who look upon the *Comedy* as a vision, and not as a journey that has really taken place—within the framework, naturally, of the artistic fiction—unwittingly destroy the prophetic force of the poem.

It is useless to rack one's brains with the object of discovering everywhere, beneath the letter of the text, recondite implications which the poet has not intended to conceal there. When he has thought it necessary to make such implications he has remembered to attract the reader's attention so that they should not be lost on him, and in other cases he has himself provided the explanation, or at any rate the clue that will put him on the way to finding it.

The explanation of the allegories must always be sought in the poet's own words. The fundamental allegory is that of the two guides, and its explanation is to be found in the last chapter of the *Monarchy*. But we must not lose sight of the fact that even the two guides are not treated by the poet as mere figures of allegory. Unlike Lucia, Lia, Rachel and the woman with the stammer, Virgil and Beatrice are not impersonal symbols, but beings whom the poet in his imagination has restored to life, endowing them with all their human characteristics. Besides being allegorical symbols they are, what is perhaps more important, creatures of flesh and blood.

If we base our inquiry into the poet's use of allegory on this criterion we may not get quite at the essence of his thought, but at least we shall not be far from it. When, for instance, we find the poet in his conversation with Forese identifying the wood in which he had lost himself with 'the life from which Virgil turned him aside' (*Purg.*, XXIII, 118), it is useless to seek other meanings for the wood than that indicated by the words of Forese. And however urbanely and subtly critics may hold forth on the subject of the three wild beasts that prevented the poet from taking the short cut to the mountain, it seems hard to credit that they have no connection with the three sparks which, according to Ciacco, have inflamed the hearts of men—namely envy, pride and avarice (*Inf.*, VI, 74–5; cf. XV, 68).

The supremely important thing is that we should not lose sight of the poetic reality through being too meticulous in our search for the right interpretation. Distinguished scholars like Pascoli, Flamini and Federzoni, despite their understanding of poetry, have made this mistake because they have looked for a vein of allegory running through the entire poem. I mention the names of these distinguished men in order that young students, with correspondingly less learning and experience, may be enabled by their example to steer clear of the danger. For the rest, I am not here putting forward explanations of symbols as though they were infallibly correct. If I did this I should be betraying the purpose of this book, which is to guide the student in his inquiry. Here I am merely stating the criteria in the light of which the symbols should be examined. The reader's conclusion should be the result of his own researches. A conclusion which is not based on the poet's words or which merely forces their meaning, or one that is not in keeping with the harmony that characterizes all his thought, cannot be near the truth even if it is supported by learned conceptual theories derived from the writings of this or that philosopher. It is not St. Thomas or St. Bonaventure or Aristotle that is important; it is Dante. St. Thomas, St. Bonaventure and Aristotle can only point the way to the understanding of the poet. Unhappily, the exposition of Dante's works has always been characterized by such theories, which have been superimposed on the poetry and so have destroyed it. It is understandable that they have aroused feelings of antipathy towards Dante criticism and towards historical criticism, as though the whole of Dante criticism amounted to nothing more than empty disquisitions on allegory, and historians as a class were responsible for a line of inquiry which those who adopted it did not pursue in accordance with the principles of the so-called historical method which they themselves professed. Yet it would be an exaggeration to think that it is entirely nonsensical. To fight shy of the methods it involves is a good thing; to feign ignorance of them is a mistake. The student's task is to discard the interpretative fantasies that have resulted from it and to pick out the facts that it has definitely established.

The books on the allegory and symbolism of the *Comedy* are legion, and I shall indicate only a few of the principal studies. In the case of the most ancient essays it is well to consult the old bibliographical inventories drawn up by De Batines and Ferrazzi, together with Scartazzini's *Dantologia*.

G. MARCHETTI, *Della prima e principale allegoria del poema di Dante*, Bologna, 1819; U. FOSCOLO, *Discorso sul testo della Commedia di Dante*, London, 1825 (also included in *Opere*, edited by Orlandini and Mayer, III, Florence, Le Monnier, 1850, pp. 83–519); K. WITTE, *Dante-Forschungen*, I, pp. 1–20 and 21–65; F. BERARDINELLI, *Il concetto della Divina Commedia di Dante Alighieri*, Naples, Rondinella, 1859; V. BARELLI, *L'allegoria della Divina Commedia di Dante Alighieri esposta da V. Barelli*, Florence, Cellini, 1864; G. CASELLA, *Della forma allegorica e della principale allegoria della Divina Commedia*, *Opere*, Florence, Barbera, 1884, II, pp. 364 *sq.*; G. PASCOLI, *Minerva oscura*, Leghorn, Giusti, 1898;

id., *Sotto il velame*, Messina, Muglia, 1900; id., *La mirabile visione* (cited above).

On Pascoli's books see L. Valli, *L'allegoria di Dante secondo G. Pascoli*, Bologna, Zanichelli, 1922.

Flamini, *I significati della Commedia di Dante e il suo significato supremo*, Leghorn, Giusti, 1903 and following years. The best edition is the second (1916). A summary of the work from the scholastic angle: *Avviamento allo studio della Divina Commedia*, ib.

F. D'Ovidio's 'Le tre fiere', in *Studii sulla Divina Commedia* (cited above) (*Opere*, I, Vol. II, pp. 3–40), is important because of its fidelity to the text. Parodi's review (*Bullettino della Società dantesca italiana*, VII (1900), pp. 281–8) is subtle but unconvincing. The writer attempts to reconcile D'Ovidio's scheme with Casella's.

G. Santi, *L'ordinamento morale e l'allegoria della Divina Commedia*, Palermo, Sandron, 1923 (including a full bibliography).

Essays V, VI and VII of F. Ercole's *Il pensiero politico di Dante* (cited above).

The student should next refer to the following studies, in which the problem is discussed from a more general angle:

L. Pietrobono, 'Allegoria o arte?' in *Giornale dantesco*, XXXVII (1936), pp. 93–134; id., *L'allegorismo e Dante*, ib., XXXVIII (1937), pp. 85–102.

L. Rizzo, 'Valore dell'allegoria dantesca', in *Atti dell' Accademia peloritana*, XLI, 1932–9.

G. Busnelli, 'Il significato morale del gran veglio di Creta', in *Civiltà Cattolica*, LXIX (1918), Vol. III, pp. 529–41, and Vol. IV, pp. 301–13; LXX (1919), Vol. I, pp. 192–201 and 454–65, and Vol. II, pp. 17–26 and 301–18.

Does the fiction of the *Comedy* presuppose a real journey or is it the description of a vision? This question is discussed by Nardi, *Dante e la cultura medievale* (cited above), pp. 311 *sq.*, and by G. Salinari, 'Che cosa è la "Divina Commedia"?' (in *Cultura neolatina*, III (1943), pp. 167–74).

The Greyhound

But if the less important symbols may be disposed of merely by the provision of bibliographical indications, enabling the

L

reader to form an opinion of his own based on a knowledge of the major studies of the subject, the Greyhound requires different treatment. This is the topic that has inspired the wildest flights of fancy. Indeed, many investigators, not to say the majority, have permitted their inquiries to be influenced by their personal predilections, or even enthusiasms, political or religious. Thus, instead of forgetting themselves in Dante, they have constructed a new Dante according to their own pattern. Hence the innumerable conceptions of the Greyhound—many of them positively absurd—that have issued in profusion from the imagination of the critics. Anyone who studies Dante without prejudice must agree that when he wrote of the Greyhound he was not alluding to any definite individual, but merely to a special envoy who, at some more or less remote time, but inevitably, would drive the she-wolf back into hell. Accordingly, any conjecture which aims at identifying this envoy with a historical character is futile. This does not mean that Dante may not at some stage have hoped, and for a moment even deluded himself, that this or that personage who had appeared on the horizon of history was destined to transform his dream into reality. But discussion of the matter can only be concerned with the general nature of this personage, who might be a pope or an emperor, and possibly neither. The prophecy, which is already obscure in itself, is rendered even more inscrutable by the fact that here, contrary to the habit and teaching of the poet, the literal meaning is swamped by the allegorical.

The Greyhound prophecy is bound up with the DXV and the Scipio prophecies, as well as with the poet's intimations and hopes that the liberation of the Vatican and of the other elect parts of Rome from the Papal adultery (*Par.*, IX, 139–42), and of the world from the greed that overwhelms all mankind (*Purg.*, XX, 13–15; *Par.*, XXVII, 142–8), was more or less imminent. More than this, prophecies and allusions are bound up with, and contingent to, the poet's religious and political vision *sous tous les rapports*. This vision naturally broadened in scope as it was reflected in passing events. The culminating moment in the evolution of his thought is signalized by the letter to the cardinals, in which Rome, Italy and the Church become in his mind one and indivisible, so that the life of one is the life of all. Incidentally, this letter, in so far as its subject is Rome, serves to demolish all the sophistical quibbles of those who have maintained that the writer of lines 22–4 of Canto II of the *Inferno* was a Guelf.

The faith which he professed was a flame over which no doubt ever cast its shadow. Indeed, it is legitimate to assert that while with the passing of the years his opposition to the Church grew more intense, his orthodoxy assumed an ever more rigorous form. His opposition to the Church grew more and more intense, his orthodoxy became more and more rigorous, and as a result his conviction of the baneful influence of clerical decadence on civil life became more and more deeply rooted. It was under the stress of these sentiments that he depicted the scenes which fill the second half of the *Purgatorio* and the *Paradiso*. Consequently, since there was to be a regeneration, and no possibility existed of its being effected through the medium of the Church—indeed, the Church itself stood in need of regeneration—the regenerating influence became personified, in the poet's imagination, in the figure of the *Dux* or of Scipio. And always his inevitable coming was proclaimed after the author had castigated the institutions of the Church. Only at the end of the canto in which he prophesies the coming of Scipio, just as he is entering the *Primum Mobile*, which promotes order in the universe, does the poet allow his mind to be entranced by what may be called a *mystical* vision of the world's rebirth, conditioned by the radiance of the heavens. Individuals leave the stage, and the influence of the stars becomes the dominant theme (*Par.*, XXVII, 142–8).

It is therefore necessary to consider the problem of the Greyhound when studying the conception of ethics, politics and religion that informs the work, and the feelings, whether of hope or of disappointment, with which the poet is inspired by the course of events. Logically, this fluctuation of feeling ought to be traced to the happenings by which it is conditioned; but none can fail to appreciate the trickiness of this line of investigation. Indeed, there are able critics who trace the same outburst of feeling back to different happenings and different years. Let the student consider Forese's prophecy (*Purg.*, XXIII, 106–11). A typical example is the above-mentioned prophecy regarding the

Dux. Some look upon this as an obscure portent of Henry's victory, which Dante hoped for and believed to be imminent, while others regard it as a no less certain indication of the hopes kindled in the poet's breast by the deaths of Clement V and Philip the Fair, which, in view of the manner of their occurrence, were, it seemed, certain to leave the way clear for history to take its course free from 'every obstacle and barrier'. In the midst of these uncertainties there is, however, one thing which cannot be doubted. No disappointment could destroy the poet's conviction that the regeneration was not far off. It could not do so because his faith rested on the metaphysical concept on which he had built his world.

A vast number of books has also been written on the subject of the Greyhound. A résumé of the various theories which have been evolved in this connection will be found in Scartazzini's *Purgatorio* (larger edition), II, pp. 801–17.

Of the older studies it is always well worth the student's while to read G. FENAROLI's *Il veltro allegorico della Divina Commedia* (Florence, Cellini, 1891; excerpt from the *Rassegna Nazionale*, October 1st, 1891) and, despite the oddity of the author's thesis, R. DELLA TORRE's *Poeta Veltro* (Cividale, Tipogr. Fulvio, 1887–90).

See also A. MEDIN, *La profezia del Veltro*, Padua, Randi, 1889; V. CIAN, *Sulle orme del Veltro*, Messina, Principato, 1897; A. SOLMI, 'Sulla traccia del Veltro', in *Il pensiero politico di Dante* (cited above), pp. 91 *sq.*; F. ERCOLE, 'Il prologo del poema e la profezia del Veltro', in *Il pensiero politico* (cited above), II, pp. 314 *sq.*

On the symbolism of DXV see in particular D. GUERRI, *Di alcuni versi dotti della Divina Commedia*, Città di Castello, Lapi, 1901, pp. 157 *sq.*; MOORE, 'The Dux Prophecy', in *Studies in Dante*, III, pp. 253 *sq.*; DAVIDSOHN, *Bullettino della Società dantesca italiana*, IX (1901–2), pp. 129–31; A. SCOLARI, *Il Messia dantesco*, Bologna, Zanichelli, 1913; ERCOLE, *Il pensiero politico* (cited above), II, p. 372; W. ZABUGHIN, 'Quattro geroglifici danteschi' (cited above), § 4.

On the mystical procession in the Earthly Paradise and the prophecy that is in a general way associated with it see PROTO,

L'apocalissi nella Divina Commedia (cited above); PARODI, 'L'albero dell'impero', in *Poesia e storia nella Divina Commedia*, Naples, Perrella, 1921, pp. 511–32.

The Moral System

Intimately bound up with the problem of allegory is the problem of the moral organization of the three realms. On this subject scholars have written, and continue to write, books that are valuable both for their penetration and for their teaching. Many of these books, however, are marred by one fundamental defect. The question is how Dante organized his realms, and their organization and its guiding principles must be deduced from the picture that he painted of it and from the explanations that he gives us. It would therefore seem that no great problems ought to arise. Anyone who desires to carry the inquiry a stage further may try to find out the source of the criterion by which the poet was guided in his work of creation, but in conducting such an inquiry one should always bear in mind that in the artist's eyes the supreme criterion is the harmony and effectiveness of his representation. Dante was not the slave of either Aristotle or St. Thomas. If he owed any allegiance he owed it to his art alone. Hence all the efforts that have been made to bring his system of punishments completely into line with the tenets of the aforesaid doctors have always failed miserably. Let the reader consider the number of arguments into which scholars have entered in order to justify the relegation to the Stygian marsh of those sinners who were missing from the list prescribed by this or that doctor. And yet the poet's words are clear: the only denizens of the Styx are those over whom anger gained the mastery. On the surface of the water are those who were quick to give vent to their feelings, while those who cherished the rancour that saddened their lives were stuck fast in the mire. These were they who, in the poet's words, carried within them a 'dull mist', in other words an anger that was powerless to express itself.

We cannot amend or complete the poet's words in order to relate them to a given system derived from the tenets of this or that sage. And when one of the shrewdest and most learned interpreters of this question, Filomusi Guelfi, writes that with the aid of some new emendations he has rendered 'the moral system which he attributes to the third realm'—the argument he propounds applies to all three realms—'more complete and more consistent with theological doctrines', it is precisely this greater completeness and consistency that increases our misgivings. No one denies that St. Thomas and the other teachers of the schools can help us to understand the *Comedy*. But to integrate poetry with philosophy, even if one is concerned with a poet-philosopher like Dante, is absurd. Our raw material is a world created by the poet; and if, for example, no part of the *Inferno* is reserved explicitly for the proud and the slothful as the theologians conceive them, nothing can be done about it. Gaps in a system which appear serious to the philosopher do not appear so to the poet; and if there are gaps the only thing left for the critic to do is to record them.

The same remarks apply to the equally great efforts that scholars have made to reconcile the system of punishments outlined in the *Purgatorio* with that described in the *Inferno*. Their arguments are like houses of cards. So eager are they that there should be perfect correspondence between the parts, and that the whole should be entirely in keeping with the doctrine of this or that teacher, that they disregard what the poet actually says. Anyone who wishes to convince himself of the unsubstantiality of these over-rigid systems may enjoy, for example, the spectacle first of Busnelli and Barone proving the inconsistency of the scheme according to which Filomusi Guelfi proposes to classify the blessed, and then of Filomusi Guelfi in his turn administering like treatment to Busnelli and to Parodi, whose theories are very similar to Busnelli's.

The truth is that in their anxious quest for an allegorical undertone and a moral system that conform to a rigid plan, the critics, through a desire to infer too much from the poet's words, have often inferred more than he implied. A familiarity with their theories is useful because they have revealed details which may easily elude those whose powers of observation are moderate. The essence of good criticism is to seek knowledge and to beware of all over-systematization.

For a general discussion of the moral organization of the three realms see SANTI, *L'ordinamento morale* (cited above); also the detailed bibliography appended.

PASCOLI, *Minerva oscura* (cited above); PIETROBONO, *Dal centro al cerchio e dal cerchio al centro*, Turin, S.E.I., 1923.

Apropos of the *Inferno* and the *Purgatorio* see K. WITTE, 'Dantes Sündsystem in Hölle und Fegefeuer', in *Dante-Forschungen*, II, pp. 121–60.

E. MOORE, 'The Classification of Sins in the Inferno and Purgatorio', in *Studies*, II, pp. 152–209.

Apropos of the *Inferno* see G. TODESCHINI, 'Dell'ordinamento morale dell'Inferno di Dante', in *Scritti su Dante*, Vicenza, 1872, I, pp. 1–114.

F. D'OVIDIO, 'La topografia morale dell'Inferno', in *Studii sulla Divina Commedia*, I (*Opere*, I, Vol. I, pp. 379–468).

G. FRACCAROLI, 'Ancora sull'ordinamento morale della Divina Commedia', in *Giornale storico della letteratura italiana*, XXXVI (1900), pp. 109–22.

W. H. V. READE, *The Moral System of Dante's Inferno*, Oxford, Clarendon Press, 1909; M. BALDINI, *La costruzione morale dell'Inferno di Dante*, Città di Castello, Lapi, 1914. In connection with these books cf. PARODI's article in *Bullettino della Società dantesca italiana*, XXIV (1917), pp. 90–104.

BUSNELLI, *L'etica nicomachea e l'ordinamento morale dell'Inferno di Dante*, Bologna, Zanichelli, 1907.

On the *Purgatorio* see P. PEREZ, *I sette cerchi del Purgatorio di Dante*, Verona, 1864 (3rd ed., Milan, 1896).

MOORE, 'Unity and Symmetry of Design in the "Purgatorio" ', in *Studies*, II, pp. 246–68. W. W. VERNON, *Readings on the Purgatorio of Dante*, London, 1889 (3rd ed., 1907).

BUSNELLI, *L'ordinamento morale del Purgatorio dantesco*, Rome, 1908.

D'OVIDIO, 'Sulla concezione dantesca del Purgatorio' (appendix to E. SANNIA's *Il comico, l'umorismo e la satira nella Divina Commedia*, Milan, Hoepli, 1909).

On the *Paradiso* see F. P. LUISO, 'La costruzione morale e poetica del Paradiso dantesco', in *Rassegna Nazionale*, CII (1898), pp. 299 *sq.*

L. FILOMUSI GUELFI, *Nuovi studii su Dante*, Città di Castello, Lapi, 1911, and *Novissimi studii su Dante*, ib., 1912.

G. BARONE, *Ancora sulla Gerusalemme celeste*, Rome, Loescher, 1911.

G. BUSNELLI, *Il concetto e l'ordine del Paradiso dantesco*, Città di Castello, Lapi, 1911–2.

E. G. PARODI, 'La costruzione e l'ordinamento del Paradiso dantesco', in *Poesia e storia* (cited above), pp. 567–607. The serious mistake in the first edition (in *Studi letterari e linguistici dedicati a P. Rajna*, Florence, Ariani, 1911, pp. 893–935) has here been set to rights.

See on the whole question COSMO, 'Rassegna dantesca', in *Giornale storico della letteratura italiana*, LXIII (1914), pp. 342 *sq.*

See also:

FILOMUSI GUELFI, *Studii su Dante*, Città di Castello, Lapi, 1908.

E. PROTO, 'La concezione del Paradiso dantesco', in *Giornale dantesco*, XVIII (1910), pp. 64–97.

G. BINDONI, *Indagini critiche sulla Divina Commedia*, Milan, Albrighi e Segati, 1918, pp. 78 *sq.*

But see COSMO, 'Rassegna dantesca', in *Giornale storico della letteratura italiana*, LVIII (1911), pp. 162 *sq.*

XV

THE *COMEDY*—II

The Fundamental Concept

The discussions that have centred round the allegorical meaning and the moral organization of Dante's world, important though they are, by no means dispose of all the problems that arise out of the study of the poem. It is no less important (if, indeed, it is not more so) to establish the nature of the fundamental concept that lies behind it—the concept to which it owes its being, on which it hinges, and from which it derives its unity. For, in the words of one of the most able students of the *Comedy*, Egidio Gorra, 'the unity of the poem presupposes a dominating idea that runs right through it and pervades it from start to finish'.

The essence of this concept is that order is the informing principle of the universe, understood in its widest sense. This concept first flashed before Dante's mind in all its vastness while he was writing the fourth book of the *Convivio*. At the time he was trying to account for the workings of history. It seemed to him that history was subject to the intervention of God. It was like a world in which freedom reigned, and hence a world that followed no predictable course. The purpose of God's intervention was to bring this world back to the ways that He had pre-destined it to follow *ab aeterno*. It had begun on that remote day when the 'most high and most indivisible divine consistory of the Trinity', with the object of 'enduing humanity with new strength', had resolved to make the whole of history culminate in the birth of Christ. Jewish history and Roman history were equally divine because each prepared the way for Catholic Rome.

The consciousness of an order that governs the physical world thus broadened into the concept of an integration of the physical world with the moral. This concept was behind the Creation and is behind the preservation of all created things. All that is, from the angels to the lowest animal, proceeds from God. Hence all things aspire to return to Him, moving with the rhythm that characterized the first steps of their journey. This aspiration and movement constitutes the supreme law and the informing principle of the universe.

Contemplating the world of nature and history from these heights, Dante felt the airy fancies which had been vibrating in his mind ever since the day of his 'wondrous vision' falling into line with this concept, blending with the new and incomparably more immense vision, and assuming an organic form. For with its harmonies, its symmetry, its rhythm—in short, with its systematic arrangement—even the poetic organism which he was creating was bound to reflect the concept to which his labours were subordinated. The journey to heaven which had as its object the glorification of Beatrice assumed the wider significance of a spiritual ascent into the presence of God. Here the poet's purpose was to discover in Him the informing principle of the universe and to inculcate into his being the rhythm of divine administration. The story of his spiritual life became the ideal of all men's spiritual lives, a pattern for all to follow. The world beyond became an enormous mirror of this world because in it the justice of God finds perfect expression. The poetic aim of transporting this world into the next so that the one might take its pattern from the other became an ethical philosophy. All problems were solved in the revelation of the heavenly order, and the whole of history was influenced by the direct experience of its working. Science and history became basic elements in the organism which the poet was creating. All the notions associated with religion and politics became part and parcel of it—the necessity of the universal monarchy for the regulation of human society, the conception of the two guides charged with the task of leading the community along the path of order, the heavy responsibility of their high office. The duty of poets—of great poets—to recall them to a sense of their obligations when they erred became a vocation, akin to the mission which at certain moments in history God entrusts to some hero—namely, to compensate for the shortcomings of the guides.

Profoundly convinced of the authenticity of his scientific knowledge, this thoughtful man believed that by his creative method he was reproducing an objective reality. Never so much as then did he become in his works the measure and the touchstone of the universe. But for that very reason his creative method was characterized by an inexhaustible lyrical fervour. Divine thought revealing itself in human effort, the object of which was the realization of ends formulated by God *ab aeterno*, human thought rising from the contingent to the absolute and finding that the prime truth and ultimate end is God—history and philosophy were one in embodying that concept, which embraced every manifestation of being. His representation of this order, however colourless it might prove to be, would fill men's hearts with a burning desire to express its marvels themselves, and would inspire in them a resolve to restore to the rhythm of history its divine quality.

Dante's creative method, then, is the product of this lyrical intuition, like his ideas on science and history and the great effusions to which he gives vent when he contemplates his world, and which are, so to say, that same world seen in the mirror of contemplation. Dante is not Monti, that we may speak of a theological romance overlaid by a collection of lyrical verses. To quote one or two examples, I would refer the reader to Canto XVI of the *Purgatorio*, in which the poet asks himself the reason for the world's disorder and finds it by going back to the metaphysical concept by which the whole work is inspired, discussing the problem right in the middle of the poem, because the very structure of the work is modelled on the order of the universe. Again, let us consider Canto II of the *Paradiso*, where the poet faces and discusses the problem of the spots on the moon. Superficially this discussion mars the effect of the great upsurging of lyrical feeling which had induced him in the preceding canto to glorify the order that informs the universe and its realization in all its perfection in the heavens. In reality it is its logical continuation. The discovery of these spots in the very first heaven seemed to confute the actual premises on which the eulogy was based. The poet promptly answers this formidable confutation with the full force of his arguments, and his inspiration is such that the existence of the spots is shown to be not a confutation but a splendid corroboration of the order of the universe. So too with the researches into the writings of those who examined the problem of the spots before Dante. These researches may in themselves prove to be merely academic, but when they have been integrated and illuminated against the background of that concept they become highly significant historical-aesthetic criticism.

Everything springs from this intuition, and everything may be traced back to it. It is behind the poet's conception of his journey; it is behind the so-called theological romance. Even the question of science appears in a different light from that in which scholars have been too readily inclined to consider it. It is easy to regard the two cantos of the *Paradiso* that are concerned with the angels as a mere theological treatise. But if we bear in mind that the scene is the *Primum Mobile*, which communicates its essence to the whole universe, that the 'movement and virtue of the holy circles' are derived from the blest movers, and that on the very threshold of the *Primum Mobile* Beatrice had indulged in a lyrical effusion in which she attributed the disorder of the world to greed, and foretold the regeneration of the world, then we see how that long discourse originated from the poet's intuition, and we can account for Beatrice's fierce attacks on bad preachers who misrepresent the word of God. The word of God is the truth that is inherent in this metaphysical concept.

On the fundamental concept of the poem see Cosmo, 'Rassegna dantesca', in *Giornale storico della letteratura italiana*, LXIII (1914), pp. 362 *sq.*; *L'ultima ascesa*, Chaps. 2, 19, 20 and 21, and *passim* throughout the book. Information as to the Thomistic concept of creation is given in the last-named volume, p. 411.

See also G. Tarozzi, *Teologia dantesca studiata nel Paradiso*, Leghorn, Giusti, 1906.

For the controversy provoked by the distinction which Croce drew in his book *La poesia di Dante* see the bibliographical references that he gives in *La Poesia*, Bari, Laterza, 3rd ed., 1942, p. 278. See also S. Breglia, *Poesia e struttura nella Divina Commedia*, Genoa, Em. degli Orfini, 1934 (but cf. *Studi danteschi*, XX (1937), pp. 72–81); W. Vetterli, *Die ästhetische Deutung und das Problem der Einheit der Göttlichen Komödie in der neueren Literaturgeschichte*, Strasbourg, Heitz, 1935; cf. *Studi danteschi*, XX (1937), pp. 64–72.

L. Russo, *La critica letteraria contemporanea*, Bari, Laterza, 1942, I, pp. 247–86; also pp. 184–8 (2nd ed., 1946, II, pp. 1–40 and I, pp. 206–10). The same essay is included in Russo's *Studi sul due e trecento*, Rome, Edizioni italiane, undated [1946], pp. 159–90.

In connection with this problem see also G. Ferretti, *I due tempi della composizione* (cited above), pp. 90 *sq.* This book is also useful for its bibliography.

E. Chiocchetti, 'La Divina Commedia nell'interpretazione del Croce e del Gentile', in the commemorative work *Scritti vari* (cited above), Milan, Vita e Pensiero, 1921, pp. 156 *sq.*

Science

Science is one of the basic elements of the poem. It is therefore fitting to investigate and to analyse these elements in order to ascertain their sources and their relationship to the culture of the time. The surest way of obtaining a clearly defined picture of Dante is to correlate every aspect of the man with the age in which he lived. Thus even a scientific inquiry becomes a historical inquiry. But this statement needs amplifying. Inquiry must enable us to find out the *vera causa* as a result of which this specific element entered into the poet's imagination, and the manner in which it did so. More than this, it must enable us to see what kind of poetry was created from this element and how it was created. And if, as sometimes happened, especially when he was treating of scientific matters, he did not achieve poetry, it must enable us to appreciate the effort that he made to achieve it.

We must rid ourselves of the preconceived idea that Dante's imagination was bemused by doctrine. (I use this word to include all forms of science.) Vico, for all his profound admiration of Dante, erred in this respect. Doctrine did not bemuse or inhibit the poet in any way; it was a source of strength, exaltation and order. The *Inferno*, like the *Paradiso*, is a theological creation. It is for a theological reason that the spirits of the damned are dark shadows, human in form, just as it is for a theological reason that the spirits of the blessed are shining lights, hidden from mortal sight. The fundamental error of those who scoff at the theological hypothesis consists in the fact that they would like a Paradise that corresponded exactly to Hell, which is merely absurd. We must instead ask ourselves whether the actual poetics of the world that Dante created made such a correspondence possible; and as to the answer there can be no doubt: it did not. By its very nature drama could have no place in the *Paradiso*; nor, for that matter, could it have any in the *Purgatorio*. If there are a few instances in which it does find a place, these are the sublime inconsistencies of the poet's temperamental reaction to the rigours of logic.

Once he has conjured up before his mind personifications of wisdom and truth, human and divine, it only remains for him to ask with the certainty of obtaining satisfaction. But if his struggles to free himself from the toils of doubt do not invest his theorization with any passionate quality, by way of compensation he finds a motive for passion in his joy at the apprehension of truth and in his consciousness of the solid foundation for the construction of his world that is provided by the infallible solution of these problems. Just as the poet would have felt his world crumbling beneath him if he had not previously solved these problems, so he is conscious that it is his ineluctable duty to inform other men of these solutions, which have by now become an integral part, indeed the very essence, of his poetic world. Thus even the cantos that seem most lifeless, far from being superfluous pieces of dialectic, are bound up with the conception and the sense of the poetic function with which Dante believes that he has been invested. By eliminating the element of didacticism as he conceives it we eliminate the man's poetic and religious mission and the prophetic and apostolic significance of his work—in other words we destroy his personality. The creator of Farinata and the propounder of theories relating to the spots on the moon are complementary.

On the role of science in the *Comedy* see:

Antonelli's excursuses on Tommaseo's commentary.

E. Moore, 'The Astronomy of Dante' (*Studies*, III, pp. 1–108), Oxford, Clarendon Press, 1903.

F. Angelitti, 'Dante e l'astronomia', in *Dante e l'Italia*, Rome, Fondazione M. Besso, 1921.

G. Boffito, 'Dante geodeta', in *Giornale dantesco*, XXIV (1921), pp. 96–119, and 'Dante misuratore di mondi', in *Giornale dantesco*, XXVI (1923), pp. 221–6.

E. MOORE, *Gli accenni al tempo nella Divina Commedia*, Italian translation by C. Chiarini, Florence, Sansoni, 1900. For a contrary thesis see ANGELITTI's article in the *Bullettino della Società dantesca italiana*, VIII (1901), pp. 209–25.

E. MOORE, 'The Geography of Dante', in *Studies*, III, pp. 144–77.

A. MORI, 'La geografia in Dante', in *Archivio di storia della scienza*, III (1921–2), pp. 57–69.

P. REVELLI, *L'Italia nella Divina Commedia*, Milan, 1923.

COSMO, *L'ultima ascesa*, Chaps. 3, 5, 9 and 19.

A. SCROCCA, *Il sistema dantesco dei cieli e le loro influenze*, Naples, 1895.

E. PASTERIS, 'Astrologia e libertà, ossia poesia e filosofia nella Divina Commedia', in *La Scuola Cattolica*, 1929–30.

B. NARDI, *Saggi di filosofia dantesca*, Milan and Rome, Società editrice Dante Alighieri, 1930.

E. MESTICA, *La psicologia nella Divina Commedia*, Florence, 1893.

N. BUSETTO, 'Saggi di varia psicologia dantesca', in *Giornale dantesco*, XIII (1905), pp. 113–55.

B. NARDI, *Dante e la cultura medievale*, Bari, Laterza, 1942.

G. GENTILE, 'Pensiero e poesia nella Divina Commedia', in *Frammenti di estetica e letteratura*, Lanciano, Carabba, 1921.

A. BANFI, 'Filosofia e poesia nella Divina Commedia', in *Studi per Dante* (*Conferenze dantesche a cura del comitato milanese della Società dantesca*, Vol. III), Milan, Hoepli, 1935, pp. 119 *sq.*

Naturally, several of the books recommended as an aid to the understanding of the *Convivio* are also useful to students of the *Comedy*. (The scientific principles expounded in the two works are identical.) The reader is accordingly referred to the bibliography at the end of Chap. VIII.

History—Depiction of Places and of Nature

Our observations in connection with Dante's scientific theories are to a great extent applicable to his interpretation of history. The extensiveness of his scientific learning and the breadth of his vision of history were together responsible for the immensity of his world, and also for his added consciousness of his own greatness. In order to understand the *Comedy* it is essential to study the history and the historiography of the Middle Ages, and in particular of the thirteenth and early fourteenth centuries, just as it is essential to be familiar with the science of the age. I say 'the history and the historiography'. In carrying out this investigation we must, indeed, always distinguish the knowledge which after decades of research we have succeeded in acquiring, and the estimate which the shrewd speculations of philosophers have enabled us to form of the thirteenth century, from Dante's knowledge and estimate of it. Just as our authorities in astronomy or natural science are named Alfragano or Ristoro d'Arezzo or Brunetto Latini, so in the matter of history the Dantologist learns more from Paolo Orosio than from any great modern historian of the Roman world, while Dino Compagni and Villani tell him more about the history of Florence than Davidsohn. To be more precise, we must refer to the chroniclers in order to find a simple representation of events, and we must integrate our knowledge of those events with the opinions of modern historians in order to ascertain the lines along which, in point of fact, they unfolded. Only through this twofold knowledge—so to style it—shall we be able to account fully for the view which the poet took of them. And we must above all account for the poet's view of events before we can wholly comprehend and genuinely savour the poetry of which, in his skilful hands, they became such a fruitful source.

A. BARTOLI, 'La storia e la politica nella Divina Commedia', in *Storia della letteratura italiana*, VI, Part 2, pp. 1 *sq.*

I. DEL LUNGO, 'La figurazione storica del medio evo italiano nel poema di Dante', in *Dal secolo e dal poema di Dante*, Bologna, Zanichelli, 1898.

E. GORRA, *Il soggettivismo di Dante*, Bologna, Zanichelli, 1899. Cf. PARODI's article in the *Bullettino della Società dantesca italiana*, VII (1899), pp. 1–36.

MOORE, 'Dante's Personal Attitude Towards Different Kinds of Sin', in *Studies*, II, pp. 210–45.

G. LAJOLO, 'Del soggettivismo di Dante' (Chap. IX of *Indagini*

storico politiche sulla vita e sulle opere di Dante, Turin, Roux, 1893).
Cf. BARBI's article in the *Bullettino della Società dantesca italiana*, I
(1893), pp. 2–11; TORRACA, *Nuove rassegne*, Leghorn, Giusti,
1895, pp. 407 *sq.*

L. LEYNARDI, *La psicologia dell'arte nella Divina Commedia*,
Turin, Loescher, 1894, Part I, Chap. IV.

F. TORRACA, *Il regno di Sicilia nelle opere di Dante*, Palermo,
1900.

G. ARIAS, *Le istituzioni giuridiche medievali nella Divina Commedia*, Florence, Lumachi, 1901; cf. SALVEMINI's article in the
Bullettino della Società dantesca italiana, IX (1902), pp. 112–22.

A. FARINELLI, *Dante e la Francia*, Milan, Hoepli, 1908, I.

H. HAUVETTE, 'La France et la Provence dans l'œuvre de Dante'
(cited above).

P. FEDELE, 'I pontefici di Dante', in *Studi per Dante* (cited
above).

R. MORGHEN, 'Libertà, gerarchia e chiesa nel pensiero del medio
evo', in *Riv. stor. it.*, LVIII (1941), pp. 439–60.

The student may also profitably consult the old collection of
lectures on Dante delivered in Milan, *Arte, scienza e fede ai giorni
di Dante*, Milan, Hoepli, 1901; *Con Dante e per Dante*, ibid.

COSMO, *Le mistiche nozze di frate Francesco con madonna Povertà*
(cited above).

There are historical implications in those passages which may
have been inspired by places the poet stayed at or visited. For
such passages see:

J. J. AMPÈRE, *La Grèce, Rome et Dante*, Paris, 1854 and 1862
(6th ed., Paris, Perrin, 1884), and *Il viaggio dantesco* (Italian
translation by E. Della Latta, Florence, Le Monnier, 1855 and
1870).

A. BASSERMANN, *Orme di Dante in Italia*, Bologna, Zanichelli,
1902.

LEYNARDI, *Psicologia dell'arte* (cited above), Part 2, Chap. II and
passim.

BENI, *Guida illustrata del Casentino* (cited above).

Dante's descriptions of places reveal his inherent feeling for
nature. In addition to what has been written on this subject by
HUMBOLDT in *Cosmos* (Part 2), BURCKHARDT (*The Civilization of*

M

the Renaissance in Italy, translated by S. G. C. Middlemore, London, Harrap, 1929, p. 294) and A. BARTOLI (*Storia della letteratura italiana*, VI, Part 2, p. 227), see STOPPANI, *Il sentimento della natura e la Divina Commedia*, Milan, Bernardoni, 1865.

ZUCCANTE, 'Il concetto e il sentimento della natura nella Divina Commedia', in *Con Dante e per Dante* (cited above), pp. 237 *sq.*

TORRACA, 'Le rimembranze di Guido del Duca', in *Nuova Antologia*, XLVII, p. 5.

CASINI, 'Dante e la Romagna', in *Giornale dantesco*, I (1894), pp. 19 *sq.*, 112 *sq.* and 303 *sq.*, and 'Toscana e Romagna', in *Scritti danteschi*, Città di Castello, Lapi, 1913, pp. 51–76.

Dante's Self-portrait

This creator of splendid poetry is also the protagonist, and indeed the dominating figure, of his own poem. Not for nothing was the *Comedy* also called the *Danteid*. Hence a knowledge of the man's life and of the repercussions of history upon it greatly facilitates the understanding of the work. We must distinguish Dante as from time to time he depicted himself—in short, the ideal Dante—from Dante as he was. He was a great idealist set in the midst of reality. His feet trod the earth, but his eyes were turned towards heaven. He was an orthodox Catholic and a fervent believer; he was inspired with a lofty sense of right and justice, and convinced that he had a great mission to fulfil—a mission that placed him in the succession of the Israelite prophets; and his mind was full of hate and thoughts of revenge. He could not forgive, he could not forget—yet he wanted to do so. But that he should realize in day-to-day life the ideal picture that he painted of himself in his poem—this was his constant dream and the goal of all his striving. Eventually he achieved his purpose, but it was a long, uphill struggle. He achieved it first in song, or, if one prefers, as a poet—that is to say, when he announced his liberation from all party prejudice; he achieved it in reality, that is in a religious sense, much later. He became a perfect Christian only when in his hymn to the Virgin he prayed that the mists of mortality which encircled him might be dispersed. And the Virgin answered his prayer. But this happened in the last canto of the poem, during the last days of his life. It was a fortunate chance. If he had obtained his freedom earlier he would have destroyed the inward source of his poetry, which derived its power from the conflict between his real and ideal selves.

On Dante's personality see:

F. DE SANCTIS, 'Carattere di Dante e sua utopia', in *Saggi critici*. See also the essay on Farinata.

T. CARLYLE, 'The Hero as Poet. Dante; Shakespeare', in *On Heroes, Hero-worship*, London, Macmillan, 1901.

N. TOMMASEO, 'Commento alla Divina Commedia', note on *Inf.*, XXVI, 21 (Vol. I, p. 284 of U. COSMO's edition (cited above) and p. xxii of the Introduction).

J. BURCKHARDT, *The Civilization of the Renaissance in Italy* (cited above), pp. 307 sq.

G. VOIGT, *Il risorgimento dell'antichità classica*, Italian translation, Florence, Sansoni, 1888–90, I, pp. 13–17.

I. DEL LUNGO, 'Dante nel suo poema', in *Dal secolo e dal poema* (cited above), pp. 300–67.

J. KLACZKO, *Causeries florentines* (cited above).

C. CIPOLLA, *Di alcuni luoghi autobiografici nella Divina Commedia*, Turin, Clausen, 1893 (excerpt from *Atti della R. Acc. di Sc. di Torino*, Vol. XXVIII [1893], pp. 372–95), reproduced in *Gli studi danteschi*, Verona, 1921.

F. CIPOLLA, 'Accenni autobiografici nella Divina Commedia', in *Atti del R. ist. ven.*, LVI (Series 7, Vol. IX, 1898), pp. 701–22.

L. LEYNARDI, *La psicologia dell'arte nella Divina Commedia*, Part I, Chap. IV ('L'individualismo di Dante').

It is hardly necessary to point out that the works by Bartoli, Lajolo, Gorra, Parodi, etc., which have already been mentioned, also serve to throw light on this question.

V. CAPETTI, *L'anima e l'arte di Dante*, Leghorn, Giusti, 1907.

COSMO, *L'ultima ascesa*, especially Chap. 13 ('Davanti alla propria coscienza d'uomo e di poeta').

With special reference to Dante's prophetic role see:

I. VON DOELLINGER, 'Dante als Prophet', in *Beilage zur Allgemeinen Zeitung*, 1887, p. 335.

F. DE LEVA, 'Dante qual profeta', in *Atti del R. ist. ven.*, VI (1888).

G. GENTILE, 'La profezia di Dante', in *Scritti vari*, Lanciano, Carabba, 1921, p. 261.

B. NARDI, 'Dante profeta', in *Dante e la cultura medievale* (cited above), pp. 258-334.

The Other Characters

Dante was thus the creator of his own character. But at the same time, with marvellous skill, he created a crowd of other characters, each one different from the rest. So deeply are these engraved on the memories of all that there is no need to mention any of them by name. It is, however, necessary to study them one by one, the more so as in getting to know them intimately we gain a more and more profound insight into the mind of their creator. For if each character is always itself, each has within it something of Dante which he has introduced. Subjectivity and objectivity combine to make great poetry.

But one has not fully understood a character until one has reconstructed it down to the smallest detail. Now the distinguishing feature of the great characters in poetry is that they radiate a force of such suggestive power that the reader never comes to know them completely. Instead, each time he contemplates them he finds in them something new. He must, however, learn how the process of contemplation and reconstruction should be carried out. There is no more helpful means to the attainment of this end than the study of the essays of De Sanctis. It is impossible at this time of day to consider Francesca, Farinata and Count Ugolino without reference to his reconstruction of their characters. His achievement in this regard will never, perhaps, be surpassed. But De Sanctis, though he was an eminent critic, was a creature of his age, and his view of Dante was coloured by the prejudices and shortcomings of his Romantic culture. Since his time other able scholars have faced the problem of these personages and have thrown fresh light upon them; here and there they have corrected and completed his work. Even before him there was Foscolo. Since, there have been Rondani, Romani and Parodi, to mention only the best among them. In order, therefore, to obtain an ever closer view of the character which one desires to study it is a good thing to integrate the essays of

De Sanctis with the researches of modern philologists. After his essays on Francesca and Farinata the student should, for example, read Barbi's studies; having digested what he has to say of Pier della Vigna and Count Ugolino he should turn his attention to D'Ovidio. By a process of correction and integration, based on a profound knowledge of the subject, he will be able to smooth away certain rough edges in the work of De Sanctis, throwing light on certain points that have remained obscure and estimating the effective worth of certain statements. More than this, the study of these authorities, and indeed of all the authorities, will indicate clearly not only the degree of imagination and the taste that should be exercised, but also the systematic precautions that should be taken, when one proceeds with one's own reconstruction of the characters.

It would be a serious mistake to employ the same criteria in studying the characters in the *Inferno* and those in the other two *cantiche*—for instance, to expect all to have the same dramatic force and to disparage them when one failed to find it. Dante, who is a true poet, is guided by the criteria appropriate to the environment in which he sets his characters. It may be said at once that as he passes from the harsh, strident verses in which he describes the pit of hell to the soft rhymes that depict the island of purgatory, so he attributes to the inhabitants of that island sentiments proper to men and women who have passed from life into the presence of a conciliated God. Pia's feelings towards her husband cannot be the same as Francesca's. The feelings of Jacopo del Cassero towards his own murderers must be, and are, quite different from Count Ugolino's. And still another distinction must be drawn. The characters in the *Purgatorio* and the *Paradiso* are often, so to say, lyrical voices that express what the poet feels. Consider Marco Lombardo. Yet even here, with sublime inconsistency, the action is liable at times to flare up with renewed intensity, as in the cantos that are concerned with Pier Damiano and St. Peter. Such is the richness and variety of Dante's art.

With regard to the numerous characters in the poem see the full bibliography in D'Ancona's *Manuale*. It is to be noted, however, that his selection was not designed to indicate the best studies of the subject, but rather to show the progress that had been made at the time of writing. It will also be profitable to consult the copious bibliography compiled by Zingarelli; I would, for instance, mention the numerous references apropos of Statius (p. 1137, note 19). Subtle analyses of a number of characters are also to be found in some of the better writings in the so-called *Lectura Dantis* (published by Sansoni), in the *Giornale dantesco* and in many other reviews. It must suffice to mention as an example the shrewd observations with which Romani embellished his own readings. Again, it will be profitable to co-ordinate observations on individual readings with the observations and corrections progressively added by Parodi in the reviews of them which he published in the *Bullettino* of the Società dantesca.

The essays of De Sanctis are so well-known and are by now obtainable in such a variety of editions that references are unnecessary. The most accurate reprint is to be found in the edition of the *Opere complete* prepared by N. Cortese (Naples, Morano, 1930 and following years); this edition contains the necessary bibliographical indications. It is almost superfluous to remark that the study of the essays should be supplemented by reference to Chap. VII of the *Storia della Letteratura*, in which the great critic summarized the best passages from his readings on Dante. For this reason the book on Dante which he contemplated so fondly was never completed. All the noteworthy things that De Sanctis had to say about Dante he had already published. That is why his last books contain very little that is new. Yet it is a good thing to consult them, for two reasons: the ideas of a critic like De Sanctis should be assimilated in their entirety, and in order to comprehend a fully-fledged notion it is above all things necessary to detect it in the process of development. Since these books are not so well-known, here are the particulars:

Esposizione critica della Divina Commedia, a posthumous work edited by G. Laurini, Naples, Morano, 1921.

Lezioni inedite sulla Divina Commedia, edited by M. Manfredi, Naples, Morano, 1938.

For the Dante studies of De Sanctis see Cosmo, 'La lettura di Dante nell'università', in *Rivista di filosofia e scienze affini*, Seventh

Year, No. 1 (1905), pp. 384–96; CROCE, *La poesia di Dante* (cited above), 5th ed., pp. 184–90.

But after perusing the chapter by De Sanctis the student would do well to read Croce's 'rapid aesthetic survey of the three *cantiche*'. Croce's purpose was not to 'deal exhaustively with all the poetry in the *Comedy*, nor to describe every aspect of it, but merely to indicate the various and diversiform stars in that vast constellation'. If one compares the master's analysis of any given passage with that of the greatest of his pupils, noting which parts they regarded as poetry and which they did not, and if one picks out the instances in which their perception was acute and those in which their researches were deficient—here the merits and demerits of both were due to their philosophical preconceptions —one cannot but profit greatly from the process. The young student can develop his intellect and his taste only in the school of the great teachers, conducting his researches in a spirit of reverence, but always preserving the freedom of his mind.

BARBI's two essays on Francesca and Farinata, which have been republished many times, should now be studied in *Con Dante e coi suoi interpreti*, Florence, Le Monnier, 1941, pp. 117–211.

For D'OVIDIO's essays see *Ugolino, Pier della Vigna, i simoniaci e discussioni varie*, Milan, Hoepli, 1907. But the student of Dante should have a knowledge of the whole of D'Ovidio's work. His *Studii su Dante* (Palermo, 1901), which includes the essay on Guido da Montefeltro, and *Il Purgatorio e il suo preludio* (Milan, 1906) are reprinted in the complete edition of his *Opere* (Caserta and Naples, 1931–2), which contains in addition *L'ultimo volume dantesco* (Caserta, 1926). For a review of the *Studii* and a general survey of D'Ovidio's work on Dante see COSMO's article in *La Cultura*, October, 1931, pp. 317 *sq*.

For general information see:

L. LEYNARDI, *La psicologia dell'arte nella Divina Commedia* (cited above). In connection with this book see COSMO's article in *Giornale dantesco*, II (1894), pp. 214–9.

F. ROMANI, *Ombre e corpi*, Città di Castello, Lapi, 1901.

M. PORENA, *Delle manifestazioni plastiche del sentimento nei personaggi della Divina Commedia*, Milan, Hoepli, 1902.

E. SANNIA, *Il comico, l'umorismo e la satira nella Divina Com-*

media, Milan, Hoepli, 1909, 2 vols. This work, and indeed the whole question, is discussed by PARODI in 'Il comico nella Divina Commedia' (in *Poesia e storia*, cited above, pp. 105–209).

Here are a few additional references:

For Ciacco: F. COLAGROSSO, *Gli uomini di corte nella Divina Commedia*, Naples, Giannini, 1900; SCHERILLO, 'Il Ciacco della Divina Commedia', in *Nuova Antologia*, Series IV, No. 94 (1901), pp. 427–40, and *Dante uomo di corte*, ib., Series IV, No. 95 (1901), pp. 114–23.

For Capaneus: SCHERILLO, 'Capaneo e il Veglio di Creta', in *Flegrea*, II (1900); reproduced in *Il canto XIV dell'Inferno* (a commentary) (in *Lectura Dantis*).

For Pier dalle Vigne: F. NOVATI, in *Con Dante e per Dante* (cited above), Milan, Hoepli, 1898.

For Manfred: SCHERILLO, ib.

For Vanni Fucci: COSMO, 'Il canto di Vanni Fucci', in *Giornale dantesco*, XVI (1908), pp. 157–67.

For Marco Lombardo: COSMO, 'Il canto di Marco Lombardo', in *Giornale dantesco*, XVII (1909), pp. 105–18.

For all the characters in the *Paradiso* see COSMO, *L'ultima ascesa*, which also contains a bibliography.

G. CHIARINI, 'Le donne nei drammi del Shakespeare e nel poema di Dante', in *Nuova Antologia*, XCIX (1888).

L. FÉLIX-FAURE, *Les femmes dans l'œuvre de Dante*, Paris, Perrin, 1902.

Formal Criticism

The analysis of character is perhaps the most exquisite part of formal criticism. All criticism, however, consists in the analysis of form, inasmuch as every idea in literary work assumes a form of its own. Anyone who studied an idea conceived by an artist, of whatever description, independently of the form in which it found concrete expression would lose himself in a bottomless well of abstraction. But to reduce criticism to the simple formula 'This is poetry and this is not', and to content oneself with the statement as though it were an epitome of the truth, without making clear why it is or is not poetry, is to depreciate criticism, and hence to follow the method of impressionism.

If historical and aesthetic criticism is to be worthy of its name it should deal with all the problems of politics, history, religion and philosophy which Dante dealt with in his poem and should aim at finding the solution which he offered in each case. The solution invariably lies in the form that the problem assumed in Dante's mind and in the sentiment that it inspired in his heart. Yet if criticism confined itself to these problems, even though it might be great criticism, it would not completely fulfil its task. The essential shortcoming of critics of the old school was that they lost themselves in a maze of details, which they detached from their context and appraised as though they were independent; but the critic cannot abandon the idea of trying to find out in what the beauty of a line of poetry or the effectiveness of an image, a word or a metaphor consists and on what it depends. The position of a word determines the musical quality of a given passage; and without music there is no poetry.

Oscura e profonda era e nebulosa—'dark, deep and misty was' the valley of the abyss from whose brink Dante peered down in an effort to examine its interior, and the iambic rhythm of the first hemistich, coupled with the hiatus and the long final word, fills us with a sense of the immense depth of the darkness. Alter the position of a single word and all the beauty vanishes. *Era oscura e profonda e nebulosa* is still a verse, but it is a verse that says nothing. In his synthesis De Sanctis, who had a sense of poetry, wrote: 'Dante often succeeds in obtaining his effect with the aid of a single comprehensive word, which evokes a series of images and feelings. Often, while the word paints a picture, if for no other reason, by virtue of its position, the harmony of the line portrays the sentiment.' This is a synthetic conclusion, only reached after a scrupulous examination of the whole work. Thus, following his example, the young student should, so to say, 'dissolve' this synthesis by analysing all the parts and particles of the poem with the idea of reaching a conclusion that is truly his own. 'In studying poetry,' says D'Ovidio, 'one should strive to discern the minutest details', and even if in the course of his minute investigation he sometimes lost his bearings, it is also true to say that his careful searching enabled him to clear up a large number of doubtful points and to reveal much that is beautiful.

N

An object, adds De Sanctis, presents itself to Dante's mind 'with the appropriate impressions and sentiments. It assumes a form, which is at once both image and sentiment—a warm, living image, beneath the surface of which we see the colour of the blood and the movement of passion.' But how are we to see this colour and movement without examining the separate parts minutely? The verbose critics of earlier days stopped short at the parts. To ignore these critics, and so to forgo the enjoyment of so many elements in the poetry, would be a mistake. In my list of references I shall therefore mention without prejudice all those studies which may prove useful to the student. But there are degrees even of usefulness. By comparing the old with the new, by noting the merits and the mistakes of both, the young student will develop his critical faculty and will learn the great virtue of discrimination.

There are a few observations still worthy of note to be found in CESARI, *Bellezze della Commedia di Dante Alighieri, Dialoghi*, Verona, 1824–6, 3 vols. There have been many reprints of this work.

There are a large number of most acute observations in the commentary of Tommaseo, who, though incapable of achieving, like De Sanctis, a comprehensive vision, was a master at observing details.

F. PELLEGRINI's school text-book, *Elementi di letteratura*, Leghorn, Giusti, also contains a number of noteworthy observations.

On the subject of similes and metaphors see *Le osservazioni alla Divina Commedia*, by the seventeenth-century writer NICCOLA VILLANI (edited by U. Cosmo, Città di Castello, Lapi, 1894).

L. VENTURI, *Le similitudini dantesche ordinate e illustrate e confrontate*, Florence, Sansoni, 1874.

G. FRANCIOSI, 'Dell'evidenza dantesca studiata nelle metafore, nelle similitudini', etc., in *Scritti danteschi*, Florence, Le Monnier, 1876. In this connection the student should also consult LEYNARDI, *La psicologia dell'arte nella Divina Commedia* (cited above *passim*).

F. OLIVERO, *La rappresentazione dell'immagine in Dante*, Turin, Lattes, 1936.

Apropos of Dante's versification see:

F. Garlanda, *Il verso di Dante*, Rome, Società editrice laziale, 1907.

F. Pasini, 'Divagazioni estetiche sulla tecnica dantesca del verso', in *Annuario degli studenti trentini*, V (1899), pp. 72–101; see *Bullettino della Società dantesca italiana*, VII (1900), p. 322. There are some excellent observations on the musical quality of the versification in M. Casella's 'Studi sul testo della Divina Commedia', in *Studi danteschi*, VIII (1924), pp. 5–85.

E. Ciafardini, 'Dieresi e sineresi nella Divina Commedia', in *Rivista d'Italia*, XIII, No. 1 (1910), pp. 888–919; id., *Dialefe e sinalefe nella Divina Commedia*, ib., XVII, No. 2 (1914), pp. 465–516.

F. D'Ovidio, 'Sull' origine dei versi italiani', in *Giornale storico della letteratura italiana*, XXXII (1898), pp. 1–89, now reproduced in *Versificazione romanza* (*Opere*, IX, Part 1, pp. 131–261).

For Dante's use of symmetry see:

F. Mariotti, *Dante e la statistica delle lingue*, Florence, Barbera, 1880.

P. Petrocchi, 'Del numero nel poema dantesco', in *Rivista d'Italia*, June, 1901.

With special reference to the origins of *terza rima*:

G. Mari, *La sestina d'Arnaldo, la terzina di Dante*, Milan, Hoepli, 1899; but see Flamini, *Giornale storico della letteratura italiana*, XXXVIII (1901), pp. 128–39, and D'Ovidio, ib., XXXII (1898), p. 55, and *Versificazione romanza* (cited above), p. 196.

T. Casini, *Per la genesi della terzina e della Commedia dantesca*, *Miscellanea di studi critici in onore di G. Sforza*, Turin, 1923.

The Language

Many of these old-time critics, obsessed by the preconceived idea of form as the garment of thought, undoubtedly exaggerated. Cesari, for example, maintained that much of the beauty of Dante's poetry consisted in the propriety and effectiveness of his language. Subject to certain reservations, it is true to say that in Dante's hands language was a potent factor in the achievement of the end which he had in view. After the linguistic criteria of the *De Vulgari Eloquentia* had grown unequal to his needs his choice of words was always dictated by their capacity to give a complete and lucid picture of what he wished to describe. The words he used were to a very large extent taken from his native dialect, but if the need arose they were drawn from all the dialects of Tuscany, especially its southern districts, from those of Italy, and from Latin, Greek and Hebrew. When no existing parlance met his needs he created new words of great expressive power. Moreover, every character was differentiated by some peculiarity of speech. Thus Bonagiunta spoke the dialect of Lucca, Belacqua used Florentine expressions, Arnaud Provençal, Friar Gomita Sardinian, while even the devils were accorded a language all their own. Dante employed Bolognese words when conversing with Venedico Caccianemico, and Virgil addressed Guido da Montefeltro in the Lombard vernacular. Always the word was made to fit the circumstance.

Clearly a thorough knowledge of the language is essential if one is to understand and savour the work to the full. Consider how the reconstitution of the text has been facilitated by the intensive research of which the language of the thirteenth century has been the subject. Just to cite an example taken from the first few lines of the *Inferno*, there is no longer any discussion as to whether we should read *Poi ch'èi posato un poco il corpo lasso* or *Poi ch'ebbi riposato il corpo lasso*, and none can fail to see how the restoration of the old word *èi*, with its propriety, in place of the modernistic emendation *ebbi*, has added to the line's realism. Having stepped out of the sea on to the shore, Dante rested a little while, he did not rest *again*.

Certainly the obstacles to the acquisition of a complete knowledge of the language and of ancient usage are by no means few. The history of the Italian language has not been studied scientifically like that of the French, and ancient usage is something of which we still know little. 'So far as the phonetics and morphology are concerned,' wrote Michele Barbi, who was an authority on the subject, 'we know something. As regards the syntax we know nothing, or next to nothing, so little consideration has been given to the question. What little research has been undertaken has generally been based on printed texts amended in accordance with modern taste, or, if reference has been made to manuscripts, scholars have disregarded what they have thought to be copyists' mistakes.' But with the right will the defect may be made good. The teacher who expounds Dante, even if he cannot work with the actual manuscripts before him, can and should acquire a knowledge of all the literature—both poetry and prose—of the thirteenth century. He should search the great catalogues, and should above all have read extensively the prose of the thirteenth and fourteenth centuries. Only through such assiduous reading of contemporary texts can one acquire not merely a knowledge but, so to speak, a sense of the ancient language. And since words are not isolated things, familiarity with them helps us to acquire a knowledge of the history, thought, sentiment, usages and customs of the age. This is the best of preparations for the study of the *Comedy*. And since this book is intended to be a guide to young students who will one day be called upon to expound Dante in our secondary schools, I may be permitted a short digression prompted by my experience as a teacher.

In my early days, when I began to expound the *Comedy*, I did not even stop to explain the allegory, as so many teachers are prone to waste time in doing. The allegory, I used to say, will explain itself in the light of the actual text. On the other hand I used to pause for quite a time to explain the language, so that young students might appreciate the essential qualities of the language of Dante. In addition, I had prepared them for this by making them read contemporary poetry and prose. As regards the line which I quoted a little while back, since some of my pupils had old editions with the reading *ebbi* instead of *èi* and *riposato* instead of *posato*, I took the opportunity which my explanation of *èi* afforded to give them an idea of the state in which Dante had left his text and of the circumstances of its critical restoration. Then, having licked my pupils into some sort of shape, I was able to proceed more quickly because they were in a position to follow me. I always noticed that they were most attentive and that they enjoyed their work.

These introductory talks were, of course, delivered at rare intervals and with discretion, but they were lucid. The teacher cannot be content with the little knowledge that may suffice for the pupil. So that he may select what he should say, the teacher should know his whole subject thoroughly, and if he is to be lucid he should first have clarified every point in his own mind. The schoolmaster should watch the progress of culture. It would be a grave error and a no less serious loss if our teachers did not capitalize the advance that has been made in the science of aesthetics in Italy by using it to bring out the beauties inherent in the work of the poet whom they expound. But if they ought to use the new aesthetics to illustrate the text that they expound, they should likewise interpret that text with the aid of the new philology. Any illustration that is not based on this interpretative principle is nothing more than idle talk. And education seeks to promote science and art, not empty rhetoric.

The books that have been suggested for the study of the language of the *Vita Nuova* naturally have a bearing on the *Comedy* as well. In addition I would particularly mention:

V. Nannucci, *Intorno alle voci usate da Dante secondo i commentatori in grazia della rima*, Corfù, 1840; *Analisi critica dei verbi italiani*, Florence, 1843; *Teorica dei nomi della lingua italiana*, Florence, Baracchi, 1858.

L. G. Blanc, *Vocabolario dantesco*, translated by G. Carbone, Florence, Barbera, 1859.

R. Caverni, *Voci e modi nella Divina Commedia dell'uso popolare toscano* (a miniature dictionary), Florence, 1877.

N. Caix, *Le origini della lingua poetica italiana*, Florence, Le Monnier, 1880.

N. Zingarelli, 'Parole e forme della Divina Commedia aliene dal dialetto fiorentino', in *Studi di filologia romanza*, I (1884), pp. 1–202; cf. *Giornale storico della letteratura italiana*, III (1884), p. 145.

I. Del Lungo, 'Il volgar fiorentino nel poema di Dante', in *Dal secolo e dal poema di Dante*, Bologna, Zanichelli, 1898, pp. 399–525.

E. Parodi, 'La rima e i vocaboli in rima nella Divina Commedia', in *Bullettino della Società dantesca italiana*, III (1896), pp. 81–156.

See also Parodi's many observations on the subject of the language which occur sporadically in his reviews of the *Lecturae Dantis* in the different volumes of the above-mentioned *Bullettino*.

F. Torraca, *Di un commento nuovo alla Divina Commedia*, Bologna, Zanichelli, 1899.

M. Barbi, 'Per una più precisa interpretazione della Divina Commedia', in *Problemi*, I, pp. 197–303; *Con Dante e coi suoi interpreti*, Florence, Le Monnier, 1941 (see under the appropriate headings in the *Indice analitico*).

A. Schiaffini, 'Note sul colorito dialettale della Divina Commedia', in *Studi danteschi*, XIII (1928), pp. 31–45; 'Influsso dei dialetti centro meridionali sul toscano e sulla lingua letteraria', in *Italia dialettale*, V (1929), pp. 1–31; 'Del tipo parofia-parochia', in *Studi danteschi*, V (1922), pp. 99–131.

The student will find it very profitable to refer to Monaci's *Crestomazia*, not only for his redaction of the texts but for the glossary (amended and greatly enlarged by Felice Arese in the second edition, which is in the press as I write).

From the student's point of view the question of the language is intimately bound up with that of the text. Accordingly, the works that I shall mention in connection with the latter should also be consulted when linguistic problems arise.

The Text

As I have observed, from the student's point of view the questions of language and text are intimately related. Critical study of the language, and therefore of its history, has made it possible to restore the text with much greater ease and certainty than before. The student need only compare an old edition, even one of the best, with the text published in 1921 by the Società Dantesca Italiana, or better still with the successive editions issued by Vandelli as an accompaniment to his commentary, bearing in mind the suggestions offered by eminent philologists and the results of his own investigations. No one, I think, will deny that some truly remarkable progress has been made. We have not yet attained that ideal perfection which the advance in philological studies foreshadows, but the text which we use to-day is not very different from the text as Dante left it. I say deliberately 'as Dante left it' and not 'as the fourteenth century knew it , because it is incredible how soon and how easily the text was altered, and what absurd mistakes—and how many of them!—crept into it.

At the very start a copyist attempted to evolve a kind of critical text from the variety of readings available, and Pietro di Dante in a revised edition of his commentary went so far as to suggest a number of emendations.[1]

The history of critical efforts to arrive at a correct version of the text is curious and of great assistance to all who wish to make a serious study of philology. It embraces the attempts made by the members of the Accademia della Crusca, who in preparing their edition of 1595 consulted manuscripts and assembled a goodly number of variants, and the researches of Foscolo; the efforts of Witte and the studies of Moore, Mussafia and Täuber; the subsequent discussions of the Società Dantesca, crystallized in Barbi's proposals for the examination of the manuscripts, and the inquiries in this connection conducted by able Dantologists and more especially by Vandelli, who was entrusted with the task of preparing the edition. But this is not the place for even an outline of the history of these endeavours. Nevertheless, without a serious grounding in philology it is useless to aspire to a complete understanding of the *Comedy*. I therefore strongly advise youthful scholars to make a special study of two works, of which one deals more particularly with classical philology, and the other with Italian. From these they may learn of the progress made by modern philologists and of the labours which precede the publication of a text—especially a difficult text like that of the *Comedy*. But if they wish to reconstruct *in toto* the history of the stresses and strains endured in this cause they will find, in the few more recent studies to which their attention is drawn below, the indications that they need to guide them in their researches.

Death begrudged Vandelli the opportunity to reap the fruits of his labours by publishing the text together with the full *apparatus criticus* which would have enabled all to appraise his work and to make corrections where it appeared that his conclusions were not justified. The manuscripts have not yet been classified with absolute certainty. So far two groups have taken shape, but it remains to be seen whether some tradition independent of these does not exist. New advice was tendered at the last by

---

[1] e.g. 'Non dicas "ad iram," ut multi textus dicunt falso, sed dicas "ad ire" ' (*Inf.*, XXIV, 69).

Barbi, whose work in connection with these studies was likewise, alas, interrupted before its time. One by one the masters leave the stage, but the way that they have opened up remains. Now we look to the young men, and to be successful they have only to follow in their predecessors' footsteps. I should be content if a few young scholars, spurred on by this Guide to gather up the inheritance of such noble toilers as these, were able, for the sake of Dante's name and for the honour of Italy, to bring their high enterprise to fruition.

The student will find it profitable, by way of a preliminary reconnaissance, to read three Appendixes by Rajna and Vandelli, viz. to the 'Testi critici', the 'Testo dei Reali di Francia' and the 'Edizione critica della Divina Commedia', in G. MAZZONI's *Avviamento allo studio critico delle lettere italiane*, Florence, Sansoni, 1907.

He should then consult:

G. PASQUALI, *Storia della tradizione e critica del testo*, Florence, Le Monnier, 1934 (cf. G. CONTINI's article in *Arch. rom.*, XIX (1935), pp. 330–40).

M. BARBI, *La nuova filologia e l'edizione dei nostri scrittori da Dante al Manzoni*, Florence, Sansoni, 1938. See Pasquali's review of this book in *Leonardo*, IX (1938), pp. 471–83, reprinted in *Terze pagine stravaganti*, Florence, Sansoni, 1942, pp. 219–49.

With more particular reference to the problem of the text the student should read:

E. MOORE, *Contributions to the Textual Criticism of the Divine Comedy*, Cambridge, 1891.

BARBI, *Per il testo della Divina Commedia*, Rome, 1891, and *Bullettino della Società dantesca italiana*, IV (1897), pp. 137–58; VANDELLI, 'Il più antico testo critico della Divina Commedia', in *Studi danteschi*, V (1922), pp. 41–98, and 'Note sul testo critico della Commedia', in *Studi danteschi*, IV (1921), pp. 39–84, and VII (1923), pp. 97–102.

CASELLA, 'Studi sul testo della Divina Commedia', in *Studi danteschi*, VIII (1924), pp. 5 sq.

See also the important edition of Casella's works published at Bologna (1923).

S. DEBENEDETTI, 'Intorno ad alcuni versi di Dante', in *Giornale storico della letteratura italiana*, LXXXVII (1926), pp. 74–99.

PARODI, 'Il testo critico delle opere di Dante', in *Bullettino della Società dantesca italiana*, XXVIII (1921), pp. 35 *sq.*

BARBI, 'Per il testo critico della Divina Commedia', in *La nuova filologia* (cited above), pp. 1–34 (from *Studi danteschi*, XVIII (1934), pp. 5–57); *Problemi*, II, pp. 435–70.

INDEX OF PROPER NAMES

189